LIVING YOUR FAITH

LIVING YOUR FAITH

Robert Nash, S.J.

PRENTICE-HALL, INC. NEW YORK

Copyright, 1951, by

PRENTICE-HALL, INC.

70 FIFTH AVENUE, NEW YORK 11

FIRST AMERICAN EDITION

Living Your Faith *was originally published in Ireland under the title* Is Life Worthwhile?

Nihil Obstat: IOANNES KELLY,
Censor Theol. Deput.

Imprimi potest: ✠ IOANNES CAROLUS,
Archiep. Dublinensis,
Hiberniae Primas.

PRINTED IN THE UNITED STATES OF AMERICA

Dedicated to

MARY

Through Whom We Have Merited
To Receive

HIM

Who Is the Author of Life

CONTENTS

PART I
FUNDAMENTALS

PART II
AN EXPERT SHOWS HOW

Part I
FUNDAMENTALS

I. Perspective

"One thing I know, that whereas I was blind, now I see."—St. John, ix. 25.

1. Beneath the Surface

Let me suppose that you decide this evening to climb some hill in your neighborhood and treat yourself to a few hours' contemplation of the view that spreads out before you. When you are nearing the summit you turn around to look: the exquisite panorama before your wondering eyes makes you draw in a quick breath of admiration and astonishment. You will probably sit down here and rest your back against a jutting piece of rock. I can see you fold your arms, cross your feet, and sigh with contentment. It is such a relief to escape from the bustle of the city, the beep-beep of autos, the stifling heat, the nerve-racking creaking of buses and trolleys. All you want is just to be allowed to remain here in silence, for we are taking it, you see, that you have a keen sense of the beauties of nature.

Time slips by but you are in no hurry. There is the glory of the summer sun, there is the hum of the bees and the song of the birds above your head, there is that wonderful blue sky, the stretch of sea in the distance—all this you want to absorb at your leisure. As the evening advances you note the differing tints of light and shade. The picture before you is changing constantly and it seems to you that each picture surpasses or at least rivals the one that preceded it. Perhaps you will take out your fountain pen and try to record your impressions. Perhaps you will reach for your brushes and paints and make the effort to transfer to your canvas the marvelous combination of color. If you are keen on photography you certainly will not have come up here without your camera, and you are not going back tonight without a few pictures.

Presently, while you are engaged with your pen or brushes or camera, a farmer passes by. He has been working hard all day at the hay or the corn, and now he is tired and hungry and eager to be home at his supper. Stop him for a minute and pour out your ardent artistic soul before him and the poor man will look at you askance, I fear, as at some strange suspected being from whom he is anxious to escape. Honest, hardworking son of the soil that he is, he is almost completely at a loss to understand your enthusiasm. What is there to be so excited about? Why, the place always looks like this in the summer! That a few twittering birds, and fields green or gold, and trees beginning to shed their yellowing leaves, and the waters of that lake below, and that sun which rises and sets every morning and every night, should evoke such encomiums from you is entirely beyond his comprehension. Soon he leaves you to your dreamings and your pretty poetry, and, sensible man, hurries down home to his supper.

> "A primrose by the river's brim
> A yellow primrose 'twas to him
> And nothing more."

Now remark that you are, both of you, looking at the very same scene, but you alone see into its loveliness. It fills you with delight and soothes your soul to bask here in the sun, far removed from the fever and the fret of life. He listens to your laudations and he too looks at the scene, but what you tell him leaves him unsympathetic and unmoved. It is the difference between a person who has developed a taste or an appreciation and one who has not.

Or take another illustration. Here is a passage of classical English—a speech from Shakespeare or an essay of Newman. Give it to one man to read and at once you perceive how keenly he relishes the beauty or the force behind the author's words. Here he smacks his lips with satisfaction as he grasps the subtlety of the argument or sees into the exquisite literary finish of what he reads. He tells you about another passage which has many similar points of style, or he remembers coming across an argument worked out on the same lines, and he promises to bring it along to you to compare with what you have just shown him. He wants to borrow your book, or at any rate write down the reference. Perhaps he comes back to you in a few days to ask if he may look up a point which he did not quite understand at first. This is a man, you say, who has certainly developed a taste for literature. It is a pleasure to you to have seen these signs of his evident power to appreciate.

Next day the trucker comes to leave you coal in your cellar or the boy comes with the groceries. Take down your precious volume today from that shelf and open at the page and ask either to read it and tell you what he thinks of it. Can he make anything of it? Not he, very likely. It is such meaningless stuff, "words, words, words." He cannot imagine how anybody could find sense in this medley, and how you can detect, not sense merely, but beauty, he fails utterly to understand. If you had given him the evening paper, perhaps, or even a detective story, he might have thanked you and gone away grateful, but what could any sensible person be expected to make out of this unintelligible jargon?

Yet he has read for you the identical passage of writing that so delighted your friend yesterday. He has read, but he has not power to appreciate. Trucking coal or delivering groceries are excellent things in their way and in occupations not so different men of the caliber of St. Benedict Labré or Matt Talbot have been fashioned. But they are not conducive to the production of literary genius, and it is nothing derogatory to your truck driver and your grocery boy to bid them good evening and dismiss them with the remark that they have no taste for the amenities of good style.

Watch the eager interest of a skilled mechanic as he investigates the improvements in a new model engine, and contrast it with the lassitude of the man to whom it is only a confused mass of bolts and steel and rivets and screws. Mark the breathless attention to the symphony orchestra displayed by the trained musician and compare it with the bored expression of the man sitting listless beside him, unable to say whether what is being played is Mozart or jazz! Consider the ease with which the spendthrift lets money flow through his fingers, and the anxiety with which the careful housewife counts out every penny.

In all these cases you will notice again that the two people concerned are dealing with the same subject. They look on the same landscape. They read from the same book. They stand contemplating the same machine. They listen to the same sounds. They handle the same money. What makes the difference in their outlook then? Simply that in one case the faculty to appreciate has been developed, and in the other it has been allowed to lie fallow.

It may be said that in the realm of the supernatural it is the possession of this power to appreciate, or the lack of this power, that marks the radical difference between the saints and ourselves. That is why St. Ignatius, right at the beginning of his *Spiritual Exercises* insists so emphatically on the necessity of allowing one single truth at a time to sink into the soul, and why he is convinced that one truth assimilated in this way will effect immeasurably more for the soul's growth in holiness, than several truths which are merely passed by in review. "It is not the abundance of knowledge," he writes, "that fills the soul and satisfies it, but to feel the thing and taste it interiorly."

It is only little by little that divine truth saturates the soil of the soul. Convictions then follow, bedrock convictions, from which are formed spiritual giants. Saints are men and women who look at the supernatural and appreciate its practical implications in the business of living, who are inexorable in applying its principles. They realize, whereas others only believe.

2. A Few Examples

The point is worth illustrating. Everybody knows, for instance, that death is certain for all of us, and every Catholic believes that his lot for eternity depends on the use he makes of time. That much he knows, but what an enormous difference comes into his life and his ways of behaving when knowledge passes into realization! Realization begins to dawn, possibly, when one day he stands over the dead body of the mother he loved. Only a few days after the death, her body may already be showing signs of corruption. So this is the world and its prizes? Has it no more than this to offer? The truth of eternity comes home in such circumstances.

It is the truth that seized upon the mind of Aloysius Gonzaga. Eternity became his lodestar. When faced with a decision to be made, he would ask himself: "What shall I wish to have decided in eternity?" When he had to make a choice, his choice was governed, not by caprice but by the same momentous question. Eternity realized, not merely believed in, dwarfed all else, and Aloysius scaled the heights.

All Catholics believe that sin is the greatest of misfortunes, and nearly all Catholics, thank God, still call sin by its right name. But when a person is living in an atmosphere in which there is no sense of sin, convictions tend to grow dull unless they be constantly sharpened. So Catholics, too, fall into sin, into grievous sin, and for years, it may be, remain slaves to habits of vice. On committing his first mortal sin, a man is indeed usually torn with remorse and filled with shame and confusion as he hastens to confess the evil he has done. Let him, however, relapse repeatedly into sin and little by little he succeeds in blinding himself to its malice. At first conscience warned him in unmistakably clear terms, but now he manages almost to stifle its voice altogether.

Realization is gone. He no longer has any sort of appreciation of the arrogance of a creature like himself deliberately and in cold blood disobeying the command of his Creator. If he does come to confession, perhaps at mission time or at the urgent and reiterated request of somebody who is filled with anxiety about his salvation, he will accuse himself of heinous crimes almost in an off-hand way, insinuating, at least by his manner, that he is no worse than many others he knows; that, if he misses Mass frequently and through his own fault, or drinks to excess, or yields to impure temptations, he is of opinion that not much more can be expected from fallen human nature. Sins like these are only natural after all!

Now turn to the saints. Open one of those wondrous books of St. Teresa of Avila and read her bitter reproaches of herself and the agony of mind she describes which is caused by the memory of her sinful past. Listen to her proclaiming that she owes it only to God's infinite mercy that she did not go to hell. From her words you would be led to conclude that she had indulged in every sort of wickedness, but in point of fact we are assured by those who knew her most intimately that she never lost her baptismal innocence. Are we then going to accuse her of insincerity, perhaps even of gross untruth? No. In the clear light that conviction gives, Teresa realizes the terrifying deformity of even a single venial sin when seen against the background of the ineffable sanctity of the Godhead.

Or consider Ignatius Loyola standing in icy cold water on a winter's night till he was nearly frozen to death, and offering this self-inflicted penance for the conversion of a sinner. Or think of Francis Xavier scourging his body till the blood flowed in order to make atonement to his God offended by sin. Or read again about the legions of martyrs who were flung to wild beasts or roasted over a slow fire or hewn with the knives of savages or hanged or burned at the stake—all because they persisted in their obstinate refusal to act against their conscience and commit a single mortal sin. Once more this heroism is the outcome of conviction as opposed to mere belief.

Unless our faith is entirely dead we believe in prayer and we make at least some effort to practise this sacred art of communing with God. But how often must we strike our breasts and confess that our prayer is a listless, lifeless, distracted jumble of words! We have to drag ourselves to it as to an exceedingly irksome duty. We have to force ourselves to go on our knees and we rise before the end for the flimsiest of excuses. While we experience no difficulty at all in spending half an hour or an hour chatting pleasantly with our next-door neighbor, or discussing at considerable length the points of a football game or a film, we feel an almost insuperable repugnance towards speaking with God. The splendid efforts to revive the devotion to Mary's rosary leave us cold. We recite it only seldom ourselves, and we have no great sense of compunction about the omission.

Now we are not trying to maintain that the saints too did not have immense difficulty to overcome in acquiring the spirit of prayer that characterizes every one of them. Nor are we saying that dryness and weariness in our prayer are an indication that the prayer is not genuine, no more than, on the other hand, abundance of sweetness and consolation are an infallible criterion of the worth of our prayer. In Gethsemani the Saviour of the world suffered intense agony and desolation. He was crushed to the ground that night by the weight of His loneliness and sense of failure. But who dare assert that His prayer was not most perfect when "being in an agony He prayed the longer"?

The point we do wish to make is that *very often* this apathy towards prayer and this state of spiritual atrophy are the result of lack of realization. We believe well enough but somehow prayer is always colorless and painful, with the result that we never become convinced *by experience* that there is a whole new world, the world of the spirit, to be opened out before us if only we can advance in the ways of prayer.

Is it necessary to insist that prayer was, for the saints, the very breath of their supernatural lives? That it loomed so very large on their spiritual horizon that, for no stress of occupation or pressure of work, would they omit it or curtail it? "Nothing great or lasting can be hoped for," wrote St. Vincent de Paul, "from those who are ignorant of the art of conversing with God in prayer." "When a man," St. John Baptist de la Salle told his sons, "called to the work of saving souls, is filled with the spirit of God, he obtains by prayer all that he desires for the success of his mission."

So we might continue to quote in this same strain from the saints till our supply of paper was exhausted. For, if there is one truth more than another about which there is absolute unanimity in the teachings of the saints, it is upon the necessity of prayer, its power with God, the ways of approach and progress in this sacred science. So true is this that prayer has come to be called the science of the saints, as though a saint and a man of prayer may almost be regarded as interchangeable terms.

This love of prayer which they show in their fervor and perseverance, this earnestness with which they exhort us to walk unswervingly in the ways of prayer despite the many obstacles besetting our path, this generous encouragement they give us to begin again to pray when we have abandoned the struggle, to what is it all due? Not merely to what they have read or heard about prayer from others, not merely to what they have been told by their confessor or spiritual director. They speak as they do about prayer because they have learned what prayer is and what it can accomplish, from their own intimate experience and most burning convictions. Once more they appreciate; they realize; like Moses they enter into the cloud and converse with God face to face.

As a last illustration of the point we are stressing, take the attitude of many Catholics towards the most Holy Eucharist. Here is a congregation of Catholics, gathered around the altar for Mass or evening devotions. Not a man or woman in this church but would assert, if challenged, their unwavering belief in the Real Presence. They have not a doubt that the all-holy God is as truly present in their souls after Holy Communion as when Mary laid Him in the manger at Bethlehem and wrapped Him in swaddling clothes. They will tell you, in no hesitant manner, that Mass is the very same sacrifice as that which Jesus offered on Calvary. They will kneel at Benediction and assure you that Jesus is truly present in that host in the monstrance.

None the less, these same Catholics will break out into complaints if the priest delays five minutes longer than usual at Mass and causes them to miss a date. Many of them will rush past the church door six days of the week and never even think of dropping in for a visit. They live not five minutes' walk from the church and they hear the bell for Mass every weekday, but, you know, they need a rest after last night's show, or they do not even try to invent any excuses, but just let the treasure of daily Mass and daily Holy Communion pass them by. They discuss remedies for our many harrowing social problems, but they are shy about fearlessly and unashamedly advocating the most effective remedy of all, the union of man with man and of all men with Jesus Christ, through worthy and frequent reception of Holy Communion.

What is the matter with them? Their faith? No, not their faith, not their intellectual assent to the astounding truth of the abiding presence of Jesus in the Eucharist, but their realization.

Once again see what this conviction effects in the saints. Look at St. Liguori bent low with age and infirmity, kneeling before the tabernacle and transported with happiness. His great heart burns within him as he kneels here and realizes the magnificent truth of it all. Read the outpourings of that mighty love as found in his little book of *Visits,* and you will see what realization does, as contrasted with mere belief. You will see there what it means to *recognize* Jesus in the breaking of bread.

Or watch Matt Talbot,* the Dublin workingman, in the small hours of a freezing morning in winter, waiting for the church to open and admit him to the first Mass. There is no need of anybody to persuade him to come. He does not require to be dragooned into the performance of his Easter duty. He realizes, he appreciates, and his realization is a magnet drawing him almost irresistibly to the tabernacle.

We have touched upon a few of the fundamental truths—some of them we propose to develop in another place—and we have seen that for the saints these are living realities, whereas for many Catholics they are only dry beliefs. Eternity, sin, the Blessed Eucharist, and prayer—saint and sinner alike we look at

* Matt Talbot was an Irish laboring man, who, after many years of incredible alcoholism, was suddenly converted to a most rigorously penitential life which was marked, as well, by a compassionate charity which led him to distribute most of his meager wages to those even poorer than he. He died (1925) with a reputation for high sanctity, and the cause of his canonization has been introduced at Rome.

these and believe them. But the gaze of the saint penetrates and he sees with the eye of the genius into the far-reaching consequences of what we all hold to be true. The refiner detects at once the difference between a true coin and its counterfeit. The artist distinguishes instantly the great master from the cheap imitation. The prospector can tell you where true gold is likely to be found. And the saint has discovered a hidden treasure, has tabulated carefully the things that are of value and the things that are of little worth. He is the spiritual genius for "he feels and tastes the thing interiorly."

We loiter on the road to sanctity because we lack conviction of the practical value and power of our religion in the affairs of everyday life. We are Sunday Catholics. Christ's enemies speed past us, borne along in a very whirlwind of zeal because they have intense conviction of the truth of fables poured into their ears by the pseudo-prophets of our times. What we want is, in the words of Arnold Lunn, "an intense preoccupation with the supernatural." How can we get it?

3. Ways and Means

Well, how do men acquire conviction, how do they arrive at a decision, in the ordinary important affairs of life? They simply think out the problem lying before them for solution. They weigh the arguments for and against, and, in the light of what they discover, they resolve on a course of action. How does a student solve a knotty question in, say, mathematics? He very deliberately segregates himself from his friends and from all distraction, in order diligently to apply his mind to think the thing out. Certain data are supplied him with the problem, and certain conclusions have to be proved. In the quiet of his study he puts his head between his hands and does a little straight thinking, and, to his great satisfaction light begins to dawn and he begins to see.

Not much more than this is required in order to set the soul straight in the way towards acquiring the strong convictions which are the foundation of the edifice of holiness. We do not grasp the reality of the supernatural because we neglect to think. "With desolation is the whole land made desolate, because *there is nobody that thinketh in his heart.*" The saints are exceptions. They refuse to be satisfied with mere dry belief. They climb courageously out of the drab valleys high up into the mountains, there to breathe deeply the invigorating air of the spiritual life. They think out the implications of what they believe, and then they proceed to *live* that faith. Everything henceforth in their lives falls right or left according as its affects the supernatural. Like Mary, they keep all the words of Jesus, pondering them in their hearts.

The Church, anxious mother that she is, has always led the way, and given her children every encouragement and facility to think things out. She has filled the deserts with solitaries who fled from the haunts of men in order to devote their entire lives to the single work of contemplation. She has built up the great monastic Orders vowed to strict enclosure and almost perpetual silence, so as to provide them with opportunity to meditate without let or hindrance, day and night on God's law. For even those Orders devoted to works of charity for the neighbor she enjoins a rule of silence and counsels retirement, as much as is consistent with the work to be done. She defines preaching by the lips of one of her greatest teachers as *contemplata aliis tradere*—giving to others what one has thought out on one's knees. For all those consecrated to God's service, in whatsoever sphere, she commands that at regular intervals some days be set aside, during which her priests and her religious, freed from every other duty, may take their spiritual bearings by thinking things out.

Nor does she neglect to instil into layfolk, also, the need of this same serious consideration. We have to content ourselves with a mere reference to the letter of the late Holy Father in which he extols the practice of closed retreats for layfolk, and urges the development of these schools of thought where men and women, "weighing things maturely and with even balance, can acquire strength and firmness for the will . . . and the soul attain to its native nobility and altitude . . . where a man hiding himself in this blessed secrecy is instructed by heavenly wisdom to form a just estimate and understand the value of human life devoted to the service of God alone . . . and may see clearly unveiled the vanity of earthly things . . ." It is not the Church's fault if her children do not ponder in their hearts.

There is a big difficulty, of course. In order to think things out, the scientist must seek the seclusion of his laboratory or study. He must very deliberately cut himself off from things that would divert his mind and hinder his power of concentration. In exactly the same way if a man is going to see beneath the surface of the spiritual life, he must, quite deliberately too, separate himself from much that attracts him at present. It is a commonplace that the world has run mad with pleasure-seeking. Speed, efficiency, rush, records, these things are the order of the day, and they leave little time or inclination for that isolation and retirement that are essential to clear thinking.

Even priests and religious, filled as they are with the desire to spread Christ's kingdom, may be in danger of forgetting the need of prayer and sacrifice—prayer which unites the soul with Our Lord, the only source from which to draw strength against His enemies; and sacrifice which empties the apostle's heart of selfishness and sin, gives scope to the life of grace to expand, and wins for souls the blessings of true conversion. If even these have to be warned against "the heresy of good works," how much more those whose lot is cast in the midst of men who are devoured by greed of money, whose only god is a "good time," whose ideals and ambitions are earth-bound? Nothing is easier than to fall into an utterly natural way of living, judging all things and measuring all things by the effect they have on our material welfare. Catholics can live a flippant, superficial sort of existence, feeding the soul, or trying to, on mere sense impressions. But they are doomed to fail, and sooner or later to understand that the soul continues to hunger, and in its hunger to cry out for God Who alone can satisfy its pangs.

If a man listens too much and too eagerly to the noises of the world, its gossip, its news, he will hardly keep his ears attuned to catch the whisperings of Christ's grace in his soul. If he fills his heart with love of what the world has to offer, he must necessarily crush out the love of Jesus Christ. If he gazes too long and too lovingly at the pleasures of the world and partakes unrestrainedly of its joys, his eyes must necessarily grow clouded and dim. He loses perspective. He loses his sense of proportion. He can no longer appreciate the supernatural truths offered by Christ through the Church, for the nourishment and satisfying of his soul. This is only to repeat the teaching of the Apostle: "If any man love the world, the charity of the Father is not in him."

Cost what it may, the effort must be made to withdraw, at least occasionally, into retirement, if a person is to preserve his standard of values unimpaired.

4. Afraid of Prayer

But this retirement is to be filled with something more than mere silence. Lay people may be inclined to take alarm at even the mention of mental prayer. They have, as a rule, only a hazy notion of what it implies, and they consider that that much justifies them in believing that mental prayer is right enough for priests and nuns, but quite unsuited for those who have to live in the midst of the world's turmoil. The truth is, however, that for all sorts and conditions of men, mental prayer—in different forms, to be sure, according to the temperament and aptitude of each—is a most powerful help, indeed an almost indispensable one, especially in times like ours.

There are many excellent Catholics who give a large portion of each day to their prayers. Few sights are more heartening than our churches, crowded at every hour of the day with men and women praying, adoring, making the Way of the Cross, saying the rosary. Though if you question them, many of them will tell you that they are dissatisfied with their progress in prayer. They have a haunting suspicion that they are not getting out of their prayer the help, the fervor, the zeal for souls that others seem to get, notably those who have aimed consistently at a life of sanctity. They go through their formulas of prayer with edifying and heroic fidelity but it appears as if those formulas had nearly worn out from such constant use. Like the young man in the Gospel they are inclined to ask, almost querulously: "What is still wanting to us?"

Now if those formulas have grown dull and insipid, if they seem to be leading the soul nowhere, it might be very well worth while making a change over to mental prayer. What does this mean? Perhaps the best answer is by way of example. Here is a man or woman, boy or girl, who is in the habit of making every day the Way of the Cross with vocal prayers only, or reading fixed prayers out of a prayer-book, or reciting by heart certain prayers learned years ago. That praiseworthy habit takes, let us say, twenty or twenty-five minutes. What change do we suggest? First of all let it be set down that the same amount of *time* is to be given to prayer; keep still to those twenty or twenty-five minutes faithfully, but spend them differently. Substitute for that period, an equal period of mental prayer. Just this time, do not make the Way of the Cross, or read those sets of prayers out of your book, or recite those formulas by heart. Instead, try some such way of prayer as the following:

You are here before the Blessed Sacrament, or in some quiet corner at home, kneeling in prayer. Give yourself a few minutes to recall the fact that the all-holy God and yourself are face to face. "Often," says Father Considine, S.J., "the best kind of prayer is simply to kneel down and let God look into my soul." If that one idea holds you, the idea namely that you are in God's presence, and you find yourself drawn to prostrate yourself before Him in love and adoration, even without actually speaking a single word, by all means follow the attraction. Spend your twenty or twenty-five minutes in such acts of love and adoration, and you have done well with your mental prayer.

But you may easily require more. So, let me suggest, that you open your Gospel and turn to the first chapter of St. Mark. In verse 35, you read that "Jesus, rising up very early in the morning, went into a desert place, and there He prayed." Very well, pray in union with Him. Kneel in spirit by His side. See Him there, very close to me, both hands clasped, the eyes closed, the body bent forward slightly, motionless, supporting itself, perhaps, by leaning against a rock. Everything is very peaceful out here in this desert place, and as I look upon Jesus, His reverence cannot but impress me, and His evident absorption in His sacred occupation cannot but awaken a desire in myself to pray like Him.

So I turn to Him and say, quite quietly: "Jesus, teach me to pray." That ought not to present any great difficulty in the circumstances, and if it comes from the heart it is a magnificent prayer. Perhaps I repeat it slowly a second time, and a third, and a fourth. I am drawn to continue to keep looking at Him, the praying Christ, and learn from His example how I too am to pray. Excellent. We have seen how the saints insist on remaining wherever I find fruit. If that one picture occupies my period of prayer, and occasionally I say to Him from my heart: "Jesus, teach me to pray," I may take it that I have done well with my mental prayer. I have not, it is true, been faithful to my fixed formulas, and there may be some who will feel a pang of regret for the omission, but the soul's realization will deepen if it does but persevere on lines like these. There will be less sacrifice of depth to surface.

This may be taken as a sample of the sort of thing we mean by mental prayer. Of course there will be times of dryness and weariness when no thoughts will come. Nevertheless, to keep at it is itself a prayer, for I go down on my knees to pray, not to enjoy sweetness and consolation, nor to look upon Jesus transfigured on Tabor. I go to prayer for one purpose only—to give glory to my God. If that be secured by dryness and hardship, it matters not at all about the dispositions of the insignificant creature, provided the struggle does but contribute somewhat to the glory of the great Creator. There is matter for endless meditation in what the evangelist writes about the prayer of Gethsemani: "Being in an agony, He prayed the longer."

Excellent books abound which will show me how to pray in this manner. If, some while before we approach the time and the place for prayer, we can read slowly over a passage in one of these, upon which we propose to meditate, it should help enormously. In a matter so important as my mental prayer, fraught as it is with immense graces for myself and for the souls of others, I may not leave anything to chance. "Before prayer prepare thy soul and be not as a man that tempteth God."

There are endless subjects for mental prayer in the life of Our Divine Lord, in the scenes of our Lady's life, in the words of wisdom and power that fell from the lips of Christ. We have just read about His prayer and tried to learn from it how to pray ourselves. In the same way I could kneel on Calvary at His bleeding feet. I could stay with Him as He sits on the brow of the hill preaching to the multitudes who look upon Him spellbound, and I could ask Him to teach me. I could visit Mary's simple home at Nazareth at that stupendous moment when Gabriel comes to her on his sublime embassy. I could place myself in the cave at Bethlehem with Mary on my left, and Joseph on my right, and the shivering little Infant on the straw before our eyes. Read over the scene beforehand, or even while I am actually trying to pray. Next place myself in the place described in my book, and try to speak with the simplicity and directness of a little child to the persons I find there. So there is no great mystery about mental prayer, and it is by no means the exclusive privilege of priests and religious.

All that we have been advocating assumes, of course, that we are in earnest about trying to arrive at that appreciation of the supernatural with which this chapter is concerned. For this, we must again insist, it is imperative that we find time to withdraw from the crowd, and, in the desert place, face to face with Jesus Christ, to think His thoughts and learn His ways. This *can* be done, even in the most rushed life in this age of bustle. It will often mean a choice between a period apart with Him, or a picture, or a game of golf, or a chat with a neighbor, or a novel or newspaper, or a listen-in to your radio, or jaunt in the car, or an extra half-hour in bed. It will mean that you must sternly insist that your period of prayer is sacrosanct, that it will always get the preference. Constant contact with Our Lord and divine things is bound to effect a radical change of outlook on life. We begin to see life as Jesus sees it, to think and judge about life as He thinks and judges. We make it our one aim to be what He wants us to be, and do what He wants us to do. This is true perspective. This is to regard the supernatural as being, what unquestionably it is, the most important thing of all.

But when everything is said and done, it is only God Who can bring about the increase. We can place the dry wood on the altar but only He can give the consuming fire from heaven. We can sow the seed in the soil but only He can send the refreshing rains to make the seed take root and bring forth fruit. In human problems we arrive at convictions for the most part by relying on the sound opinions and judgments of prudent men. But in the sphere of the supernatural the light comes, no doubt, from our own painstaking efforts, but also from a loving God Who sees our efforts and never allows Himself to be outdone in generosity, He deigns to give such a faithful soul an occasional flash of truth. These flashes become more frequent and of longer duration, according as the soul keeps perseveringly to its program, till there results a habitual frame of mind, a habitual way of seeing and judging all things from the standpoint of the supernatural. "Let that mind be in you," writes St. Paul, "which also was in Christ Jesus."

The soul acquires, through constant living close to Christ, His outlook on life. Such an outlook gives insight into the purpose of life, an instinct for right and wrong, a very clear perception of the hollowness of much upon which men set their hearts and expend years of time and energy trying to achieve. This is to have the mind of Christ. This is to have a true sense of proportion. This is the perspective which the following chapters will endeavor to help us to acquire.

II. Stating the Problem

"God takes note of our least services with supreme exactitude; if it were only to raise our eyes to heaven to think of Him, there is no fear of His leaving this act unrewarded." —St. Teresa, *Way of Perfection*, chapter 24.

1. What the Experts Say

It is good to have an expert near you if you have a problem to solve. You wake up one morning with an acute pain in your side. You do not want to worry the rest of the family by talking about it too much, so for an hour or two you say nothing and try to carry on as if everything was as usual. But by midday the agony is no longer endurable and you have to tell. Your wife or husband or father or mother or child insist on your calling in the doctor and following whatever instructions he sees fit to give. He is the expert, you see.

Or a friend comes to visit you, and, while you are chatting, his attention is attracted by a picture hanging over there on the wall opposite to where he is sitting. He asks you to allow him to examine it more closely. He goes across the floor and stands looking intently for three or four minutes in silence. "Now I may be mistaken," he says, as he sits down again, "but my impression is that in that picture of yours you possess a most valuable work of art."

If you consider that there is even a remote chance that his surmise is correct what will you do about it? Why, of course, you will at once consult an expert, some man who knows about painting all that there is to be known, and you will believe him unquestioningly. If he assures you that your picture is a real old master, worth thousands of dollars, you rub your hands with glee; if he smiles good-naturedly and tells you it is only a very inferior imitation, your face drops; but in either case you take him at his word.

If the schoolboy cannot unravel his passage of Cicero, he will discuss it with his teacher, an expert professor of Latin. If you are looking for sound advice about an important business venture, if you need accurate information as to the quickest way to send a letter or a package through the mail, if you are anxious to make certain of the hour your bus or train departs or arrives, if your car breaks down and you cannot find out why, if you want to estimate the value of a house you contemplate buying, you know exactly what to do. You will seek out the expert, the man who can give you professional information at first-hand, and you will obey his directions with implicit confidence in whatever he tells you.

Now the supreme task laid on the shoulders of every man walking across the stage of time is to live the kind of life he is put here to live. "The wisdom of a discreet man is to understand his way." For, as we shall soon see, life may not be frittered away in pursuance of one's whims. Life is a tremendously important affair in which there are at stake issues of such overwhelming consequence as to leave us baffled when we try to express them, and stammering before our task like children who cannot master the difficult page.

Why am I here? What is life for? Self-appointed experts abound to supply all the answers. Look at this man whose heart and soul are centered on one ideal, to make money, and still more money. He has a farm, or a factory, or a business, which is a going concern. Night and day he is excogitating ways and means of pushing his wares, of extending his buildings, of securing supplies of commodities that are rare and expensive, of ingratiating himself into the favor of men possessed of influence to advance his business. Tell him of a good chance that is coming his way of piling up money, advise him to make contact with a city magnate who seems disposed to help him, and watch the glint of pleasant anticipation in his eyes, and listen to his quick eager questions and proposals, and you will not long remain in doubt that the man before you regards life from one angle only. For him it is an opportunity to make money. For him this standard determines its success or its failure.

There are centuries behind him to prove that wealth has never succeeded in satisfying man's cravings. Instances abound to show that excessive riches have ruined many an otherwise splendid career. Very frequently there is, beyond measure, more contentment in the cabin than in the rich man's palace. Tell these things to your man. Do you think he is listening? Not he. All this he brushes aside and rushes from you in hectic pursuit of his ambition. And so-called experts stand all along his pathway applauding him, clapping him on the back, hailing him as a man of sound common sense.

Or it is the unbridled passion for amusement. "What use is life, anyway," ask the experts this time, "if you do not have a good time? 'Eat, drink, and be merry, for tomorrow we die.' Man has five senses which clamor for gratification. Let them have whatever they look for, and you solve the riddle of life." So before the fascinated gaze of the pleasure-seeker, there is drawn up an attractive program to supply one thrill after another. "Plunge," say those who profess to know. "Plunge into this whirlpool existence and taste the delights of seeing and hearing and eating and drinking and talking and going about. There are deeper pleasures, too, to give you a feeling of very ecstasy. Seize upon them all. Never you mind about my restraint. Forget the ten commandments. Do not worry about a future life which, if it exists at all, can very well afford to look after itself. Have a good time. Why not? What else is life for?"

So the expert takes you by the arm and brings you to the door of this brilliantly-lighted dance-hall, and its lilting music makes your heart beat wild with excitement. He introduces you to the very pleasant people who have gathered here for the night's fun. What do they talk about? They have all plans made for a hiking expedition next Tuesday. Sure you are coming. Over the cocktails they discuss in detail the delightful week they had at the seaside resort. They ask if you have been to the latest film or read the latest best-seller, or have you met that interesting lecturer or heard his advanced views. Arrangements have just been completed for another big dance over the week-end, and they supply you with the list, pat, of the people who will foregather there.

As you sit between the dances resting, puffing a cigarette or sipping your glass, or as you glide about with your partner, you realize, do you not, that this is the solution of life's problem?

When the eye sees everything it craves for, and the ear hears what it loves to hear, and the heart is all of a flutter, is it not difficult to imagine that there can be any other philosophy of life? Young people easily abandon themselves unrestrainedly to this butterfly existence and forget there is any other. They even poke fun at any other solution to the riddle of life. Get all the excitement and thrill you can out of life. Anything else is waste of time, sheer loss of opportunity.

Even those who are no longer young will ape the ways of youth and share youth's views about the solution of the riddle. Veteran females of sixty-five and seventy will attire themselves like girls of twenty; they will make-up and giggle and assume an attitude that is meant to mark them as being frivolous. It is all rather silly, this vain attempt to recapture youth which has departed forever. Why do it then? Because the conviction still persists that there is no other purpose in life than to give the senses whatever they demand.

Before we proceed, be it well noted that it is not our contention that there is necessarily much positive evil in a life such as we have been describing. With that aspect of it we are not concerned at the moment. Our only point is that it is foolish, unsatisfying, superficial; that it leaves its votaries' hearts empty; that no sooner is one thrill passed than it is forgotten and the heart knows no rest till a new one be found. In this ceaseless chase, life is lived and at the end it leaves the mind vacuous, and the heart dry of affection or the power to give it or receive it, and the hands empty—hands which could have been laden with eternal goods if only opportunities had been availed of. No, not positive evil, possibly, but a most saddening and truly lamentable blindness and waste.

Sin, too, comes forward with expert advice. The attractiveness of sin is an admitted fact. Passion that stirs in every human heart is insatiable in its demands. "Very well," whisper your counselors, "yield and be happy, and you have your problem solved. Life is going to be a strait-jacket existence if you try to control those cravings. Far more sensible to take what you long for. Open your eyes and look around you and see the jolly time those men and women have who throw aside all restraint and let things take their course." It is not always so easy to discredit this very alluring theory, either, of the purpose of our life here.

Individuals, too, if you ask them, will proffer other solutions which they have thought out for themselves. A few years ago a priest put the question to an earnest non-Catholic, a chance companion in a railway. "Why am I here in this world? Now that you ask me, I'm not so sure that I can answer right away. But I should say that I am here in order to help my fellowmen. I see around me plenty of poverty, and sickness, and loneliness, and cruelty. If I can do anything to relieve suffering mankind, I think I am living for a worthy purpose."

A Jesuit was teaching a class of pagans in China. "And where is so-and-so today?" he asked, referring to a boy of fifteen who was attending the college. "Father, so-and-so is dead." "Dead! But he was here yesterday in school." "Yes, Father, but he took poison to revenge himself on his mother. He wanted to go to America and she would not allow him." This was told with a dispassionateness that shocks the Christian but is logical enough for the pagan for whom life is a blind alley ending at death.

Over twenty years ago a priest offered himself for work in a leper settlement. His offer was acknowledged at the time, and since then he heard no more about it—until quite recently, when his bishop writes that now it is accepted and he may face the work if he still wishes to do so. The priest begs his friends to pray for him, as he takes up the pen to reply. Will he accept? Of course he will, and does. "Here is a wonderful chance. I must not miss it!" It is comforting to remember that Our Lord has friends like this, in these times when so many walk no more with Him. That letter signs the priest's death-warrant. It will mean complete isolation, nauseating work amid most distressing cases of the dread disease, possible infection for himself, and possibly the death of a leper in a leper settlement. What is life for? That noble priest has found an answer that satisfies him. "Here is a wonderful chance. I must not miss it!"

The visitor was being shown over the monastery, a place where the monks live in very complete solitude and almost continual silence. "We do not know much about what happens outside," said the monk who was guiding him, "but we hear that communism is gaining ground. If it comes this way, we are hoping to be asked to shed our blood for Christ." The visitor inclined to the view, that in that particular district anyhow, the danger was rather remote, and he noted how the monk's face fell at once. What is life for except to grow in the love of Christ, and what greater proof of that love than to die for Him? He was hoping that soon that proof might be asked for, hoping, you will observe, and sadly disappointed to hear even the expression of a contrary opinion.

Why am I here? The question this time is put to a nursing nun in charge of a large cancer hospital. Many of the cases she treats can hardly be less dreadful than what you would find in a leper settlement. "Yes, sister, why are you here? Do you never grow tired of it all, the same dreary round for seven days of the week?" "Well, to tell the truth, I do. But I remember it is all being done for Him. I try to see Him in these poor afflicted people around me, and do for them what I would do for Him if He was in their place."

Some of these solutions are wide indeed of the mark, and there is the test of experience to prove that they do not solve. Others are much nearer the truth, but these express the conclusions which follow, rather than the fundamental answer which goes right to the root of the riddle of life. What then is the ultimate reply to our searching query? What is life for? Why am I here? Some answers have been considered and propounded, but the fundamental one is quite important enough to claim an entire chapter to itself.

2. The Key That Fits

Why am I here? Clearly the question has baffled the self-constituted experts. They leave us stumbling in a land of fog. So at this juncture Jesus Christ steps into the midst of the darkness and contradiction, and, high above the babel of voices, His words proclaim to the world that He can answer with infallible assurance and divine authority.

It would indeed be a pleasure, before listening to His words, first to take His credentials into our hands and examine them and establish firmly the proofs of the claims He makes to be heard and obeyed. But such examination would lead us outside the scope of this book. All we can allow ourselves here is to state that Jesus Christ asserts that He is God, equal in all things to the Eternal Father Who created us, and everything round about us, and upholds all by His divine power. Therefore Christ's word about the riddle of life must be final, once we grant that His claim to be true God is an incontrovertible fact. Elsewhere Catholic writers have provided lucid expositions of Our Lord's claims, and the irrefutable arguments which prove them. Here, we have to assume these and confine our attention to the answer He gives to our question.

He is the divine expert, and His answer briefly is, that man belongs to God and that therefore he has only one business to do in life—to obey God. Man is not here just in order to enjoy himself or amass wealth; still less to wallow like an animal in the gutter of sin. Even the doing of kindly deeds, or the heroic life among lepers, or the service of cancerous patients, or the prayer and penance and solitude of the monk's cell, do not constitute the ultimate purpose of life. These are of value in God's eyes in so far as they are the expression of what He wills to be done, and He wills them because they are objectively right in themselves. To build up a successful business, to provide handsomely for one's family, to enjoy the natural pleasures of life—the sunshine, the beauty of a winter landscape, the companionship of those we love, reading, dancing, movies, radio—such things are laudable and therefore permitted, if, and only if, they are in full accord with God's will.

And why? First because man belongs to God. In order to get some idea of the absolute nature of His claims on man, we propose, in company with the divine expert, to turn over the pages of a most wonderful story. It is the story of *my* soul, a story very easy to forget, for the simple reason that I never see or touch my soul. If I look into a mirror I do not see any soul of mine reflected there. If I have an X-ray taken it will show me much but not a sign of the existence of my soul. Let me subject a living man to the closest scientific analysis, and no scrutinizing of mine will ever reveal to me the sight of his immortal soul. That is why it is so easy to forget I have a soul at all, especially when my lot in life is cast among those who never stop to think about it. Incidentally, it is also the reason why the tendency to become a willing slave of the senses is so strong.

But Jesus Christ is absorbingly interested in the soul of man, and He holds in His hand the key to life's problem, and judges all things with the sure discernment of an expert who is at once divine and all-knowing. A priest, on the day of his ordination, was walking with a friend down the main street of a large city. He realized dimly the immensity of the powers that had been conferred upon him that morning and the privilege that it was to be irrevocably consecrated to the divine work of saving and sanctifying souls. As he walks along he sees the madding crowds, lining up outside the movie houses, rushing for trolleys or buses, buying, selling, chatting together, dining in restaurants, smoking, sipping their drinks, reading their papers or glancing through the pages of an illustrated magazine, and for the most part thinking of everything and anything except the soul, talking about every subject except the soul, interested in innumerable topics but listless about the soul. All this, notwithstanding the fact that the soul is eternal and the things on which they spend so much time are merely passing! What blindness it is! "The wisdom of a wise man is to understand his way." How little they value—many of them at least—those treasures of grace flung open to him, as a priest, so lavishly this very morning!

When Our Lord passed down the streets of His day, or climbed the slopes of the Galilean hills, or stopped on the roadside or at the seashore to speak to the men, or walked into the hamlets of the country people, He too found many of them insensible to the message He longed to teach them. Their eyes were turned towards the earth and Jesus sought to lift them to heaven, but, so immersed were they in what concerned their temporal well-being, that there was no inclination left for His doctrine or the capacity to understand its force and importance. "You will not come to Me," He complained of them, "that you may have life." "What doth it profit a man if he gain the whole world and suffer the loss of his soul? Or what shall a man give in exchange for his soul?" They heard but heeded not. They only passed Him by. So many other things which were really important and pressing claimed their undivided attention, that, at the moment anyhow, they could not spare time to stand here listening to Him, still less to allow His words to sink into the deepest places in their hearts and provide for the remainder of their lives the standard by which to shape their conduct.

Suppose we get away from these crowds, Jesus and I. It is clear that I must learn from Him what I can about my soul, if I am to understand His answer to the riddle of life. Away in some desert place, where all is quiet and conducive to calm consideration, He and I propose to read between us the story of my soul. We open out the volume in which it is written and get ready to study with care the different chapters of a story which, being as it is so personal to me, should hold me enthralled.

When you are reading a book, you usually like to commence at chapter one. So, as soon as Jesus and I are settled down, I want to open out the first chapter also. But presently I make a very surprising discovery. No matter how many pages I turn back, I do not seem, somehow, to be getting any nearer to the beginning. With a puzzled expression I lift up my eyes and look into the face of Jesus Who is bending over me, and gradually the truth begins to dawn upon me. In point of fact there is no beginning to the story of my soul!

No beginning? Suppose I force my mind backwards? Let me wander again, in imagination, amid the earliest memories of childhood—a tiny infant toddling around that room, learning at the cost of innumerable bumps and falls, the difficult art of standing up straight or walking a few steps. Will that bring me to the beginning of my soul's history? Not at all. Nor even if I try to envisage, not myself but my parents before me, in the days of their early childhood; though that be ever so much farther back, it is still removed by an immense distance from chapter one of my soul's story.

Our Lord Himself was once like that too—a little child learning to walk about the floor of Mary's home at Nazareth. Does my soul's story, perhaps, begin here? Still farther back must my mind travel, back past the pages of the Old Testament, past the patriarchs and prophets, past Isaias and Jeremias and Ezechiel, past the garden of Eden, and the creation of Adam and Eve, past the angels, past the beginnings of heaven and hell and land and sea, back so far that the mind almost reels in the effort to force itself. Finally it comes upon God, the ever blessed and adorable Trinity, "reaching from end to end mightily and disposing of all things sweetly." Only God. As yet there are no angels or men, no time, no created light, no birds in the air nor fishes in the sea, nothing—only God in His eternity.

There, in eternity, God is thinking about *my* soul! There He plans to create, on a definite day and at a given moment, this soul of mine. Why did He plan? Because, perhaps, He needed me, or at any rate could need me when the time would arrive to call me forth from nothingness? Not so. For eternity God lives in ineffable bliss, the Father knowing the infinite perfections of the Son, the Son knowing the infinite perfections of the Father, and, Father and Son knowing in this way, expressing between them an act of infinite mutual love which is the Spirit of love, the third adorable Person. God plans to create me, simply because He is good, and goodness wants to share with others the good things itself possesses.

Name any perfection that can be named and you find it in this wonderful Being, God. It is in Him in so absolute and complete a manner that He constitutes its very essence and is Himself its source and fountainhead. "One only is good, God." In God is the fullness of life. In God is the fullness of knowledge. In God is the fullness of love, of power, of wisdom, of strength. The reason God plans to create this soul of mine is, that He may pour into it a share of these marvelous perfections. My soul will be a capacity to contain some of God's life, some of God's love, of God's knowledge, of God's power and strength and wisdom. This is His plan, devised in eternity, and the reason He makes it is that God is love and love longs to give of its goodness to others. "Yea, I have loved thee with an everlasting love."

Have you ever sat down to discuss with an architect or an artist a scheme you have cherished for a long time? You want a new house built, or a statue erected, or you tell him about a picture you saw once in Paris or Rome, of which, from the description you offer, you would like him to reproduce a copy as best he can. Some weeks later he returns and presents you with a rough plan, just to give you an idea of how the work is progressing and get your opinion. You spread it out flat on your table and both of you sit down to consider it in detail. With the tip of his pencil he indicates various points to show how he has tried to meet your wishes. But you are dissatisfied on the whole. He must go back home and draw up another plan, and perhaps a third and a fourth. He is, to be sure, more successful now, but after all, your building or your statue or your picture is going to last a long time and you want none but the best. When finally he turns up at your house with his sixth or seventh attempt, your eyes glisten with pleasure. "Well done! You have got it this time. This is the one we select. This is our preference. Build or paint according to this design and we shall be delighted with the result. As for the other plans, you can scrap them; put them in the fire or your waste-basket."

When God makes His plan in eternity, there arises before His divine mind, not one or two or a hundred possible creatures whom He might call into existence. He sees as it were spread out before Him an *endless infinite number* of such possible creatures. (In parenthesis we have to remind ourselves that this is to speak in our own human way, for no change is possible in the changeless God. He *is* making this plan in eternity; He never *began* to make it; it *is* in His divine mind always.) There is, then, an infinite number of creatures from whom He might select, in order to give some of them the marvelous gift of life and with it the power to share in His divine perfections. Here He selects; here He rejects. Back there in His eternity I see Him today, very deliberately placing His finger on one such possible creature and I hear the Blessed Trinity declare that this is the creature whom they prefer. To be preferred by God, and preferred before an infinite number of others who are rejected, who never will share in the divine life—to whom is this stupendous privilege accorded? If the plan is astonishing to contemplate, the answer to my query is overpowering. *I* am God's choice. In eternity He prefers *me*. From eternity the thought of my soul is in His mind; there never was a moment that He does not remember me. From eternity He decides to give to me this wonderful gift of life, with its possibilities of growth according to His plan. Why? "Wit it well," writes Mother Juliana. "Wit it well—love was His meaning."

This stupendous plan, conceived by God in eternity, becomes a reality in time. God decides that at a given moment He will call me forth from nothingness and that I shall obey His summons. That moment arrived a certain number of years ago—eighteen or twenty or fifty or seventy. Having decided upon it from eternity, my Creator, as soon as that moment strikes, fashions with His own omnipotent hands this soul of mine. My body, which also comes ultimately from God, I received from my parents according to the laws of His Providence. But my soul He creates Himself. It will be His own special handiwork. Whether it be possible or not for God to give to another the power to create, in point of fact He never has actually done so. It is as if He would guard this power as His own special privilege. Straight from His hands, then, my soul comes forth, the masterpiece of God's fashioning. He infuses it into my body and the person I now know myself to be begins to exist.

There is chapter one, the first page of my soul's story, written in eternity. It is well calculated to make me think profoundly and to stir my heart with a deep sense of abiding gratitude. It might be well worth my while to cease reading further for a few minutes in order to give this first chapter time to sink into the soil, for it is a seed that should bring forth fruit a hundredfold.

3. The Last Chapter

Sometimes little children grow restless while reading a story, especially if the story is particularly exciting. They do not have the patience to wade through the chapters, so they skip to the concluding pages in order to find out at once how all is going to end. Perhaps we may allow ourselves to imitate them in this, as we sit here, far removed from the haunts of men, face to face with Jesus Christ, looking now at the book open on our knees and now at Him to instruct us in its mysterious contents. What then is to be the end of my soul's story? This time I proceed to turn the pages in the other direction in order to get at the concluding one, and once again a surprising discovery awaits me. For, just as I found that the story had no beginning, so now I learn that there is no final chapter, or rather that the last chapter will never end.

No end to the story of my soul? I close the volume, keeping my finger in the place I saw last for I shall want to refer to it again in a few minutes. I look up into the eyes of Jesus questioningly, and, with His wonted condescension, He prepares to explain. He lifts up both hands and draws back a veil, the veil separating earth from heaven, and bids me look. Here is the last chapter, the reward prepared for this soul of mine as soon as ever the journey is finished here. "To some of My saints," He seems to say, "I have given a glimpse of the happiness awaiting the soul in heaven, and, as a result of even this momentary flash, they were intoxicated with joy."

"I reckon," cries out St. Paul, "that the sufferings of this present time are not worthy to be compared to the glory to come that shall be revealed in us. For that which is at present light and momentary of our tribulation, worketh for us, beyond measure exceedingly, an eternal weight of glory." To possess God, to be able to rest in the unshakable assurance that no power on earth or in hell can take Him from me, or endanger the security of my hold upon Him; to contemplate, no longer in a glass darkly but face to face, the splendors of the Godhead—the ineffable purity; the ocean of infinite love; the knowledge He has of all things past and present and future and of what would have happened in other circumstances; the vast power of God, sustaining all, ordering all things sweetly; the ravishing beauty of God, a fleeting sight of which, vouchsafed to men here below, was enough to set their hearts burning within them, enough to change the sweet things of earth into bitterness and unreality; to know with a certainty that excludes all possibility of doubt that this God, being Who He is, gives Himself to me, being what I am, what I see and understand myself to be; that He bridges the wide chasm between His own essential Being and my nothingness, and actually deigns to assure me of His personal love of me, and His craving for a return of love from me, the thing He has fashioned; eternity with God, with such a God, this is the last chapter in the story of my soul; the last chapter, but not the end, for no scribe will ever be found to place the final full stop.

What a mockery is language when it grapples in this hopeless manner with the task of expressing the truth about my soul! Even St. Paul throws down his pen in despair. "Eye hath not seen, nor ear heard, neither hath it entered into the heart of man to conceive, what things God hath prepared for them that love Him." "How insipid this world grows to me," cried St. Ignatius of Loyola, "when I lift up my eyes and look at heaven!"

Heaven—but what *is* heaven? Nobody can give a full answer, but, with the divine expert to guide us, we may at least attempt a few halting, stammering sentences. First of all then, heaven is a state the *raison d'être* of which is to inundate the soul with happiness. Just as hell is terrible to contemplate precisely because it exists only to punish, so much the thought of heaven stir up hope and joy, because, were there no souls to make happy, heaven would have no purpose to fulfil. It would be like a sumptuous banquet without guests, an artist's masterpiece with nobody to appraise it, a delightful melody being played with nobody to listen.

In the planning and construction of heaven, the divine builder employed *omniscience, omnipotence,* and *infinite love.*

An all-knowing God, to speak once more of God in the incorrect and inadequate terms necessary for our limitations, conceived the idea of creating a place which would have only one object—to give happiness. Because He is all-knowing, He understands in His omniscience just exactly what is suited to this plan He has formed. Were we to set ourselves to think out such a problem we would necessarily make mistakes. In every age man has been trying to build up an earthly paradise, and the result has been one ignominious failure after another. Why? Because man does not know—although he is persuaded he does—what will certainly contribute to his own happiness. He is the sport of extravagant fancies; his knowledge of what is good for him is cramped and altogether incomplete.

But God is not hampered like that. When His divine mind exercises itself upon the task of thinking out a place of perfect happiness, He enjoys the fullest possible understanding of what to include and what to exclude. Everything that would militate, even in the least degree, against perfect happiness must be rigorously excluded, and God knows exactly, because He is omniscient, what things these are. Included in the plan must be everything that would contribute, in a greater or lesser degree, to man's well-being, and again omniscience understands perfectly what these are. In this way we conceive of the all-knowing God thinking about the work He had set Himself, so that the resultant idea in the divine mind must express the very acme of unalloyed happiness.

Many a man makes plans in his mind which he never can hope to see actualized. He can form a picture of a beautiful country home; he can visualize a magnificent pageant; he can summon up in his imagination ideas of what he would do if he inherited a large fortune. But all the time he knows that this is idle dreaming. It will never be possible for him to see these plans exist, except on paper.

But when the all-knowing God ordained in eternity to execute His scheme about heaven, He could not be hampered in this way. For He is not omniscient only, but omnipotent too. So, when He began to construct that place of perfect happiness, there was nothing capable of hindering His work. A man may be held up in his building by lack of funds, but at God's disposal there is infinite supply to draw from. A man may have to deal with workmen who disagree, he may be impeded by shortage of material, but no obstacle of this kind, or of any kind, can get in the way of a God Who is omnipotent. His omnipotence, then, calls into existence the place of perfect happiness conceived by His omniscience. What a place of ravishing delights it must be, and how Christ, Whose eyes were ever fixed upon it, must have longed to make all men follow His gaze!

There is nothing more congenial to parents than to wish for the contentment of their child and to do all they can to secure it. It is a source of sheer delight to a parent to watch the light of joy in the child's eyes when it comes upon the pleasant surprise prepared for it by the love of the parent. In later life distance may separate parent and child, but, where ideal relations exist between them, distance serves only to weld all the stronger the ties of affection. With what eagerness the parent looks forward to the child's homecoming, and how anxiously the child counts the days and the weeks that still intervene until the great moment of reunion!

Our Lord's revelation of almighty God teaches us that He is

our Father—"our Father Who art in heaven." Now if an earthly father loves to make his child happy, can we not well argue to the same trait in the heavenly Father? So all that we have seen Him do in the laying out of heaven, in which omniscience and omnipotence combined, was done with a great love for His child surging up in that Father's heart. "Wit it well—love was His meaning." For after all, to know what to do and to have the power to do it, might avail little if the knowledge and power were not supported by love. And Jesus, the divine expert, assures us of this love. "Fear not, little flock, for it hath pleased the Father to give you the kingdom." Having conceived and planned and executed heaven, an infinitely-loving Father flings it wide open to His children and bids them enter and enjoy the things He has prepared for them. "Possess the kingdom prepared for you from the foundation of the world. Enter into the joy of your Lord."

That little word *possess* is worth noticing. It would seem to imply that absolute security of tenure which we have considered already. Let the child of God once enter the portals of heaven, and there is absolutely nothing that can ever, by any sort of accident or possibility, jeopardize his possession. In this life there is no such guarantee. Today a man may be in excellent health and before the week is ended he may be hanging between life and death. Today he may be in easy circumstances, and in six months hence he may be reduced to beggary. But, let him once enter heaven, and behind him on this earth things may go all wrong—there may be wars and rumors of war, there will be poverty and strife and misery and sin, there may be earthquakes, and disasters at sea and on land and in the air—but, *whatever happens,* it is sheer impossibility that that man could lose the ecstatic joy that inundates his soul on going into heaven today. "*Possess* the kingdom."

Jesus, the divine expert, assures us of the absolute truth of all this. As the Object all-satisfying to the eager soul God gives Himself, His fatherly, familiar, intimate presence and companionship, a share in His very life, to be the source of the soul's inexhaustible bliss. No wonder that Our Lord Who saw this always, Who was ever looking on this Beatific Vision, yearned to make all men let in this light of heaven into their dull minds.

To many people, especially perhaps in these times of ours, this may read like a pious fairy tale. Even to us Catholics the story is so stunning as to seem too good to be true. Moreover, the thought of it is crushed out when we move constantly, as often we must, among those whose only paradise is on earth. Besides, life is so full of trials and disappointments that it is hard to lift up our thoughts and desires to a heaven, which, at such times anyhow, seems remote indeed and unreal. For all that, we know in Whom we trust. Incredible though the fairy-tale may seem to be, we know it is most marvelous of all in this, that every word of it is the truth. For it is the solution given by Jesus Christ, Who neither can deceive nor be deceived.

And, as Jesus Christ stands in our busy streets and watches the crowds go up and down, can I now be surprised any more at the expression of pity on His face as He regards them all, or nearly all? So long have their eyes been fixed on the glitter of tinsel that they cannot now discern between the real and the counterfeit. So long have they listened to the lies dinned into their ears by the self-constituted experts that they give no hearing to One Who is divine, and divinely-commissioned to solve the riddle of life.

As for myself—why am *I* here? He has not yet given me the full answer, for all we have done so far is to try to read the opening chapter of my soul's story and the last one. What about the intervening pages? They will occupy us in our next section—for the most part, though not exclusively.

4. The Pages In Between

My soul came from God because God freely chose to create my soul. My soul will go back to God at a moment determined by Him from eternity. It is worthy of note that in all this wonderful scheme of things God did not consult me. He exercises over me the rights of a lord and master whose authority is absolute. He did not create me and then ask me if I would like to continue in existence. He does not ordinarily reveal to us the hour decided upon by Him when we shall deliver back our souls into His hands. When that moment comes, I shall have to yield instant and unquestioning obedience to His summons. Another summons I might disobey or put off—from my employer, from an importunate visitor, from a salesman. But when it is God Who calls me, I drop everything else from my hands and go.

From all of this it follows, with irresistible logic, that I belong to God. He owns me by every sort of right and title. My very existence is His gift, my continuance in life goes on because He sustains me from one moment to the next. Did He forget about me for a split second I must instantly lapse into the nothingness from which He drew me forth. Did He take away His supporting hands I must inevitably fall. All of which goes to illustrate the absolute nature of His rights over me. I am nothing and He gives me existence. I am tending to dissolution and must surely return to my nothingness only that He continues to sustain me. I am facing death and it will summon me, at the time and place and manner ordained by God, and at that time, and at that place, and in that manner, I shall obey.

Why am I here? What is life for? Clearly it must be to do whatever He wants me to do. As His claims upon me are absolute, so my one business is to find out His will in my regard and then spend myself in its perfect accomplishment. "The Lord thy God thou shalt adore, and Him only shalt thou serve."

If you paint a beautiful picture and give it as a present to your friend you will rightly be pained if you discover he has chopped it up to make firewood. If my watch gets out of order and you, at the cost of much trouble and time, take it to pieces and succeed in mending it, and you hand it back to me in perfect condition, you will be indignant if I give it to a three-year-old child to play with. If you sow in your garden a tree that is valuable and rare and you are keenly interested in its development, and, just when it begins to thrive I come out and wantonly pull it up by the roots, you will follow after me and hotly demand an explanation.

And God, Who has created my soul in love, Who plans about

my soul from eternity, Who has designed such a marvelous destiny for my soul, Who has reserved for His own creative hands the fashioning of that soul, shall God be indifferent to the use or misuse I make of His gift?

I must do God's Will, because I am His property, His servant, His creature. I must do God's Will because of the stupendous love He has shown toward me, because of His concern about me and what I do or fail to do with my immortal soul, the masterpiece He has entrusted to my frail keeping.

I *must.* Yes, that is correct. God has a perfect right to tell me what to do, to order me to do it, and even to force me to obey against my will. He presents me with His will in the ten commandments, and He might in all fairness say to me: "Here are your orders. Fulfil these to the letter. I am your master and lord whom you are to obey."

Earthly masters normally act in this manner and everybody considers that in doing so they are quite just and fair. You hire a man to plow your field or bring home the hay or the wheat, and you certainly will object strongly if he spends most of the day leaning leisurely over the fence discussing the news with the passers-by. You promptly tell him that he *must* obey, that he *must* spray those potatoes, or cut that wheat, or mow that meadow. That was the purpose for which you engaged him, and if he continues to neglect the task assigned him you will soon find another to take his place and do the work instead.

Or you advertise for a maid to help you with the housework. You will by no means be satisfied if, when you tell her to wheel baby out into the park, or sweep the stairs, she settles down instead in your best drawing-room armchair and proceeds to light a cigarette and peruse a novel.

Now God would act quite justly if He dealt with us in the same way, indeed with a justice immeasurably more reasonable than the owner of the farm or the mistress of that house. But, as we shall see at greater length on another page, He does not force our obedience, for one of the most precious gifts with which He has endowed us is our free will. What He wants from us, His children as well as His creatures, is that voluntary submission to His will which is given from the motive of love.

But suppose a man refuses to give that which he is bound to give by a thousand titles? Suppose he flagrantly disobeys, making complete topsy-turveydom of God's plan for his soul? For being free, he can do so. God, Who is infinite justice as well as infinite love, owes it to Himself to see to it that His claims will be fully vindicated. Hence if that man or woman refuses obedience which justice demands and dies in that perverse state of mind, God must exact in eternity the penalty that fits the crime. Since the servant in time refused to meet his obligations, it is only fitting that in eternity the supreme and absolute claims of God be satisfied. Hence the soul which on earth freely prefers mortal sin to the service of God, and dies still preferring it, must expiate the crime in hell. It must now give a forced obedience. If it would not obey out of love, as a child of the heavenly Father, the balance must now be restored by obedience through constraint, to an inexorable judge of infinite justice.

As the divine expert looks at life He does not minimize either the fact of hell or the appalling nature of its sufferings. God's claims are absolute. "The Lord thy God thou shalt adore, and Him only shalt thou serve." It is very easy, today more than ever, to shut one's eyes to the terrible alternative to this service. Many men make merry over the notion of hell and toss it aside as a sort of bogey. It is a simple matter to formulate specious arguments against even its very existence. "If *I* had a child whom I loved, and that child offended *me,* I certainly would not send that child to hell. . . . It is silly to think that an offence against God, which takes only a minute or two to commit, should have to be atoned for by punishment that is never-ending. . . . Who ever came back to tell us there is a hell, anyway? . . ." In such wise do men argue against hell, and admittedly they can work up a case that at first sight looks fair enough. Certainly, too, it would be a great convenience to a person who wants to persevere in his career of sin if he could succeed in disabusing himself and others of all belief in even the existence of a hell, or at least an eternal hell.

But he must first dispose of the clear and reiterated teaching of Jesus Christ, the divine expert Whose credentials to give the answer to the riddle of life have already been considered. It is true that Our Lord was the most lovable and kindest of men. It is true that every sinner, no matter how black his record, was received by Him with wide-open arms, provided he repented truly of his crimes. Indeed He was dubbed by His enemies the friend of sinners, and, so far from denying the accusation, He gloried in the charge and it called forth two of the most beautiful of His parables—the Prodigal Son, and the Good Shepherd. It is true that little children loved Him, this Jesus of Nazareth, that they wanted to follow Him everywhere.

Because these things are true, because He is habitually so gentle and so restrained, when from the lips of such as He there fall weighty warnings about hell, and His eyes flash fire as He speaks, so moved is He by the fearful emphasis He wants to lay on His message, we realize all the more the urgency of paying heed to His words. "Fear not them who can destroy the body, and after that have no more that they can do. But fear Him Who, after He has destroyed the body, can condemn both body and soul into hell. Yea, I say to you, fear Him." And again: "If your right eye scandalize you" (that is, if it lead you to commit sin), "pluck it out and cast it from you. It is better to enter into life blind than, having two eyes, to be cast into hell, where their fire is not extinguished and their worm does not die. And if your right hand or foot scandalize you, cut it off and cast it from you. It is better to enter into life maimed than, having two hands or two feet, to be cast into hell, where their fire is not extinguished and their worm does not die."

Our limited minds may be incapable of grasping the justice of eternal punishment. Our sceptical age may sneer at the arguments which support it. But, whatever be the case we try to bolster up in favor of disbelief, it goes down in face of the definite teaching of Jesus Christ, the infallible Son of God. *He,* at least, had no sort of doubt about the fearful nature of the punishment, about its existence and its eternity, and He can neither deceive nor be deceived. Man belongs to God. He has most solemn and sacred obligations to do God's Will, therefore. These he can sidestep, if he wishes, for a time, but justice demands imperatively that the balance be restored hereafter. God is a God of justice Who owes it to Himself to vindicate those supreme rights which man, in his arrogance, has dared to despise.

"Thou *shalt* serve." If it be not the devoted and willing service of a child here on earth and hereafter in heaven, it must necessarily be the forced obedience of a servant, not because God is cruel, but because man has freely abused and misused his free will; not because God is unjust but precisely because He is infinite justice.

One sees, too, in these warnings of Our Divine Lord about hell yet another indication of His love for us. They are indeed intended by Him to make men look into the depths of their souls and scrutinize their consciences and put their accounts right with God before it is too late. But does He not also reveal here the love of His Sacred Heart? If a friend of yours was unknowingly driving his car towards a yawning abyss you would certainly cry out loud in warning—because of your love for your friend. Jesus, the divine expert, looks at the souls He loves, the souls with the destiny He has already unfolded for us. But there is terrible danger ahead; there is that yawning abyss, and all that loves in Jesus Christ lifts up its voice in tones of anxiety for the welfare of those He loves.

The mother will snatch her child from the pathway because she sees a truck coming that threatens the life of her child. The father will risk all he holds most precious in order to beat away the wild beast prowling around the tent where his infant son lies sleeping. And Our Lord, Whose love of souls is throbbing within Him, will He keep silence, or can He refrain from warning, when He sees the imminent danger?

It would be a very sad mistake, however, to focus our attention exclusively on the motive of fear and justice. Fear is an emergency motive to fall back upon only "if ever my love of God should grow cold." For God is not merely master and lord. He is also the most loving and most tender of fathers. What loving father ever wants to have from his child a stilted and strained obedience, rendered only because the child trembles with fear of the punishment that surely awaits disobedience? God lays His yoke upon us, but it is a yoke that is sweet. He asks us to carry a burden, but in the same breath He assures us it is a light one. So He would have us accept it, not with a scowl on our faces such as may be endured in a serf, but with a smile of gladness with which a loving son welcomes the opportunity of pleasing so loving a Father.

If a bird is imprisoned behind a window-pane you will not find it too easy to set him free. He will resist your well-intentioned efforts and dash himself violently against the unseen obstacle. He is seeking for freedom, the environment natural to him, but he does not understand that if he is to attain to it, he must first submit to you. He must allow you to take him into your hands, bear him to the portion of the window that is open and let him speed forth out into the sunlight.

Your only desire is to guide that little creature into the liberty he longs to possess and you must insist that he permit himself to be so guided. It is true that the sinner struggles against God's will because he fails to understand that to serve God is to reign. God does not ask for our obedience in order to curb or restrict unduly. His commandments are like signposts along the road that leads to the heavenly country, placed on the route by a loving Father Who desires to consult man's best interests. Let a man wander as he wills up and down that road, and he may vaunt his liberty, he may boast that he is doing just what he likes, but everybody with sense sees clearly that he is deceiving himself. Not that way does true freedom lie, no more than for the bird dashing itself against the pane of glass in its vain struggle to escape.

It gives much pleasure to a father to reward generously the child's obedience, even though he might have reasonably exacted that obedience in strictest justice. Our Heavenly Father, as we have seen, is like that. "Eye hath not seen, nor ear heard, neither hath it entered into the heart of man to conceive, what things God hath prepared for them that love Him." He does indeed employ the motive of fear, and it is a truly salutary one, but only when the motive of love is in danger of failing. To foster that love He holds out a reward surpassing great, even here on earth. For, just as submission to you leads the little bird out into the light and glory of the summer sun, so, even here, does obedience to God's will secure for the soul a measure of deepest peace to which the votary of the world is an utter stranger. The peace of God, surpassing all understanding, is not only unknown to the worldling and the sinner, but it is incomprehensible to him. He cannot understand the contentment with so little, the rejoicing even in the midst of hardships and persecutions, the joyousness surrounding the death-bed—things which are the ordinary concomitants of a life lived in faithful obedience to the will of God.

But that peace of soul in this life is the merest foretaste of what lies ahead. Times there will be when even the dark land of exile seems flooded with sunlight. Moments will come for that faithful soul, perhaps before the Blessed Sacrament, when the truth of the story we are reading with Jesus begins to dawn, and the realization that it is all indeed so, will inundate the heart with a joy not of this earth. The fact of God's eternal love, the assurance that the soul is indeed on the road that leads straight to Him, the vivid truth that very soon it will be no longer exile but home forever, the thought that the trials of yesterday and the day before, the months before and the years, are all gone and that the soul will never again have to endure these, when things like these break in on the mind with fresh forcefulness, the result must be a deep joyousness that cannot be ruffled or disturbed by what is merely of the earth, earthly.

If even here there can be such solid comfort, even here where we understand so dimly and see the viewpoint of the divine expert only through a glass darkly, where sin so often masquerades in the garb of happiness and the service of God seems at times so irksome, if even here, in spite of all these handicaps we can still rise at times to heights of great spiritual joy, what then must it be to be at home with God, where all these marvelous truths are not believed merely, but where they are clearly seen and securely held in possession?

The first chapter and the last I have seen in the story of my soul. The intervening pages are being filled in each day I live. The first chapter is entitled: God's Choice of My Soul, and the last is called: The Final Destiny of My Soul. In between the two covers the leaves are being fitted in, and each slips into its place quite naturally and logically if each day is a sincere attempt to yield perfect obedience of God's will.

You will sometimes be told that man is placed on this earth to save his soul. Perhaps the statement needs qualification. Man is not placed on earth primarily in order to save his soul but to do God's will. If he is faithful in doing this, his salvation follows as a matter of course. "Man was created," writes St. Ignatius, "to praise, reverence, and serve God, *and by this means* to save his soul."

5. Jesus and the Will of God

Part of the reason why Our Lord came into this world was to serve as a perfect model by which to direct our conduct. "Learn of Me," He says; and another time: "I have given you an example, that, as I have done, you should do also." These latter words, it is true, He made use of to inculcate the lesson of humility after He had washed the feet of His disciples, but they may also be regarded as capable of a wider and more general application to all the events of one's daily life.

He has shown me that I am placed by God in this world, that I am to return soon to Him, and that therefore my one business is to find out God's will in my regard and spend every moment of my time in fulfilling it. By this means I am to attain to that reward exceeding great which my heavenly Father has prepared. This is the gist of what the divine expert has been explaining to me by way of answering the riddle of life.

If now He comes forward and points to Himself as a perfect model whom I am to imitate, it would be most reasonable to expect that in His teaching and example He Himself will lay much stress on the importance of doing God's will. For this end I am here and He offers to show me the way; therefore it is to be expected that He will throw much emphasis on this fundamental principle.

He does. First of all, away back in the pages of the Old Testament the prophet foretells the coming of the Messias. And what will be one of the characteristic notes of the Christ by which all men may recognize Him? "In the head of the book," says the prophet, speaking as it were with the lips of Our Lord, "in the head of the book it is written of Me that I should do Thy Will, O God. Then said I: 'Behold I come that I may do Thy will.' " If men were looking for the promised Redeemer let them seek in Him an unqualified acceptance of and obedience to the will of God.

Actually when He did come, Jesus took care never to swerve a hairsbreadth from the path mapped out for Him by the will of that heavenly Father. At least three times in His Life He summed up in a single sentence the aim and object of all He did and taught and said, and each of the three times He pointed to the will of the Father as the great norm which directed all. "The things that are pleasing to Him [My Father], I always do." "I came down from heaven," He says again, "not to do My own will, but the will of Him that sent Me that I may perfect His work." Lastly, when all is nearly over, and He is seated for the last time with "His own" at the supper table, He lifts up His eyes in prayer: "Father, I have finished the work *which Thou gavest Me to do.*" Thus, on Our Lord's own testimony, repeated three times over, His whole life is like a straight line; it is one long act of unquestioning and unqualified obedience to the will of His Father. When death has come, the Apostle remembers this, and in his turn gives his own summary of Christ's life. "He humbled Himself, becoming obedient unto death, even unto the death of the cross."

At a glance then, one sees immediately the importance He attached to the fulfilment of that will. But if we go more into detail in His life, and examine especially the high-points of those thirty-three years, we find Him being most careful again to lay stress on the same principle. Once only in the first thirty years is He recorded to have spoken. One sentence is remembered and written down, out of all He said during that long period. And what does it express? He spoke it to our Lady when she found Him in the temple at the age of twelve. "How is it that you sought Me? Did you not know that I must be *about My Father's business?"*

He comes out of the obscurity of Nazareth when He is thirty and enters upon His life of preaching the gospel. In His first great sermon, delivered on the Mount, to the general multitude, one of the salient points is once more the will of the Father. "Not everyone that saith to Me: 'Lord, Lord' shall enter into the kingdom of heaven, but *he that doth the Will of My Father* Who is in heaven, he shall enter into the kingdom of heaven."

Presently He picks out, from this concourse of people, a little group of men to be trained with special care for the work of spreading His gospel. It is most worthy of note that the very first lesson He impresses upon them is the importance of doing God's will. He had been speaking to the Samaritan woman at the well of Sichar and His Apostles had gone into the town to buy food. On their return they pressed Him to eat but He refused. They wondered, for they knew He had been fasting and He proceeded to explain: "I have meat to eat that you know not. My meat is to do the will of Him that sent me."

In His first defence before His enemies Jesus turns to the same principle. They accuse Him of breaking the sabbath by healing a man on that day. No, He replies, it is no breach of the sabbath, because He is God, and therefore one with the Father Who is Lord of the sabbath.

In Gethsemani Jesus prays that the chalice might pass from Him, but He is careful immediately to add: "Nevertheless not My will but Thine be done." In obedience to that Will He accepts that bitter chalice and empties it to the dregs, and on the cross bows His head in sign of His complete acceptance. "All is finished." He has done all that the Father willed Him to do, and done it perfectly.

So whether we view His life as a whole or in its details, whether we examine His teaching given to others or His own mode of action, we are forced to the same conclusion. Jesus' whole life was governed entirely by God's Will. Whether He remained in the hiddenness of Nazareth or moved about in the midst of men, whether He worked or slipped away into the desert or up the hillside to pray, whether He argued with His enemies, or spoke at His ease to the simple people, or took His twelve apart to instruct them, in short, whether He lived or died, Jesus did all because every detail was just what was most pleasing to His heavenly Father at that moment. "The things that are pleasing to Him I always do." His teaching and His conduct both emphasize the one truth—that man has no reason for being here on earth, except alone to find out what God wants him to do, and having found that out, to bend all his energies to that one task. In this, as in everything else, the divine expert stands before the whole world as the perfect model of mankind. "Jesus began to *do* and to teach." His practice here, as always, is perfectly consistent with His teaching.

6. An Eye to Business

Thus it is clear that reason, and faith, and the example of Jesus Christ, all combine to impress upon me the same philosophy of life. All three provide the same basic principle upon which to raise the structure of a life which will be a success judged by the standards of the divine expert.

At this stage we insert a chapter that may be regarded as an interlude. We want to pause and consider a homely example which will help, it is hoped, to enforce our fundamental principle further. So we suppose that, down our street, about four years ago a new large business house was opened. For weeks before, while the renovation work was in progress, the enterprising business-man had displayed a huge advertisement on the window-front. He informed all and sundry that he was soon to make a start and he begged them, in their own interests obviously, to save their money for the astounding bargains he was going to offer. But he did more. During those weeks of preparation he was most careful to explain all his plans to his friends. He canvassed among the well-to-do and the influential, leaving no stone unturned to win their patronage.

Apparently he has done well, too, for as we pass by this afternoon, we notice that he is already enlarging the premises. The place is all boarded up and a crew of carpenters and builders are busy down there, though the proprietor is careful to tell the world that "business is being carried on as usual during the alterations." It would be a fatal mistake to lose the contacts he has made, or run the risk of missing others.

It is worth our while to drop in. At once the keenness of the man impresses us. The slogan "business as usual," indeed, is evident before we have well reached the interior, and we are not long talking to him before we recognize that he is a live-wire. If we are on terms of intimacy he will tell us, perhaps, about the competition with which he has to contend—lower prices and better value, apparently, offered by other stores in order to draw away his customers. He expatiates on all the help he has got from friends of his who deal here and speak about him to others. He apologizes for the condition of the shop today, covered with dust and shavings, but he invites us to come back in a month's time and see how *chic* everything will be, when once he is out of the workmen's hands. A final evidence of his keenness is his readiness to give us as much of his time as we want, his care to show every mark of civility, and his pleasant smile as he holds the door open and bows us out.

All of which is easily applicable to the one work we have to do in life—the unqualified obedience to God's will.

Just as this business-man has to face competition, so we have to withstand the attacks, repeated and violent, of the world, the flesh and the devil. Opposition only toughens the will that is bent on success, and a man resolved to render to God the willing service of a loving son, is positively glad when he encounters a difficulty. He is sore pressed by a temptation to break his pledge, or to go back, under the guise of some specious pretext, to meet a sinful companion. He knows in his heart and soul that if he does so, he will swerve from the fulfilment of God's will; he will fall into grievous sin. But, because he loves, he welcomes the opportunity of proving his love. "What doth he know that hath not been tried?" When the struggle has passed him by, leaving him perhaps breathless and panting, but still on his feet, he finds that now he experiences a sense of exaltation and rejoices in the testimony of a good conscience. Yes, the fight was worth while. Victory over persistent temptation is sweet indeed.

It was thus that the great Apostle St. Paul hewed his way through the thick of his enemies, and found a deep peace in his soul even when the battle was raging most fiercely. "I am filled with gladness; I rejoice exceedingly in all our tribulations." Loyalty to God's will means war to the knife, but Christ's soldier would not have it otherwise.

That business-man of ours, we remember, took good care to enlist the patronage of the great and the influential. Here, too, we take a page from his book. To secure the courage and the strength required to guide our conduct by our principles, we have at our beck and call all the invincible forces of heaven to help us. It is worth while counting them up on our fingers. First, there is God Himself Who has created my soul, and Who, as we saw, cannot therefore be indifferent as to what I do with such a gift. Then there is Jesus Christ, Who loved me and delivered Himself for me, Who has taken me apart in these pages in order to impress me with an understanding of my value in His sight. There are the angels and the saints, who burn with the desire to promote the glory of their God, and who see clearly the immense glory accruing to Him from the life of even one person who labors to render Him perfect obedience. While they were in this world the saints toiled incessantly to make Him known and loved. Surely when now they see Him in the beauty of the Beatific Vision, when now they understand so much more clearly the enormous possibilities for good in a soul, surely it is fair to argue that now their eagerness to help that soul has increased proportionately. Do we need to insist upon the love of Mary, the mother of God and the mother of men, and her eagerness and readiness to save us from the pitfalls on our way and to lift us up again, if, despite her motherly warning, we fall? "Nobody ever called upon Mary and was not graciously heard by her."

To secure powerful patronage the business-man has to go round and canvass; he has to write letters; he has to advertise and talk up his goods. But all the wealth of heaven is at our elbow. We have only to ask for it in fervent prayer; we have only to steep ourselves in the spirit of prayer and at once all these powerful friends at court use their influence on our behalf.

Next, our shrewd man of business sees to it that his shop is kept spotless. No customer worth while is going to deal with him if the counter is covered with dust, if the windows are dirty and filled with cobwebs, if the man himself is habitually unshaved, with hands always soiled, with clothes that are stained and in tatters. No. He understands well that he and all around him must be spick and span.

Here, too, the man who makes God's Will the law of his life will find a page to ponder for his guidance. He understands that his life must be free, first from all stain of serious sin, but also he will labor to acquire an ever-deepening sense of the hideous nature of even venial sin. He realizes that his soul is God's dwelling-place; the abode of a divine guest. Just as the efficient man of business is careful to have everything spotless upon which the eyes of his patrons will fall, so the man of God has a horror of any stain in his soul, realizing that all is naked and open before the eye of God. He will be most assiduous in removing every trace of cobwebs and every speck of dust, for the simple reason that he understands so well the dignity of his soul in which so great a guest has deigned to make His home. "If any man love Me, My Father will love him, and We will come to him and make Our abode with him." The man of God often recalls this stupendous promise and it is a powerful incentive to him to make no truce with deliberate sin, even venial sin.

A business-man who wants to succeed will be very keen to keep his shop well stocked. In times of emergency he will redouble his efforts, for the very fact that a given article is difficult to procure, ensures that it will bring him a better price. Hence you will hear him speak of his care to keep up his supplies.

And in the spiritual order, what are the "supplies" except the man's stores of sanctifying grace? He knows that if he possesses this treasure he is on the straight road that leads to God, here and hereafter. But he is not going to be satisfied with mere possession; he is always on the watch to increase what he has. So you will see him regular and fervent in his reception of the Sacraments, frequent and persevering in his prayer. Why? Because through prayer and the Sacraments he is adding to his supplies. These are the divinely-appointed means by which grace is borne into his soul.

It is wise in the affairs of this world to keep up your supplies; it is infinitely more wise in the affairs of your immortal soul. It is true that every man who passes out of this world in the state of sanctifying grace will possess God throughout eternity. But, although everyone in heaven will be perfectly happy, not all will be by any means equally happy. One man dies after a life of sin, but on his deathbed he makes a really good Confession; another dies after having watched his opportunities all throughout his life to increase his supplies. He, too, will save his soul, but one may assert that ordinarily his reward will be immeasurably greater than that of the other. He has done God's Will more perfectly, and that, as we have insisted all through, is his only reason for being here.

So our visit to the new premises down street has given us headings, general principles, by which to direct ourselves in our life's task. The shrewd business-man is alert, he misses no chance of securing an order or patronage, he keeps his place spotless, he seizes upon every opportunity of getting in fresh supplies, especially of rare commodities. If men who profess to be earnest followers of Christ were as keen as he, what gigantic strides would be made in the work of extending His kingdom in souls! But today, as in Our Lord's day, it is still true that the children of this world are wiser in their generation than the children of light.

7. "The Sacrament of the Present Moment"

These general principles are excellent, but it remains to see how they can be applied to the needs of our daily lives. Since my only task is the performance of God's will, I have to understand how that will can be made to influence every action of mine, even the most insignificant. And I find an admirable guide in Père de Caussade, a French Jesuit, who wrote a remarkable book entitled, *Self-Abandonment to Divine Providence.**

Poets are fond of pointing out that we live in either the past or the future, rarely in the present. Regrets for the past and its mistakes haunt us; or dreams of pleasant days now gone forever obsess our minds; or else we spend our time building up rosy expectations of good things to come, or we live in a state of dread of possible calamities which may never befall us. And meantime, what becomes of the present moment, which is the only one we can turn to account?

Père de Caussade, at this stage, comes forward with his doctrine about "the sacrament of the present moment." What does he mean? He teaches that the present moment, with all the varying circumstances it brings to different people, is *God's arrangement.* The task of the present moment, or the pleasure of the present moment, or the interruption or obstacle or annoyance of the present moment—the present moment and whatever it brings, he regards as a kind of sacrament, and our task, if we wish to do God's will in every detail, is simply to "receive" this "sacrament" by a ready and loving acceptance of whatever God permits to befall here and now.

How does this work out in practice? Somebody snubs you in the street. He did that because God permitted him to do so. An

* de Caussade, Père, *Self-Abandonment to Divine Providence.* London, Burns Publishing Company, 1934.

intruder comes in to interrupt you when you are busy making up your accounts and when most of all you want to be left alone. You are very keen on the picnic party you have organized for next Thursday, but the rain comes down in torrents and keeps you locked up at home—because God saw fit to send the rain. A letter arrives for you in today's mail. It is scathing in its contents and naturally you are inclined to boil with indignation. But consider, that that letter would never have been written and never sent to you, only that God allowed it. Your work or your children are made the butt of a cynical joke; a cutting remark is passed in your hearing, about the stupidity of your son in college, or a physical defect of your own, or an idiotic line of conduct you took which made you the laughing-stock of everyone who saw you—these things were said through God's permission.

So I am to believe then, am I, that all these acts of ingratitude or harshness are pleasing to God? By no means. Those who perpetrate them may indeed be doing or saying something that is sinful, even grievously so. But "the sacrament of the present moment" shows me clearly that this wrong thing, though evil in itself, is still ordained to a good purpose by God Who foresees it and permits it. By such means He would train the generous soul to the sanctifying habit of sweet and ready acceptance. To recognize God's hand beneath such occurrences and, for this reason to bow to them without a murmur—this is to practise Père de Caussade's teaching. The soul which learns, especially in these and other trying circumstances, the lesson of silent endurance—and for the reason just stated—will grow marvelously in divine love.

And it is not only the hard and unpleasant events of life, little or great, which can be "received" in this way. When God sends the glorious sunshine after weeks of clouds and rain, when a friend you love turns up unexpectedly after ten years of absence, when the postman brings you a letter freighted with good news, or the phone or wire informs you that your friend's critical operation has been a wonderful success, when a loving Lord has deigned to comfort you in prayer and make you realize the fact of His personal love for you, when a soul you have been trying to help proves to be responsive and you hear of a heroic stand he or she has made against a violent temptation—in all such cases, too, the "sacrament of the present moment" is to be "received" with loving gratitude. Here once again is God's hand at work, permitting all, ordaining all, arranging all, in the manner calculated to advance your soul in love and true sanctity.

Whatever be the circumstances of the present moment, they are rich in possibilities, for they come to us from God's hand, and they are grace-laden. Think again how far-reaching is this doctrine. The bus-driver takes you a few hundred yards past your stop, and on a day, too, when the rain is heavy—would you scowl at him and rebuke him so sharply if you recognized God's arrangement in the passing annoyance? You have been trying for twenty minutes to get a call through on the phone. First you dial a wrong number, then the number you want is busy, and finally when you do get through it is to be told that the man you are looking for left the house just five minutes earlier. If you had not made the stupid mistake of dialing the incorrect number, you would just have caught him. All most aggravating—until you begin to see it in the light of Père de Caussade's doctrine. As you come out of the phone booth, you will begin to explain to a friend you meet how exasperated you are and you will go into all the details—but if you see God's hand behind them, perhaps you will begin to talk about the weather! Or you will listen for the seventh time to the story of his funny adventure, and smile or laugh when finally he does get to the point as if you never heard it before. Why? Perhaps Père de Caussade will be able to tell.

Nor would Père de Caussade by any means have us concentrate exclusively on mere submission to what God ordains or permits. There is also the fulfilling of God's will by doing whatever duty is assigned us in the state of life in which He has placed us.

Times there may be when even the best of us suffer from the monotony of life. It is not so easy to keep on, starting out each morning for business and spending the day poring over ledgers, or smiling pleasantly at exacting and inconsiderate customers. It takes grit to keep patience with the children, to get meals ready and have the home tidy, and to be at the beck and call of all and sundry—as the mother has to do in the family. It is hard enough to settle down to a grinding study when the sun is shining gloriously and all nature urges you to go out and have a swim or a game. Even when you can discover no cause for weariness, it is quite true that often enough it presses down upon you and makes you sick of life.

Now in all such circumstances the doctrine we are considering is like a ray of heaven-sent light. Not all of us can imitate the saints in their mighty achievements for spreading of God's kingdom on earth. Not all are meant to work miracles, to impose rigorous fasts upon themselves, to leave home and friends, and toil upon the mission-fields. "Abraham," wrote St. Francis de Sales, "left home and family in order to do God's Will, but the eternal Son of God found the Father's Will in the midst of His own kinsfolk, and in working for them and with them." It is not because he went to the Indies that St. Francis Xavier became a saint, but because he fulfilled the Will of God by going to the Indies.

A most comforting doctrine, ensuring a cheerfulness and optimism which the soul will bring to the accomplishment of what is drab and ordinary.

And here, as in everything else, the example of Our Divine Lord is our model and our encouragement. In another place we have stressed the truth that His entire life was one long act of unswerving obedience to the will of His Father. Now out of the thirty-three years assigned for Him to live on this earth, thirty were spent in the obscurity of Nazareth. Nazareth was a byword among the Jews. "Can anything good come out of Nazareth?" Never once in the whole Old Testament is Nazareth even mentioned; the first we hear of it is that Mary was living there.

Into this drab little place the Son of God descended to spend thirty years of toil that was uninteresting and monotonous, years wasted, as men might consider, in doing the most commonplace things—standing in the midst of shavings and sawdust to learn the trade at St. Joseph's bench; taking the pail at the bidding of

His Mother to fetch water from the well; sitting in the synagogue with the other boys of the town to be taught by the local rabbi.

For Him, too, naturally speaking, all this must have been monotonous and boring. He knew much more than St. Joseph or the rabbi, for His divine mind was filled with the treasures of wisdom and of knowledge. But all is held in check and He appears in despised Nazareth, just as the ordinary son of these very ordinary people. But—and this is the tremendously consoling truth—in these ways Jesus did the Will of God perfectly. It is this fact which enabled Him to subject Himself to the trivialities around Him, to put into the humdrum task of the present moment the same zest He would later employ when surrounded by the multitudes and preaching the Word of God. In His eyes preaching and working miracles were not one whit more important than washing dishes or hammering in nails or using the plane or the saw or mending a broken plowshare.

There have been men and women who followed Jesus closely in His hidden life and who have sanctified themselves and others by the art of supernaturalizing everything. And there have been men and women who worked eagerly and incessantly, who were powerful organizers, who could sway whole multitudes to their will—and they have gone down into the grave and their so-called achievements have perished with them. This is not to advocate apathy in God's service—far from it—or to utter a syllable that might be construed into censure of external works for His glory. But it is to prove that the only reason I am here is to do God's will, and that that can be done as perfectly in a hovel as in a palace; it is often accomplished in a life which the world rates a failure, and it is often lost sight of in a life which the generality of men would call a success.

Where, then, does the divine expert teach me to find the will of God? Obviously, in the first place, in God's commandments and in the commandments of the Church, and after that, in the duties of my state of life. These constitute what spiritual writers call "the will of God signified." Then comes His "permissive" will, in all the details that He allows to befall me from morning till night, all the chance happenings, like those we have instanced, that come to me each day and each hour. Underneath all these "the sacrament of the present moment" teaches me to recognize God's "signified" will, or His "permissive" will, and to accept them all in that spirit of docility and bless the hand that orders or allows them.

There is a passage in the writings of the late Archbishop Goodier which makes an admirable summary of the doctrine we are trying to elucidate. Here it is:

> "To have as little as possible to do with the making of my own career. What God wills, let it be done to me.
>
> "To be ready, so far as I may, for anything and everything. For this, to make the best of myself, so far as opportunity allows. There will always be something wrong, always there will be something to be done.
>
> "To do the duty of each day as it comes, for its own sake, because it is a duty, the gift of God to me, not looking too far into the future, not looking too much for results. Fidelity in the present spells fidelity in the future. If the duty is done, the fruit will come.
>
> "To know that God, almighty and all-loving, is behind all, with His hand on every thread, personally interested in all things, in me, in His own great design, in that portion of it for which He has particularly made me.
>
> "To trust Him blindly, knowing well that His vision is more comprehensive than mine, His goal different from, grander than, mine. His ways not as my ways but infinitely more sure.
>
> "To recognize this again and again in my everyday experience; how underneath seeming failure success is constantly attained, my failure His success; of another kind, it may be, from what I had anticipated, but in the end far more real and important. To see how, in an instant, He restores or replaces what seems utterly to have collapsed, how for all the ends He has in view the means are always found."

This, briefly, is the doctrine of Père de Caussade. He is especially insistent that many fail to reach holiness of life, in spite of much good will and earnestness, because they do not seize in this way upon the present opportunities. They allow a gigantic amount of spiritual treasure to slip through their fingers because they have never schooled themselves to recognize God's hand shaping all, directing all, permitting all. "To those who love God *all things* work together unto good."

8. Hours Off

Oftentimes the present moment will be left to me to dispose of. I am free to work or to rest, to go down town or to remain inside, to read or to pray, to visit a friend or to write a letter. What becomes of "the sacrament of the present moment" in such times? No duty is assigned me; there are no urgent calls on me just now; this is "time off."

Père de Caussade proceeds to explain in detail three principles to guide me aright in such circumstances. First, as is clear, whatever task or employment I select must be free from sin. If sin enters in, and in the measure it enters in, in the same I am deviating from the doing of God's Will. This we can take for granted, and anyhow we have stressed it already.

Secondly, if we are to apply his doctrine to our "free time" we must cultivate great "purity of heart." This purity leads to a close and careful analysis of the motives by which we are influenced in our decisions, and a ruthless insistence with ourselves on uprooting selfishness when it is discovered in them. *Why* do I tell that funny story—is it just to secure the spotlight for myself? *Why* do I go to see that picture? *Why* do I read that book? It is not always easy to answer, but at least the man or woman sincerely trying to do God's Will in all the details of life will make a consistent attempt. Much light from above will be granted to such a sincere heart, and in this light will be discovered, little by little, a fund of selfishness, the existence of which was for years unsuspected. "I have many things to tell you," said Our Lord, "but you cannot bear them now." It is only gradually that the soul sees into these depths of selfishness; if they were seen earlier the sight might paralyze all further effort. But the light is proportioned to the soul's progress, and this explains why the saints use expressions of self-contempt which at times surprise us who do not know our sinfulness as they know theirs.

Lastly, we must use prudence in deciding how to choose our occupations in hours off. This does not by any means imply that we must play for safety. When St. Francis Xavier was warned by his friends that if he visited a certain savage tribe he would be devoured, he took no notice but went to the tribe just the same. But prudence, teaches Père de Caussade, is the virtue which shows me what course of action, in this present moment, will contribute most to God's glory. Some people who pride themselves on possessing the virtue of prudence remain all their lives silent witnesses to the truth; they contribute little or nothing positive or constructive, by word or act or work, to the building up of God's kingdom. So they never make mistakes, and seldom anything else.

This is not the "prudence" advocated by Père de Caussade. He would have me, in free time, examine the various possible occupations in the light of God's glory. Shall I work, and if so in what manner? And from the different works which offer themselves, all useful, which shall I choose to do in this present moment? Or, on the other hand, perhaps I ought not to work at all; perhaps instead this is an occasion for a "break"? What is going to determine my choice? Caprice? Impulse or whim certainly does determine many people in such circumstances. But if I am out to live a life of entire consecration to doing the will of God, I will not allow myself to be led by my whims and fancies. Life is a "sacrament," and the question facing a man who regards it as such is "Which of these possible choices do I sincerely believe is most calculated to please God, to contribute to His glory?"

And here once more the light of grace shines into the mind of a faithful servant of God enabling him to see his way clearly.

Thus, the three principles laid down by our guide may be summed up. First, your choice must be without sin. Secondly, your motive must be pure; you must train yourself to discover unworthy motives, and having discovered them, to supplant them by supernatural motives. And lastly, prudence must determine your selection, that is, you must choose what you sincerely believe will give most glory to God. Live thus, he would add, and your whole life will be without sin; your intention will be upright; and your actions will be most pleasing in God's sight. In other words, you will spend your days doing God's Will, and that is precisely the purpose God had in view when He gave you this wonderful gift of life.

This consoling doctrine about the value of the present moment, however, rests upon an even greater authority than that of the saintly Jesuit who has written about it so fully and so illuminatingly. It can easily be derived from the teaching of Our Divine Lord Himself.

In one of the most beautiful passages of all Scripture He invites men to look at the little birds flitting across the sky. These have no sense or foresight to provide for the winter, to gather into barns. But our Father in heaven knows all about them for they are His creatures, and not one of these tiny things drops to the ground without His permission. Let His hearers observe those lovely lilies growing over there wild in that field, swaying so gracefully in the summer breeze. It was the same heavenly Father Who clothed them with all this splendor. It is true, of course, that in a few days or weeks they will shrivel up and be good for nothing except to be flung into the fire. Still, during their brief existence, the great Father thinks it worth while to embellish them in this marvelous manner.

Now, concludes Our Lord, if you have a Father Who is so prodigal in beautifying the mere flowers which last but for a season, if you have a Father Who watches so carefully over the insignificant creatures which do not even know Him—what may you not reasonably expect will be His solicitude for you who are His own children, His sons and daughters, chosen by Him before He laid the foundations of the world and destined to live with Him forever? "Be not solicitous, therefore . . . for your Father knoweth that you have need of all these things. . . . Seek ye first, the kingdom of God and His justice and all these things will be added unto you."

This teaching of Our Lord would seem to be the foundation of the lesson we have tried to learn in the school of Père de Caussade. It teaches the highest sanctity. To trust God thus when from a human standpoint everything seems to be going against us; to acknowledge that He knows best and to submit wholeheartedly, without a murmur even in our own secret soul; to see all our cherished plans fall to pieces, and those of our enemies go forward; to accept contradiction and misrepresentation and misinterpretation of our motives and our actions; to bow low before sickness, and disappointment, and separation from those we love; indeed to give even in advance our unqualified "Fiat" to whatever God sends, and our "Amen" when He takes us at our word—who ever said that these are easy things to do? But they embody that childlike abandonment to God's Will, in all things great and small, which Père de Caussade is at such pains to recommend and expound and which Our Lord Himself lays down as the essential condition of true holiness of life.

St. Francis Borgia arrived late one night at a Jesuit College. The rain was falling heavily and he knocked several times in vain, for the hour was late and he was not expected and everybody was in bed. Next morning there was consternation and many of the community expressed regret at the unfortunate occurrence. Francis only smiled. He was quite happy all night at the gate, for was it not by God's permission that the rain was falling, and was it not He Who had allowed the mistake to take place? Francis wanted one thing only—to do God's Will perfectly in every detail of his life. And he finds it here as he stands in the rain, in the darkness, before the gates barred in his face. So there was nothing to be annoyed about; on the contrary he was quite happy to recognize exactly what, for him, "the sacrament of the present moment" was bringing, and he "received" it with immense peace and joy, and growth of grace to his soul.

9. Happiness in the Will of God

To recognize God's Will in the events of life, on the lines indicated by Père de Caussade, must necessarily prove to be a powerful help to happiness. In the light it sheds into a man's mind he must see a wonderful example of God's love for the soul He has chosen from eternity and created in time. To think that He is thus continually occupied with the work of the soul's advancement in holiness; to remember that there is not a single thought, word, or act done by me or to me, which affects my life remotely or proximately, but it is permitted by Him with a view to helping my soul; that the Lord is indeed solicitous for me, and that His solicitude is constant; to recognize this, to be convinced of this, gives me at least a faint idea of my true importance as being loved thus by the heavenly Father.

You have watched, I am sure, the care with which a mother looks after the needs of her little child. Look at mother and child making a long train journey together, and you must marvel at mother's patience, and at the ingenuity she shows in discovering ways and means of keeping the little one entertained and amused. She dare not forget. She must put aside all other occupations and focus all her attention on the one task of looking after this little child.

It is thus that God attends to the needs of my soul! "Can a mother forget her infant so as not to have compassion of the child of her womb? And, even if she should forget, yet will not I forget thee." So it is He Who arranges my whole life, He Who plans all the details and circumstances of each day and each hour, always with a view to cultivating in my soul the seed of sanctifying grace sown therein on the day of my Baptism. Why am I here? To try to discover what He wills, and without asking why, to submit like a little child. Often, like the child, I do not understand why He allows certain things to happen to me, often it will seem to my childish mind that I could manage things much better myself. But if I deepen my spirit of faith I will see His hand guiding all, and the vision revealing such loving and such constant care for me cannot but flood my heart with joy.

A very strong protection against sin is the remembrance of the source from which it emanates. Every suggestion to evil comes from my deadliest enemy; therefore it is condemned in advance. It is true that sin can look attractive, but, from the mere fact that it is from *him* it comes, I know with certainty that despite all fair appearances it is bound to make me miserable.

I can argue, in like fashion, to the happiness which must result from practising the "sacrament of the present moment." It is true once more that people may say sharp things to me, that I may be misunderstood, or laughed at, or that sickness or failure may pursue me relentlessly. But God permits these things. They emanate from Him. And God loves me with an eternal love. If these "misfortunes" seem hard and difficult to understand, I have only to remember that never would a loving Father allow them to come my way, unless He saw very clearly what an immense blessing would accrue from them to me whom He loves. And this attitude towards them must necessarily bring joy into my life. "Wit it well; love was His meaning."

Moreover, the soul filled with the spirit of faith sees well that this purification is a prelude to eternal bliss. The soul's aspirations are all heavenward, and every blow of the chisel, how painful soever, is welcomed if it will serve to make the material more perfect. "Let no other ambition be mine but this," wrote the saintly Father Michael Browne, S.J., ". . . to live in order to satisfy the divine craving for love, to burn out my life as a living candle before the shrine of the Eternal Lover. May my life be burned out, second by second, in the flames that leap from the Sacred Heart of Christ!"

Once more let us try to see how this works out in practice. You have a young growing family, and you own a business that is thriving. Prospects for the future are very bright—till one day you fall seriously ill. You are forced to take things easy, perhaps to close down your shop or factory at the very moment when it was shaping up so excellently. And your children, and the good education you had hoped to give them, and the rosy dreams for their future which you and your wife often discussed together? All these ambitions you must lay aside. You and yours have to face instead the grind of poverty. It is heroic to accept all this sweetly, to stifle every breath of complaint—even to yourself—because you recognize that it comes to you straight from the heavenly Father's hand Who would never have permitted it if He did not see what a blessing lies hidden underneath the sting. Heroic, yes, and a saint is God's hero who sees life as having one only purpose—unquestioning acceptance of God's Will.

Or you are an apostle. You have heard and read for yourself the Pope's repeated calls to Catholic Action. Your own contact with the world has brought home to you the crying need of zeal and initiative in work for God and for souls. But your efforts and your enthusiasm and your appeals for co-operation are treated with good-humored amusement or undisturbed complacency. No doubt you mean well, but as you grow up you will learn sense, and—prudence! Hard? Of course it is, and let no apostle be daunted by it! But if cynicism threatens to freeze your enthusiasm, may we suggest that again you recall and apply Père de Caussade's doctrine about the "sacrament of the present moment?" It is above all in difficult circumstances such as these, if they be sweetly accepted, that divine love develops wonderfully in the soul of the apostle, and spreads—perhaps in ways he never knows or sees—from his soul into the souls of many others.

10. Mary's "Fiat"

There is only one command put on record as having fallen from the lips of Our Blessed Lady. At the marriage of Cana in Galilee she told the waiters: "Whatsoever He [my Son], shall say to ye, do ye." Now that command may well be taken as summing up all Mary's teaching about the reason why I am here, and as a very trustworthy index of her own attitude towards life.

When the angel visited Mary at Nazareth he asked her if she would freely consent to be God's Mother. "And Mary said: 'Fiat mihi . . . ! Be it done unto me according to thy word!' "

Throughout all the subsequent years she ever regarded herself as God's little serving-maid, whose only reason for being in life was to discover what He wanted her to do, and having discovered it to perform it in all details with a most ready and unquestioning obedience.

This obedience of Mary to the Will of God directed her into many hard paths. These she did not seek out for herself. She let herself, rather, be guided by His hand wherever He led the way. It was very hard to set out for Bethlehem at such a critical time in her life—a long journey of eighty miles, in winter, and at a season when both Jerusalem and Bethlehem were crowded with visitors, crowded out, indeed. It was hard to be compelled to take refuge under a shed intended only for beasts, and there to give birth to her Child, and almost immediately afterwards to have to flee before the naked sword of a tyrant into a country unknown to Mary herself and to Joseph.

The privations of the hidden life were hard, and it must nearly have broken the Mother's heart to say farewell to such a Son, on that memorable day when she stood at the door of the little house at Nazareth and watched Him walk down the street for the last time, turn the corner and leave home forever. And Mary returns to her empty home. Never again when she looks out through the window at the back will she see Him, as she often did, bent over a piece of carpentry, with a saw in His hand and His knee on a plank. Never again will He sit in this chair where He often sat beside her, and they talked together when the day's work was over. He is gone, and over the little house of Nazareth He has left behind Him the shadow of the Cross.

What words can tell how hard it was to remain waiting for Him as He came up the street of Jerusalem on Good Friday bearing His own Cross to Calvary, to follow close in His footsteps traced in blood, and to stand for three hours watching His death-struggle? But Mary did "stand"—the valiant woman, enduring it all, lovingly and sweetly repeating the "Amen" to her "Fiat."

Often, when the cross presses heavily upon our own shoulders, we are inclined to cry out that God is very hard on us, and we ask querulously what have we done to deserve such treatment at His hand. We probably do not quite mean it, for, though the spirit be willing, the flesh is weak indeed. Still, if we want the answer to our complaint, we find it when we examine the life of Mary. What did *she* do to deserve all this? Like her divine Son, Mary did all things well.

But she is destined to be queen of all the saints, and therefore she had to show us, in her shining example, that the perfect acceptance of God's Will is the perfection of sanctity, and that such unqualified acceptance leads the generous soul to the heights, but the heights are surmounted by a cross, and the climb thereunto is steep, and before He reached the summit even Jesus fell several times.

III. "Sin Doesn't Matter"

"We have erred from the way of truth . . . we wearied ourselves in the way of iniquity and destruction, and have walked through hard ways, but the way of the Lord we have not known."—Wisdom v. 6, 7.

1. First Offence

Our present Holy Father has declared that one of the greatest evils today is the world's lack of the sense of sin. This does not mean merely that sin abounds—for men have erred since the days of Eden—but rather that today vice is condoned and the opinion finds ready acceptance that every person is expected, more or less, to walk the ways of sin. Let him step clear and the world regards him as a freak. Let him show that he reverences the ten commandments and the gay worldling turns from him with a commiserating smile and shrug of the shoulders. Every sensible person nowadays understands that Christ and Christianity are out of date. His views about life and its purpose have failed to keep pace with our modern enlightenment.

Our twentieth-century world, while it may pardonably pride itself on its progress and its knowledge in other spheres, has grown deplorably ignorant and forgetful of even the meaning of sin. Time was when men sinned and were ashamed, when they sinned and acknowledged that their action was wrong. But the appalling change that has come takes sin as a matter of course, considers that normal men and normal women indulge in sinful habits, almost as normal people eat and drink and sleep. Sin is part of man's natural make-up.

Must we prove all this? On tonight's radio program a play is announced. Suppose we listen in? It is funny all right, the plot is clever, and the characters are well drawn. But, on re-considering it, do you not see that it all turns on sin? The hero of the piece came out smiling at the end, having carried his scheme through to enrich himself handsomely. But his methods? Now that you think of them, they were flagrantly in violation of the seventh commandment. Besides there were false oaths sworn in court, and to perjure oneself is, in God's eyes, a heinous crime. Do you think your playwright and his principal character are going to allow a trivial circumstance like that to weigh against the chance of winning notoriety or getting a good box office? Sin is a note that jars, so please let us forget it and get on with our play.

Anyhow, this is *only* a play, meant merely to amuse. All right. It is not a direct attack on God's law. It only leaves God out. It only takes for granted that God is not worth considering. The propaganda does not become ineffective by being subtle. Imperceptibly it contributes its quota to the formation of a mentality that thinks sin does not matter.

Your spicy novel offends in just the same way. Frequently the writer will not bother to direct his shafts straight against what we are taught as Christians. Once more he only assumes that God's point of view does not hold any longer. He leaves the impression, by an innuendo here and a half-truth there, that, while it is true that a few credulous Catholics still believe in and practise what Christ taught, the vast majority of people have outgrown His doctrines, as they have grown up and outlived the stories of nursery days. You cannot have a good time and be a practising Catholic, so, once given that enjoyment is your *raison d'être,* automatically you laugh out of court Our Lord's stern denunciation of sin. "For," says your gay writer, "what He calls sin is really your main avenue to happiness. If He insists on closing that absolutely to you, and you are intelligent enough to see that life without thrills is unendurable, it is evident that He and you must part company. But do not allow that to worry you. There are compensations, plenty of them."

Another night you sit at the movies. Examine many a film and again you find the same easy readiness to ignore God. There may not be a frontal attack, only the calm assumption that what God has set down as His law and His will no longer deserves mention, still less observance. The film smiles indulgently at old-fashioned notions of morality and wonders that anybody can be found to take them seriously nowadays. If the new morality happens to clash with what was thundered forth on Sinai, who is so silly as to bother about that? Let us fall down and adore our golden calf. Conscience is a bogey. Sin does not matter. Forget it. Everybody does today.

What is the result of this insidious propaganda? You have it in the mentality that regards sin as "only natural." Everyone does it, why not you? You can gather as much from the screen or the thriller. You are no worse than anyone else, and why not join in the fun? It cannot be too bad, and anyhow God is merciful and we can hope to fix up things before we die.

Sentiment overrules reason and the teachings of our faith. The world subtly invites us to sympathize with the husband who is unfaithful, or bids us admire the skill with which the crook makes a get-away, or sends us home laughing and amused at the forgeries by which a criminal evades the law. It does not take trouble to add, but rather takes quite a lot of trouble to omit, that this free and easy conduct is sin, mortal sin, a flagrant and insolent refusal on the part of the creature to do what we have seen him to be bound by a thousand claims to do—to render obedience to God's Will. The world never bothers to point out that there is a fearful sanction for that law. If God be not obeyed here from the motive of love, His justice will assuredly be vindicated by an eternity of punishment in hell.

Childish, sneers your smart modern. Old wives' tales, hoary with age, dead as the dodo, or at least decaying fast and moribund. We have grown up, thank you.

How are we Catholics going to preserve our sense of perspective in the midst of all this distorted thinking? Or strengthen it for ourselves if it has bent before the storm? Suppose we come again and consult the divine expert? Bring sin to Him, as you would bring a picture to be examined by a skilled artist, or a curious piece of stone you have found to get the opinion of an acknowledged authority on archaeology. What does God think of sin? What does Jesus Christ judge of its real nature? For, despite the world, His standards are still the correct ones, since truth is eternal. Sin does not matter? Does the divine expert corroborate this easy sentence? Does *even one* mortal sin not matter? Let the divine expert take into His hands even one mortal sin and show me what it is in the scales of God.

One mortal sin. This time Our Lord leads me by the arm and guides me down the street till both of us come to a halt in front of a courthouse. We make our way in and sit down and look on at the trials which are in progress. In the dock there are three sets of prisoners. The judge is on the bench, but I notice that there is no jury. There is no need of a jury, for this judge is unique in this, that He knows beforehand every jot and tittle of the evidence for and against the prisoners. This judge is God Himself, and each set of prisoners brought in here before Him has committed *one* mortal sin.

An earthly judge may make a mistake through lack of prudence or through ignorance of some point of the law. God sees at a glance how far the sinner is responsible, how much he was influenced by passion and temptation, what allowances are to be made for innate weakness.

An earthly judge may sometimes compromise his conscience; he may be open to a bribe. Not so this judge. An earthly judge may act without due consideration; swayed by the impulse of the moment, he may decide in anger against his prisoner, and afterwards he may have regrets and remorse of conscience. Not so the judge before us today. Here there is no danger of impetuosity. Here everything is weighed most carefully in the scales, and with a certainty incapable of error the punishment is measured out with nicest accuracy to fit the crime.

Turn from the judge to the prisoners. The first group in the dock are the angels who rebelled. I know their story. They were created by God in beauty, with the purpose in the divine mind that, after a period of trial, they should enjoy forever the happiness of heaven.

What happened? These angels committed a sin. It was, as we should say, *only* a sin of thought. It was their first sin. It was their only sin. A thought of pride in the mind of Lucifer led him to rebel against God's will and to gather around him a third part of the angels. What does the modern world think of the story? If it deigned even to read it and consider it, the world would certainly make light of the offence. Only a stray thought! And a first offence! But God, what does He think of it? He takes that sin, a mortal sin, and puts it in one pan of the balance. In the other He places the punishment it deserves. When the two pans are equally poised, so that one does not weigh a fraction of an ounce more than the other, you have, in one, a single mortal sin, and in the other, eternity in hell. Remember that in this judge there is no impulse of passion, no desire of vindictiveness, no lack of knowledge. Such a judge is bound to pass this sentence on an unrepented mortal sin, only because He sees that it is, quite objectively, what the sin deserves.

One mortal sin. At this stage Jesus Christ, sitting by my side, bends over to ask if ever *I* committed even one mortal sin. Can I recall the circumstances? By day or by night? Alone or with a companion? In early life, or later on? While on holidays, or while employed with such and such a person? In married life or before? There it stands before me today, like Banquo's ghost, a deliberate mortal sin committed by me, an act of known disobedience to God in a serious matter. If I had died then! If, after I had lain down to sleep with that fearful guilt on my soul, I had wakened in eternity! Why did that not happen? Why did He pass sentence on the rebellious angels after their first sin, and why did He spare me after my first mortal offence? Even more astounding if the offence was repeated, if, as is possible, I went on for whole years offending Him, emboldened by my repeated escapes. He spared me—why? "Wit it well; love was His meaning." "It is the mercies of the Lord that we are not consumed."

Our first parents are in the dock, too. Like the angels they committed a sin, as far as we know, their only sin. Once again the judge takes that sin, their first sin, into His hands to weigh its malice in the scales before me. All the miseries that flesh is heir to have been let loose upon the world as a result of that one mortal sin. The gay world makes merry over the childish tale, but Adam's disobedience to God lost him all right to heaven, brought into the world the tidal wave of immorality, the countless diseases that crowd our hospitals, the hatreds which make men snarl at each other like wolves and spend their brief lives in devising ways and means to exterminate each other, the poverty and squalor of our slum areas, the constant struggle against the threefold concupiscence, death itself.

Adam and Eve were punished immediately on committing their first sin. Once again Jesus Christ bids me remember the debt I owe to the infinite mercy and patience of the judge in my regard. "Wit it well; love was His meaning." "The mercies of the Lord that we are not consumed."

The third prisoner is a person my own age. He has committed a mortal sin, his first mortal sin, and died in the act. He is entering hell *now*. Or, if I imagine that God would surely spare him and give him time to repent if this was only his first mortal sin, at least I can very well conceive a man or woman going today into hell, for fewer mortal sins than I have committed. Why? It is as if both of us were brought up here for trial. He is condemned; I am given time to repent. Had death come when I was in the midst of that sinful act, instead of sitting here reading these pages, *I* would have been in *his* place. Why am I not? The answer I know.

Sin doesn't matter? The divine expert thinks it does. It is for me to decide who is right—the world with its record of lying and hypocrisy and insincerity; or Jesus Christ, the light of the world, the lover of all mankind, Who hates sin, and must hate sin, because He sees it with the perspective of the expert.

2. Look and Learn

One of the trials of our school-days was looking up vocabularies. As, with wrinkled brow you plowed your way through your First French Reader, or blessed Hannibal for crossing the Alps, you came upon a word that was unfamiliar. To this day you can recall that your excellent teacher would never allow you to slur over that strange word or merely hazard a guess as to its meaning. No, he rightly insisted that you should fix it in your mind by turning to your dictionary or to the vocabulary at the end and discovering for yourself what it meant. And if you failed to recognize the same word when you happened upon it another day and in another context your inexorable master would refuse point blank to help you out. He knew the value of finding it again for yourself, so once more there was nothing for it but to obey his orders and search the columns of your dictionary.

The very same orders are repeated today by the divine expert who would teach us the meaning of sin. He, too, would have us look and learn, by consulting an open book that will teach, very vividly and very impressively indeed, what sin is.

There is a striking picture of St. Thomas Aquinas kneeling in prayer before the image of Jesus crucified. We have, all of us, at least some hazy notion of the colossal amount of work Thomas did for Catholic theology by his pen. Popes have vied with each other in trying to discover words that will express adequately the genius and the sanctity of this "perfect doctor and perfect saint." The picture referred to illustrates the story told about Thomas and his friend, St. Bonaventure. "Where, my brother," asked the latter, "do you learn so much? Whence do you draw all your wonderful doctrine?" By way of answer Thomas pointed to his crucifix. "This is my book. At His feet I learn it all."

We might suggest that from the same book we could derive a correct definition or description of sin. What Hollywood happens to think of sin need not detain us, or what attitude towards sin is adopted by the writer of a modern best-seller. But the divine expert, what does *He* think? He has already shown me the judgment of the eternal God upon the malice of sin. Now He invites me to Calvary, where He is dying in disgrace on a cross, for here, perhaps more surely than anywhere else, I can see sin in its true colors. So it will repay me, like St. Thomas, to kneel down here at His bleeding feet and clarify my notions about sin. Every wound in that racked body in front of me is like a tongue to instruct me. The book is open wide before my eyes and all I have to do is to look and learn.

Before listening to those different tongues speaking, it is well to let the truth first sink deep into the marrow of our being that this sufferer is God. When sin is permitted to work out its malice in full, against a victim who is the sinless Son of God, Calvary is the result. "*He* was made sin," says St. Paul, with his customary vigor, implying that Jesus is its victim. Here is the result, Jesus writing in His own blood the answer to the question we are pursuing. Despite the metallic laugh with which our moderns dismiss sin, it must indeed be an evil the depths of which we may never expect to fathom, if Calvary is God's way of making us realize its cruelty, its base ingratitude, its insolence, its insatiable hatred in hounding to death the Man-God. Sin doesn't matter? Doesn't it? Sin, which did *this* to *Him!* To Him Who is suffering, not for His own sins, but for ours. "If *this* be done in the green wood, what shall be done in the dry?"

What is sin? As we kneel here with the book spread out before us, we observe that there are nails in the feet of Jesus Christ—a nail in His right foot, and a nail in His left foot. Here is His first answer to our query. To all who look and learn, those two nails are a reminder of the price paid for sins which men commit with their feet; sins which I, who am kneeling here, have committed too.

Our feet used to sin, how? People will walk into places full of danger, where they are aware their immortal souls will be seared with the guilt of grievous crime. There is that dark haunt where deeds of shame are done, hidden from every eye, except God's eye. There is that public-house or lounge bar where men and women have drunk to excess and left themselves exposed to the imminent risk of falling into other vices which need not be named. This may be old-fashioned language for the smart set who squat here, but it is true, as true as it was on the day when the Son of God bore nails driven into His feet to expiate the vices of those who use their feet to walk into such dens of sin. If it is not good form to speak like this and spoil the fun, no apology is offered. If we do not like thinking along these lines, it is just too bad but we shall have to do so, here or hereafter. That, at least, is what the divine expert teaches.

What is sin? Suppose that, before going into that place where sin was morally impossible to avoid, you had paused to contemplate those two nails in the feet of Christ, I wonder if you would so easily absolve yourself and placidly assure yourself that sin doesn't matter.

Sins committed by the feet? Any qualms, have you, on the score of dancing? Has it been, possibly, to you or your partner a cause of sin? It is easy to dismiss the question as silly, but at the same time you ought, perhaps, not be too cocksure. There were two feet pierced with nails, you know, to remind you to search your conscience, and form your judgment, not by the standards of our neo-pagans, but by those of the divine expert. They were the feet of the Son of God. Never thought about it just that way, did you? Never caught on to the idea that, by sinning with your feet, you were joining with those who used their feet to walk to Calvary and, while following Him along the road, jeered Him and called down His blood upon themselves and their children?

Sin doesn't matter? From your position here at those bleeding feet, lift up your eyes a little higher and, before the darkness falls, notice that the sacred body of Our Lord is naked. Such an indignity to God's divine Son! Yes, but men must understand and women must learn, the lessons of Christian modesty. No sane person expects or wants girls today to dress as they did in the "good days" of Queen Victoria. But there is a limit in the other direction, too, and Christians, kneeling here on Calvary, have to ponder in their hearts the solemn words about modesty spoken so frequently by the Vicar of Christ. One wonders if many girls ever sit back and try to realize the truth that, by their *blasé* attitude concerning dress, they may be permitting themselves to be a pawn in the devil's game to stir up men's passions. Or if many parents understand the harm they do by allowing their children, even little children, to depart from the standards of

Christ in this matter and follow slavishly where the ultra-moderns lead.

These things need to be said, and said very plainly. Once again you may curl your lip and hear them with a supercilious smile. You may dismiss them as echoes of medievalism. But the divine expert went to Calvary and hung on the cross to impress on you and me that they are the truth.

Shortly after His death Our Lord was pierced with the lance and His heart was opened. Here, too, is a most moving and eloquent answer to the question we are proposing. The heart is the seat of affections, and the open heart of Jesus is a tongue crying out to warn all who gather here about the heinousness of allowing the heart to become enslaved by unholy desires and unchaste love. The married man who pays sinful attentions to the young girl typist in the office with him; the wife who is silly enough to allow her vanity to be flattered by the notice she receives from the man living across the street, or the man who calls to collect the money, or to deliver those parcels; the girl who knows perfectly well that she is a thief and a robber, stealing from her employer, not his gold or silver, not his tea or sugar or coal, but the love which he solemnly vowed before God's altar to give to another alone—do these dare to affirm, in the light of Calvary, in the sight of the pierced Heart of Christ, that sin doesn't matter? That they are just carried off with the spirit of our times, and are no worse than anybody else?

Look and learn. This time your eyes rest upon Christ's swollen lips and upon the tongue that is dried and cleaving to the roof of His mouth. And we blandly tell ourselves that foul and suggestive talk is of no great consequence? We have indulgent views about taking the Holy Name irreverently, have we? We do not attach much importance to our growing habit of criticizing our neighbor harshly and broadcasting his faults, real or imaginary or exaggerated? The tongue of Christ here on Calvary has a different lesson to teach.

Sin doesn't matter? You were up in a court case, and you *had* to swear that false oath. All the others around you were doing so at that same trial, and you stood to lose the whole case if you did not follow suit. So you were *compelled* to call the all-holy God to bear witness that your lying tongue was speaking the truth. Jesus went to His death, to *this* death, because He stood by the truth and refused to swerve from it when solemnly adjured in court to answer in the name of the living God. Look at His tongue and learn from the divine expert the malice of all lying, and perjury, and uncharitable gossip, and tale-bearing, and irreverence for the Holy Name, and those filthy stories which you calmly assure yourself and others are just the order of the day.

Christ's lips are parched, for He is undergoing an excruciating thirst. I wonder what those lips have to say to our cocktail parties if they lead to sin, especially to mortal sin. Does this girl, on her high stool at the bar, as she laughingly raises this glass to her lips, ever pause for a moment to consider the lengths *He* went to, in order to warn her of the terrifying possibilities of the habit she knows she is contracting, a habit which is part of our modern "emancipation" of woman? Is it sufficient justification to tell herself she must be a sport and do as well as the others? If, when she wakes up late next morning and immediately recalls how she degraded herself the night before, will she, even then, look and learn from the swollen parched lips of Christ the true nature of her sin?

This Christian man who squanders his week's wages on drink, who breaks his wife's heart, and terrifies his children, would he ever be guilty of such insanity if he gave himself time to think of what drunkenness cost Christ on Calvary? Jolly companions tell him at the dance that he is a real sport, "decent" fellows will take him by the arm and treat him to drink, and still more drink. The eyes of the divine expert look on at it all. With a tongue that is dried and lips that are thickened He defines the foulness of excessive drinking. Above the blare of music in that dance hall, He tries to make Himself heard. He speaks in the very midst of the coarse jokes and inane shrieks of laughter and He refuses to allow His message to be drowned by the chorus of cheap songs that fill the saloon or the bar on Saturday night. When will the sinner stop and listen? Whether man hear or not, the word of truth is there, proclaiming in unmistakably clear terms the malice of vices which are so readily condoned.

What is sin? When the same voice of Christ summons the sinner next morning to fulfil his sacred obligation of Sunday Mass, is the sinner too sodden and too stupefied to obey, as a result of all the "fun" of the previous night? Sin doesn't matter. It is certain that Jesus thinks it matters a whole lot.

What is sin? What is drunkenness? What is filthy talk, what are lies, and tale-bearing, and irreverence for the Holy Name, and uncharitable gossip, and suggestive stories and songs, and false oaths? What are these things? Just part and parcel of modern life, that's all. Nothing very much to get excited about, since every normal person nowadays does them. Our callousness can become galling even to think about. Are we purblind that we cannot look and learn what the lips and tongue of the divine expert have gone to such lengths to teach us on Calvary?

The eyes of Jesus Christ are weighed down with blood and spittle. And our eyes? Are they ever used to commit sin? Are we not just a bit ashamed as we kneel here and think of that reeking volume over which we gloated, devouring its garbage with our eyes? And we passed it on to another who in his turn feasted his or her eyes on the sight of the same cesspool.

Sins with the eyes? What about that show the other night when you sat there bolt upright with eyes glued to the screen or stage? What was it that held you spellbound in this way? Have you the courage here on Calvary, in the light of His all-seeing eyes, to wax eloquent about it as you did to your friends after it was over? Of course you were all agreed that is was a great show, a splendid picture, a clever plot, so true to life, you know. But bring it up here to Calvary and find out if *He* is of the same mind? His verdict about it is the only that matters after all, since He is the divine expert.

There are other ways of sinning with the eyes, but their malice we can look at and learn for ourselves. No need to be more explicit. Jesus Christ, with those two eyes of His now opened and looking straight into the innermost places of our souls, provides light in which to read and understand what He thinks of vices so casually dismissed by a world that has lost its sense of sin.

What about sins of thought? Here more than ever the world smiles at your childish scruples. Why, of course, you can think as you please. Provided you preserve a veneer of outward respectability all is well. The important rule is to "play the game," to avoid getting "caught," to remember that certain things are "not done" in good society, and certain subjects (many of them discussed in these pages) are taboo. But in your mind and heart foster all the depravity you wish for. Feast your thoughts without any restraint on any subject that happens to attract you. Nobody is going to bother about that, for nobody sees what takes place in the inmost recesses of your mind.

But on Calvary I learn that *He,* once more, does not share these easy views. I remember that He taught that a man, if he merely look on a woman with evil desire, has already sinned with her in his heart. To enforce this lesson He wears today a crown of thorns, pressed tight into His temples, and causing Him exquisite torture. It is a forceful reminder of the evil of impure thoughts—not involuntary thoughts, indeed, for, in the present state of fallen nature, it is impossible to avoid these entirely. But when the temptation to consent to them grows strong, to sit back and allow their poison to saturate the mind—then to look up and learn the lesson from His crown of thorns must surely prove a warning and a deterrent.

We have still to contemplate the ears of Jesus Christ which were assailed with cries of blasphemy and mockery. These He would suffer in order to teach the malice of using our ears to commit sin. We may, if we will, bend our ears to listen eagerly to the smutty story, but one wonders if we ever take time to remember the price our sin is costing Him. It is indeed a sad commentary on our sinful condition that those ears of ours are always so ready to listen, time after time, to the same shady story. Tell a man a good clean joke today, and repeat it to him tomorrow and the chances are that he will remind you he heard that one before. It has lost its point when it has been heard once. But introduce a smutty story and it will be listened to and rehearsed time and time again. It will go on its rounds of devastating work, ruining the souls for whom Christ has bled and died. Is this silly and gross overstatement? The divine expert does not think so, nor do those whose privilege it is, like Him, to work directly for souls.

In the hands of Christ, as in His feet, there are two nails. Let me stretch forth both my hands and look at my two palms, as I kneel here. Were those hands of mine ever used for sinful purposes? Men think themselves smart if they can rake in money with their hands, quite irrespective of the ways and means. The prevalence of theft and dishonesty, even among juveniles, grows apace. The modern gospel is to swindle right and left provided you can get away with it. One almost despairs at times, of trying to awaken our dormant consciences to a sense of the gravity of dishonesty. Everyone is taking advantage of the poor man's necessity, why not you? Everyone tells "business lies," so you may as well use light weights; sell that load of coal or wood for three times its value if your purchaser is simple enough to imagine that you still respect the seventh commandment; dip your hand whenever the employer's back is turned, into his cash-box; sell what belongs to him at half-price to one of your friends; or increase the price by a dollar or so and pocket the extra bit for cigarettes or a ticket for the dance. It's all part of life, you know. You need to be a wide awake to get on in these times. Sin doesn't matter.

Still keep looking at those hands of mine. Are they ever used to sell drink over the counter, or in the lounge, to people who have already had more than they can carry? Those hands are co-operating in the sins of others. If that man on his way home is knocked down by a passing truck and killed, in the state of mortal sin, it will be poor consolation to say that it was his own affair to take too much drink. If he is incapable of getting up for Mass tomorrow, Sunday, it will avail little in sight of the divine expert to exonerate oneself by saying it was his own fault.

Sins with the hands? Copying out dirty stories with those hands, and passing them on, and instructing others to copy them and circulate them too? And this in full sight of the nails piercing the hands of Jesus on Calvary? "O senseless Galatians," cries out St. Paul, "who hath bewitched you, that you should not obey the truth, before whose eyes Jesus Christ hath been set forth, crucified among you?"

Look and learn here the meaning of theft, of co-operating in another's sin, of crooked dealings in business, of acts of impurity. We do not need to insist, do we, that the gay world looks on with amusement and perhaps slight irritation? But it cost the Son of God this price to set before our eyes the gravity of using our hands for sinful purposes.

Earlier in these pages we pleaded for the habit of reflection. "With desolation is the whole land made desolate, because there is no one that considers in his heart." At this point it is worth while putting the recommendation into practice. What more we have to say in subsequent places can wait over. Meantime? Meantime it will repay us to slip away into a quiet spot, take out our crucifix, kneel down, and study at our leisure each of the answers given to our query about the meaning of sin. Look and learn. Touch those two nails in His feet, what is their lesson? Consider the poor naked body, how does His nakedness contribute to impress upon us the meaning of sin? His heart is pierced, why? His tongue is parched with thirst; His lips are swollen; His eyes are heavily laden with blood and spittle, how does all this help to clarify our notion of sin? There are thorns round His head, there are nails in His hands—look at them and learn, feel them and let them speak. They all unite in proclaiming that there is one evil in this world, one only evil from which, as from a running sore, all other evils emanate, and sin is its name.

The longer we remain here the better for our realization of the meaning of sin. No matter how long we stay, no matter how carefully and prayerfully we ponder over those signs in Christ's body, we shall never probe the depths of the malice and abomination of sin. But we can do much towards acquiring this realization. Efface for these few minutes every other image except that of Christ crucified and He will shed much light into the mind and at last we shall begin to see. Men sin because they do not think, because they do not look and learn, because they are always so rushed that they do not give themselves time to reflect. This is especially true at the moment when temptation presses hard. The urge is fierce, it may be, to taste this forbidden pleasure, cost what it may. Suppose instead, in the strength of divine grace, that the tempted person knelt here at Calvary and allowed those wounds to speak their message, for even five minutes? Mary stands here under the cross to point out all we have been considering. If we take the time to stop and listen, it is not easy to believe that we shall next rush from her into the haunt of sin.

St. Vincent de Paul was trying, without success, to bring back to God a notorious sinner. His pleadings and warnings alike fell upon deaf ears, till he bethought him of a new way of approach. He came with a large crucifix and made a bet with the sinner. He challenged him to place the crucifix on his mantelpiece, look at it steadily three times every day, and say to himself very slowly while looking: "I do not care." Yes, to be sure, the sinner would take on the bet—and win. But he lost. In less than a week he returned to St. Vincent. "Father, you win. I cannot do it. I *do* care. I never realized before what my sins meant. Beg Him to have mercy on my sinful soul."

3. A Story Retold

A priest was sitting in a railway coach, waiting for the train to start. Presently, on looking out of the window, he saw standing there on the platform, a peasant woman with a shawl over her head and her husband by her side. Their son, poorly dressed, was leaning out from the window next to the priest.

That young fellow was no good, and everyone knew it. He had brought disgrace on the heads of his decent father and mother, and it was as a result of his misdemeanors that he was being forced to leave the place and go to jail.

Three or four minutes before the whistle blew the poor mother broke down badly. She was a mother and he was her son, wastrel though he had proved himself to be, and she loved him still. She began to sob as if her heart was about to break. She turned up the corner of her check apron and wept into it, leaning helplessly against the side of the train. The husband looked up and down the platform, obviously ill at ease as he stared and fidgeted in his shy and awkward way, evidently dreading a scene and wishing from his heart that the train would move off and end this agony and suspense.

From his quiet corner the priest was taking it all in. But now came a shock of horror. The young man proceeded to produce his own handkerchief and actually began to mimic and ridicule the sobs of his broken-hearted mother. Not satisfied with having brought down in shame her grey hairs to the grave, not content with having repaid all her years of love with cruelty and crime, this boy now devises yet another insult. The last memory she will have of him, before the train takes him away from her perhaps never to lay her eyes upon him again, will be that, when her heart had already more grief than it could well bear, he left her standing on the platform behind him, with a mocking grin on his face and a cry of mimicry in his voice.

Think of it—her own son, her own flesh and blood, with a heart, you would say, like a block of granite. No wonder the priest was furiously indignant.

That was twenty-five years ago. Before we see what bearing this anecdote has on our theme, we turn for a moment to another scene. In one of the books of the Old Testament (III Kings), we find the prophet Nathan telling David about two men, one of them very rich and the other poor. The rich man had "exceeding many sheep and oxen, but the poor man had nothing at all but one little ewe-lamb." One day a friend dropped in to visit the wealthy man, and, in order to spare his own goods, he seized upon the poor man's one lamb, killed it and had it cooked to make a meal for his guest.

At once David's anger blazed up. He swore that that rich man should die, having first restored fourfold to the poor man "because he did this thing and had no pity." But Nathan turned on him and dumbfounded him by declaring: "*You* are the man!" For David had sinned mortally, nothwithstanding all the blessings heaped upon him by a loving God.

"*You* are the man." As we come back to that railway station we may now, perhaps, be warned to pocket our indignation against that boy and direct it to ourselves instead. What that boy is doing to his mother, the sinner has done, and is doing, to Jesus Christ, "crucifying again the Son of God and making a mockery of Him."

"*You* are the man." "Imagining Christ Our Lord present before me on the cross, to make colloquy with Him, asking myself what have I done for Christ, what am I doing for Christ, and what ought I to do for Him. Then, beholding Him in such a condition, and thus hanging upon the cross, to make the reflections which may present themselves." These are the words of another man who looked long and learned deeply the meaning of sin. That picture which St. Ignatius Loyola gives us at the close of his meditation on *Three Sins* has suggested the thoughts which have been occupying our minds on Calvary. Because men shut their eyes and refuse to look and to think, they go on crucifying the Son of God.

But there are many who open their eyes and look and learn and they are filled with an irrepressible longing to make others look and learn also. "What ought I to do for Christ?" With that searching question we propose to round off this section of our book.

Twenty-five years ago that incident took place at the railway station. But today the crime is repeated, only today its magnitude is more extensive and it is perpetrated, not against an earthly mother, but against God the Father and Jesus His Son. Think of this. Within the next twenty-four hours that infinitely-loving God, Whose plan for men's souls we have already dwelt upon, will be offended by innumerable mortal sins. Tonight the stench of these crimes will rise up into the sight of the all-pure God, as of old from Sodom and Gomorrha. There are men and women round about us now, probably not half a mile from where we are sitting reading this book, and if they die tonight in their present condition of grievous sin, there is no alternative for them other than eternity in hell.

"What ought I do?" We have seen that, were it not for God's extraordinary mercy I would have been sentenced myself in the courthouse; surely then the least I ought to do in gratitude is to try to help other souls, so dear to Christ and in such imminent peril. "Deep mystery this," writes our Holy Father, Pius XII, "*subject of inexhaustible meditation*, that the salvation of many depends on the prayers and voluntary penances which the members of the Mystical Body of Jesus Christ offer for this intention. . . . This must be held, marvelous though it appear, that Christ wills to need His members . . . Heavenly gifts will surely flow more abundantly if we not only pray fervently . . . but if we also set our hearts on eternal treasures rather than on the passing things of this world, restrain this mortal body by voluntary mortification, denying it what is forbidden, forcing it to do what is hard and distasteful, and finally humbly accept as from God's hands the burdens and sorrows of this present life. Thus according to the Apostle 'we shall fill up those things which are wanting to the sufferings of Christ, in our flesh, for His body which is the Church.' "

Our Divine Lord atoned abundantly for all sin and merited all graces for us. But in order that the fruits of His Passion be produced in men, it is necessary that all who have reached the age of reason should co-operate with Him, doing what He does in so far as that is possible consistently with their weakness and imperfection. In regard to ourselves we must, says St. Paul, "die to sin and live to justice." In regard to others our Holy Father has just instructed us to "restrain this mortal body by voluntary mortification." What this means in practice we shall now try to learn as we continue to look on the wounds in Christ's body on Calvary.

"What ought I to do for Christ?" Once more we direct our

gaze to the nails in His sacred feet. Those feet that walked the hard ways of life in search of the sheep that were lost can walk no more now. So the apostle, asking what he ought to do for Christ, sees that he can show genuine sympathy with Christ by continuing the journeys He began. Like Him he walks into the slums and alleys to bring to Jesus the souls He dies to save. He walks into the homes and estates of the rich and the powerful and speaks out fearlessly if he knows they are living in sin. He will use his feet to walk to early Mass and Holy Communion, to visit the tabernacle, offering his steps for the conversion of sinners. Christ's feet are suffering. The generous apostle will often be weary and footsore, too, but in this he glories, for this is the way to fill up what is wanting to the sufferings of his Master.

The body of Jesus is racked with pain as He hangs on the Cross. The body of Christ is naked and cold. The body of Christ is hanging in a position of acute discomfort and excessive agony. Here once again, the faithful apostle learns what he ought to do. His body will suffer too, like Christ's body, in reparation for sin. As an antidote to the pleasure-seeking, comfort-loving world around him, the apostle will, with Our Lord, hang on his cross and make his own sinful body feel the smart of pain. Jesus can no longer suffer in His physical body, but the true apostle cannot stay here on Calvary and look and reflect, and then go his way and forget. If that innocent body goes through this anguish to save souls and repair the damage done to them, the lesson is plain to read. Only by voluntary penance can the Passion be continued and souls won from the thraldom of sin. That is why generous souls long to endure fasts, to make their bodies feel pain, to spend their energy and wear out their bodies in toil which they undertake joyfully, urged as they are by their craving to be like Him. When sickness comes and prostrates them with agony, you will find in them a marvelous submissiveness. Here is a chance, sent direct from Him, to enable them to extend the fruits of His Passion. The worldling stands by, perhaps cynical, certainly uncomprehending.

The spear pierced His side and opened His heart. The heart of the apostle, too, will be opened wide. The open heart of his model is a challenge to him to embrace in the love of his heart the souls of all men without exception. Like Jesus, the apostle cries out: "Come to me, *all you* that labor . . ." That love of Christ for all men must continue to pour itself out on mens' souls, through the co-operation lovingly given by the apostle. Accordingly, he must keep his heart close to the Sacred Heart and fill it continually from this source.

The eyes of Christ have taught us much already, but there is more. This time the apostle understands that he, too, must use his eyes to expiate sin. You will often find him on his knees, perhaps far into the night, keeping vigil with those eyes of his fixed upon the tabernacle. You will discover a kindliness in the expression of those eyes which instinctively reminds you of the look from the eyes of Christ that nearly broke the heart of Peter with sorrow and with love. You will find a look of sympathy creeping easily into the eyes of the apostle and it recalls to you that the eyes of Jesus filled with tears as He stood before the tomb of His friend Lazarus.

The lips of the apostle he will consecrate to the sacred work of filling up what is wanting to the sufferings of Christ. Those lips will often move in prayer; they will champion Christ's cause; they will speak out fearlessly against the sophistries by which His enemies deceive men who have not the mental ability to detect the falsehood; they will attract by the sweetness of their charitable utterances, even as the words that fell from His lips drew men almost in spite of themselves. Men indeed sin with their lips, but generous souls will be found, many of them, who will seal their lips in perpetual silence, and, hidden away in monasteries and secluded places, offer this silence in reparation for those who use the tongue to blaspheme.

Jesus wore a crown of thorns from which we have already learned the malice of evil thoughts and desires to which free consent is given. But that same crown is the inspiration of the apostle. It leads him to ask himself how he can use his mind in the work of atonement. There are men today who offend God grievously by misusing that gift of His which makes them most Godlike—their intellect. There are others whose minds revel continually in those foul thoughts we have considered. That very fact lends wings to the apostle who wants to find out what he can do for Christ. For there are many men too, thank God, who have consecrated most brilliant intellects to the cause of truth, who have written and spoken valiantly in its defence. There are men and women round about us and they are ever occupied in their minds with one only problem—how to bring souls to Christ and Christ to souls.

From such consecrated minds have sprung forth organizations like Mary's Sodality, which, for four hundred years has been fashioning men and women to high sanctity and sending them into the field of Catholic Action to inflame the souls of others. From such intellects evolved, one hundred years ago, the great Apostleship of Prayer—a tiny mustard seed at first, sown in the obscurity of a Jesuit classroom—and behold, its branches have extended till they have become co-terminous with Christianity. From minds that have studied with minute care the mind of Him Who is wearing the crown of thorns, have come forth the Society of St. Vincent de Paul, and, in our own days, the world-wide Legion of Mary. If there are men and women whose minds are steeped in sin, it is good to remember that there are others which are full of light, and their brightness is kept alive by constant contact with the mind of Christ on Calvary.

Others there are, also, whose minds are full of divine light, though they are less well known to the world. For not all who drink in the ideas and ideals of Christ are endowed with the ability to organize great works, or to write in His defence, or to travel far and wide founding schools or hospitals or havens and homes for the poor and those exposed to grave dangers. But, though they cannot do such things, these souls are a source of deep consolation to Christ, for, by their hidden apostolate of prayer and sacrifice they exercise an influence over the world which may very well far excel that wielded by others who are more conspicuous. For these Jesus has not worn His crown in vain. They, too, have looked and learned the thoughts that lie hidden in that divine mind. Beyond all question, they are helping to fill up what is wanting to the sufferings of Christ.

His ears had to listen, on Good Friday, to jeers and taunts, and we saw that many men use the gift of hearing to offend Him. But the apostle will consecrate this gift of God to His service. He will resolutely close his ears to uncharitable gossip, but he will open them wide to hear, with Christ-like sympathy, the story of sorrow or shame. You will find him generous with his time whenever he comes upon trouble of mind or body, for Jesus was like that, and the apostle's ideal is to be as it were Jesus over again. "I live, now not I, but Christ liveth in me." It is an ideal so exalted as to be never attainable, but he will keep trying. So he will use his ears to listen, as he knows Jesus would listen; he will be deaf to hear in circumstances in which he knows Jesus would be deaf also.

What can he do with his hands to press them into Christ's service? Men sin with their hands; what then ought the apostle to do with his? Our Lord's own hands were nailed to the cross on Good Friday, but time was when they were roughened with toil, time was when they were employed to touch healingly, when they rested lovingly on the heads of innocent children, or busied themselves to wait on His disciples, or wash their feet, or cook their meals. These things the hands of Christ can do no longer now, for in each of them there is a nail keeping it fastened to the cross. But the hands of His apostle can be consecrated. They can become, in their turn, as it were the hands of Jesus Himself.

So he learns to "apostolize" the tying of a parcel or the washing of a dish, by offering that trivial action as an expression of his love. He understands when using his hands to attend to the needs of that patient, who is sick indeed but possibly ungrateful and unreasonable too, that he is continuing the apostolate of his Master and Model. If he earns his living by breaking stones, or digging ditches, or sweeping the street, he understands that no labor is too menial to be sanctified since Jesus used His hands to ply the trade of an artisan. If a poor woman goes out to collect firewood and bends wearily under her load on the way home, she draws strength and encouragement from the thought that His hands clung to the cross on the way to Calvary, and His shoulders bent still lower underneath the weight.

What can the apostle do with his hands? One looks at the magnificent output of Catholic literature in our day, in which men use their hands so effectively to carry on the apostolate of the pen, with its incalculable potentialities for effecting lasting good in souls. One hears of and knows about the sewing, and making of vestments for the missions, and clothes for the poor. One watches the apostle's hands as they cook meals for the needy and distribute food generously to those who are hungry or starving. One kneels before the altar and sees the hands of the priest raising for our adoration the immaculate Body of Christ that hung on Calvary, or exposing It for our veneration in the monstrance. One thinks with gratitude of the many times those same hands were lifted over the bowed head of the repentant sinner, to absolve and to heal. One remembers the hands that guide the blind, the hands that open a door to the destitute or the fallen, the hands protecting and directing the early steps of childhood.

If there are some, many even, who use their hands to commit sin, there are others who have learned from His hands the sublime art of supernaturalizing everything they touch. It is not such a difficult lesson to master if only we look and try to apply our minds seriously to learn. When understood and put in practice, the lesson has a wonderful power to elevate the most commonplace action to the plane of the supernatural. Mere external achievement, devoid of the pure motive of love, is of no value in the sight of the divine expert. He regards, not so much what we do, as why we do it.

A mother was watching at the bedside of her dying son. "Mother," he gasped. "Water! I am tortured with this thirst!" And the mother held the glass to his lips. Just at that moment the clock in the town outside struck three. "My son," she whispered, "it is three o'clock, and today is Friday. It is the day and the hour of Christ's death. He thirsted too." The boy put the glass of water, untasted, back into the hands of his mother.

Which of them displayed the greater courage? It is difficult to know, for a mother's heart feels the pain endured by her son more than her own. But one truth is clear to be seen—both mother and son had learned on Calvary what sin is. They understood that sacrifice is the most effective weapon by which to check its deadly work against the souls for which such a price was paid.

IV. Little Sins

Venial sin "produces the same effect upon the soul as a lasting, though not deadly, disease produces upon the body. It cripples the powers of the soul."—St. Thomas Aquinas.

1. Who's Right?

If you break the pledge against strong drink taken so earnestly at the parish mission, it is likely enough that you will experience some tinge of remorse afterwards. But you will take comfort in the thought that, though it be true that you did indeed take drink to excess, still you were quite well able to walk home or even drive your car through the city traffic. You committed a sin, but it was only venial and nobody nowadays has time to be bothered with such trivialities.

Little six-year-old Tommy accidentally spills ink on your clean linen table-cloth and instantly you fly into a rage and possibly you punish him severely. When you cool down of course you are sorry. You realize you were unjust, and Tommy's red eyes look over reproachfully at you as you vigorously apply some stain-remover to the cloth which you had intended to use this evening for guests at dinner. Your conscience smites you but you deafen your ears to its censures by telling yourself that young people must be trained, and you had frequently warned the lad to remove the cloth before placing his bottle of ink on the table. Anyhow, at the worst your outburst of temper is only a venial sin, and we cannot all be saints.

What is the most satisfactory angle from which to view that nagging employer of yours, whose exactions, you tell me, would exhaust the patience of Job? Is it not when you observe him, from out the corner of your eye, take his hat and coat off the rack and strike for the street door? Such a relief! You peep through the window to see which direction he has taken and you sigh contentedly. Whenever he goes that way, he never returns to the office under two hours. Here is your chance of a little surreptitious dive into that favorite novel, or for a pleasant twenty minutes' chat with the boy or girl at the other typewriter, or perhaps even for a cup of coffee or a coke not provided for in the original bond.

Of course in your heart you know it is not quite right. But what harm anyway? The others all do it and you do not want to be considered a queer one. To waste or misuse your employer's time is a sin. Yes, but only a venial sin, a thing of no consequence, and you take it, good-naturedly, that the Lord will readily condone your easy views.

It was all hours before you reached home after that dance last Saturday night. You just fell into bed exhausted and never heard a sound till the bell was ringing for last Mass next morning. To do you justice you did then jump up and you tried to make haste. But it took you no small time to retrieve that collar-button which had fallen down behind the dressing-table, or to tie your shoe-lace which *would* snap just at the wrong time. Your landlady, to be sure, had insisted many times that she would call you, and anyhow there is that alarm-clock of yours which never fails to arouse you on weekdays when it is a question of being in time for work. You make sure not to lose your job, but the Lord does not matter! So you reach the church just as the priest is beginning to read the Gospel. You observe that you are not the only late arrival and you give a knowing smile to the chap entering with you whom you met last night at the dance. You feel a sense of comfort in having a few companions with you. You hear a Mass that abounds in all sorts of distractions, having begun with such a heavy handicap, but when you come out and light a cigarette you dismiss the whole affair from your mind. At any rate you have fulfilled the essentials of your Sunday obligation, and if your laziness, and your late-coming, and your bad example, and your deliberate distractions constitute a venial sin, you certainly are not going to let a triviality like that weigh heavily on your conscience and spoil the remainder of your free day.

Not quite sure, are you, how you reacted towards that suggestive book borrowed from the public library? A friend had told you it was pretty hot stuff, and your morbid interest was aroused. But after all one cannot be a prude, and you must keep in step with your generation. No great harm in reading anything, at least for one who likes to be considered grown-up, not more than a venial sin at most. Incidentally, are you *quite* satisfied that it was no more?

Then you tell your pal about it and he in his turn wants to read it too and get the thrill. So you pass it on. Had you not read it yourself and spoken about it, the chances are that he would not have bothered. But as things now are, he is all out to lay his hands upon it and drink in its poison. You and I have heard, haven't we, about the responsibility of those who co-operate in the sin of another? Yes, to be sure. But what on earth is the use of making such a fuss about a small matter like a book that is a bit spicy? Perhaps the co-operation was not all it should be. It might be a venial sin, but if it is, who cares?

In that said little volume, by the way, there was a killingly funny situation developed. It gripped you as you lay in bed and you could not bring yourself to turn off the light till you read it right through. Granted, it was not just the sort of thing that would edify the holy nuns at your sister's convent school of three or four years ago, or would please the ears of your venerable parish priest. But everyone knows that he is too strict, and, as for the nuns, well, they are excellent in their way, but they do not understand modern life!

So this funny situation you rehearse, in a whisper perhaps, for your companion, and he or she feels it is up to him or to her to cap it with another. Soon you find yourself drifting, almost imperceptibly, into the habit of shady talk. Your tongue, consecrated by contact with Christ's immaculate body in Holy Communion, is now made to serve a sinful purpose. "Oh, I can't stand exaggeration," you exclaim impatiently. "What's the use of making a mountain out of a molehill? My talk was not pious twaddle, I admit, but there is nothing to get excited about. It may be a bit questionable, but I'm sure it is no more than a venial sin, and who is going to bother about that?"

Conversation with that chance companion you met on the trolley yesterday was somewhat strained—until the name of a third party came up for discussion. And then? Why, you both found yourselves, between two stops on the route, developing the eloquence of Demosthenes spiced with the sarcasm of Cicero! There was an incessant flow of talk. Moreover, you pounced upon this golden opportunity to verify a rumor you had heard about the neighbor. No doubt your own whispered little tale does no good to that neighbor's character, and the confirmed rumor shows him up in a positively vicious light.

As you drop off the trolley and part company with the chatterbox, you recall vaguely a forcible sermon preached last Sunday on charity. The priest stressed especially the truth that what we do to another, is, on Our Lord's own word, done to Himself. Viewed in this light, your recent conversation does not soothe your conscience, but then you know, everybody says that that priest is an idealist. You *must* talk, or people would begin to think you were odd. All the same you know that this time you spoke too freely, and indeed, now that you begin to think it over, you exaggerated the fault out of all proportion. You regret it, I suppose, and you hope chatterbox forgets it and does not pass it on. You were definitely uncharitable, but your sin was only venial, and with that salve for your conscience, you turn into a shop to purchase cigarettes or candy, and the unpleasant memory glides away quite easily.

A word about that half-dollar which has been lying there on that mantel-piece for the past three days. Would anybody blame you for taking it? It is not yours, of course, but you may as well have it as the next person. Or you have the handling of a goodly amount of cash every day. An occasional quarter or two would never be missed, and times are hard, and everyone is out for himself, and there is that show you want to go to and bring your friend. But the money does not belong to you and it is a sin to steal! Forget it! Such a small amount is only a venial sin, and you are not going to be such an idiot as to miss a chance like this!

It is only a venial to say you were sick and unable to go to school when you were hale and hearty all the time; to avow that you knew nothing at all about that accident which you had witnessed; to affirm stoutly and with an air of injured innocence that you had not even seen that missing pair of gloves which you know are safely stowed away in the hidden recesses of your pocket; these things are only small lies; you cannot expect to get through life without them. It is only a venial for a child to answer back mother or father, or to stamp with rage and sulk in the corner. It is only a venial for a boy or girl of eighteen or twenty flagrantly to disobey when told by father or mother to be in by a certain hour. Only a venial to permit or encourage conduct with a partner at a dance or on the way home, concerning which those who love your soul have warned you many times. And, once again, in these cases can we be quite sure that, in point of fact, some of these sins *are* no more than venials?

So we make nothing of these little sins and we consider our attitude the sensible one. But I remember that St. Catherine of Siena wept for two continuous hours over her sins, no one of which was more than a venial. I recall again that St. Teresa of Avila always spoke of herself as a most wicked sinner and, though she never sinned mortally, she had constantly a cry for mercy on her lips. I read that St. Aloysius, on account of two slight faults, was so overcome with sorrow and shame that he fainted at the feet of his confessor. St. Alphonsus Rodriguez would kneel down in the hall before going out and earnestly beg of God that he might die there on the spot, rather than that he should offend Him while outside by even a venial sin. There is that scene in the life of another St. Alphonsus, the founder of the Redemptorists, to show what he thought about the malice of even a venial sin. He was a bishop, you see, and one day, while presiding at a ceremony in all his pontifical vestments, he had a thought of pride and vainglory. How well he looked, arrayed like this! A few hours later you might have met him, armed with a small whip, making tracks to a room at the top of the house. He is going there to scourge his body in order to exorcise himself on the demon of pride!

Clearly the saints do not share our indulgent views about venial sin. Something is wrong somewhere. Whose view is the correct one? Suppose, as is our way, we bring the question to the divine expert?

2. The Expert Again

Before He decides for us, Our Lord would remind us that there is need of a distinction to be kept in mind regarding venial sins. Some of these are semi-deliberate only, and these even the greatest saints do not always succeed in controlling completely. They spring from surprise, from man's innate weakness, from an impulse that asserts itself almost without our advertence. A sudden gesture of impatience when a door bangs, a slightly uncharitable conversation into which one slips almost imperceptibly, a bitter remark spoken on the spur of the moment, a statement made—in itself of no importance—without sufficient investigation, a harshness in judgment of another's conduct because it differs from one's own; into faults such as these even the most faithful of God's friends fall from time to time.

These are not always possible to eradicate. They do not seriously hinder the soul's progress, and He leaves them with us for reasons which will presently appear. As the soul grows in fervor and watchfulness over itself, the tendency is for even these semi-deliberate sins to decrease. But in even those who are most earnest in God's service there is at times to be found quite a plentiful crop of such weeds in the garden, which not all the efforts of the gardener succeed in uprooting.

But fully-deliberate venial sins are in a very different category. Such are, for instance, an habitual aversion towards my neighbor of which I am perfectly conscious, which I show on every possible occasion and make no effort whatever to curb; a habit of telling lies to extricate myself from any awkward corner; a habit of behaving in a testy, nervy, impatient manner which others find so trying, and I know they do but I make no effort to improve; a laziness at my prayers, unpunctuality at Holy Mass, slovenliness at my work, waste of time in gossip or newsmongering, too-great absorption in the care of my health. What does the divine expert think of these, and the legion of other venial offences which the world regards as part of our normal life?

First of all He begins by making a few suppositions. Suppose then, you have a dearly loved mother at home who is lying grievously ill. Suppose there is a certain medicine which will infallibly cure her if it can be procured. But in order to get it, there is only one way open to you—you must commit a venial sin. You may reasonably enough object that in such an extreme case a way out could be found by which to avoid the venial sin. That, I should say, would be likely in the circumstances. But that is not our case. Our case supposes that if you are to get your hands on that bottle of medicine, you must, let us say, tell a lie, a cold-blooded deliberate lie. You must commit a venial sin, therefore. You may compromise, just this once? May you brush aside the troublesome circumstance in the anxiety that is eating your heart out to see your mother well again?

It has to be asserted, and firmly, that, rather than commit what we suppose would be only a venial sin, you must continue to watch your poor mother stay in pain. You must even allow her to die before your eyes rather than save her life, if a deliberate venial sin be the price to be paid for recovery.

Admittedly this is an extreme case, but we have made it so designedly, in order to bring out the more clearly the frightful nature of venial sin. It might indeed, in such a case, be possible to sidestep the circumstance quite lawfully. But *if* it is not possible without venial sin, there is nothing for it but to permit even the death of the mother you love.

Another supposition. We have just come out of the throes of the most devastating war ever witnessed. Suppose that a unique opportunity comes your way to guarantee to the world that never again within the lifetime of the present generation, will there be a re-occurrence of such a catastrophe. Need we expiate on the immense blessings that must follow? No more black-outs, or bombings, not another shot to be fired, men can settle down with easy minds to the occupations of peace, for all is guaranteed for at least another eighty years. But in order to secure such a happy result, you have to pay a price. All this will happen, provided you tell just one deliberate lie. May you do so? It is only a venial sin after all, and think of all the good it will accomplish. The answer once again must be definite and unhesitating. It has to be maintained that to tell a lie is always a sin, and nothing can ever make it lawful.

In the very extreme case we have imagined it might be possible to find a form of words capable of two interpretations, one of which will save the situation. If so, it might be lawful to make use of that form with certain safeguards. But if there be no choice except to commit a venial sin by telling a cold-blooded lie, then the wonderful prize of a permanent peace must be allowed to elude you. You may not tell a lie even to secure the temporal welfare of the entire world.

I feel sure you are on the point of wanting to expostulate. Does not this rigid doctrine seem altogether silly and exaggerated? Is not this the kind of thing that causes the Church to be accused of unreasonableness, that keeps many fair-minded non-Catholics from entering her fold or examining her claims? The reason we make light of venial sin is that we are always comparing it in our minds with mortal sin. We have the wrong background. Catholics readily enough admit that mortal sin is the greatest of all misfortunes, and the mere fact that a sin escapes being so grievous makes them inclined to minimize its malice and its heinousness. But in point of fact venial sin is the greatest possible kind of evil imaginable, excepting only the foulest and most revolting crime conceivable. Venial sin is just something less disgusting than the most loathsome, slimiest act which man is capable of doing. Can it be possible, then, that venials are not serious?

Instead of using mortal sin as our background—against which the malice of venial sin does not stand out sufficiently in relief—the divine expert would have us substitute the infinite holiness and purity of God against Whom venial sin is committed. Moreover, that insult is offered by a person towards whom we have seen this God bending in a love so condescending that the thought of it almost paralyzes when we begin to think out its implications. We have glanced at a few pages of the love-story His hand has written. The stupendous gift of creation, of grace, of forgiveness, the entrancing promise of heaven, the minute directions He gives lest we lose our way home—is it a negligible offence to belittle such proofs of divine love? "Every best gift and every perfect gift" flows down from His generous hands into the souls of the men and women He loves. Is ingratitude to such a benefactor not so serious? Can the creature slight such a Creator, even in a lesser matter, and take the slight in his stride as something beneath his notice?

You will see, under the guidance of the divine expert, more clearly still the ingratitude of venial sin if you make the case your own. A friend of yours, a great friend whom you have known and loved since childhood, gets involved in very serious difficulties. At once you are full of concern and you tell him that any help in your power to give is his for the asking. He needs professional advice in order to understand his own case and discover the most effective means of extricating himself, and you go to no end of trouble to secure it for him. He requires the help of men who are highly placed, and, at great inconvenience to yourself, you write to them, you obtain for your friend several interviews, and assurance of further assistance if required. This friend of yours has to make a good many journeys in the effort to solve his difficulties; these cost money, and you, most generously, put your hand in your pocket and give him as much as he wants. He has to leave his family behind for days at a stretch, but you allay all his anxiety by telling him they will be well looked after in his absence.

You have surely proved yourself a staunch friend. While his case is still in the balance let me suppose that you have to go away yourself to a very remote part. You are there a full month and to your surprise not a word reaches you. You write to ask how things are faring, but you get no reply. Six months and a year pass without a line from the man you helped so much. After sixteen months you are sitting in a bus one day, and a chance fellow-passenger tells you in the course of conversation that the case of your friend has come out all right. Everything is once again in apple-pie order. It has been proved clearly that he was quite innocent of all the charges, or that the accusations were all based on a false supposition.

Glad, are you? Well, I expect you are, though it would be hard to blame you if you did not feel a sting at the man's ingratitude. After all you did to help him out, when everything has turned to his advantage, he did not think it worth his while to send even a postcard to thank you and tell you the good news.

But venial sin is ingratitude to God. There is, most literally, nothing of good in us except what He has given. "What hast thou that thou hast not received?" If love proves itself by deeds, then indeed does the love of God for my soul stand this acid test. Search the history of the most noble friendships and the most holy and most generous loves, and find, if you can, any one of them that can bear comparison with the friendship and love of God for the soul of man. Now, venial sin spurns that love, at least in a measure, but in quite an appreciable measure. You are indignant, and I suppose rightly, at the thankless and thoughtless attitude of your friend, but in the same breath you speak about venial sin as not being serious. To show unmistakable signs of ingratitude to the advances made by an infinitely-loving God Who has loaded the soul with every blessing; to lay down conditions for the Creator, the creature of His hand dictating to Him; to feign deafness when He asks for a sacrifice as proof of your love, a sacrifice that is obligatory, indeed, though in a lesser matter, a sacrifice asked from His son or daughter with a view to enriching the soul with a yet greater abundance of His graces; when God says to the soul, "I am come that you may have life and may have it more abundantly," to reject His offer and decline with an insolent refusal! Of course the soul does not refuse entirely to co-operate with Him, but it cannot just be bothered with fidelity in lesser matters. Are we beginning to understand why the saints had such a horror of venial sin? Venial sin is ingratitude to a God Whose heart loves His creature with an infinite love, and longs for a full return of love.

But it is also insolence and arrogance on the part of the sinner. God is not only a God of love, but of power, too, and of infinite sanctity. "What is God?" asked the thoughtful boy at school, and, as he grew up into manhood he probed deeply into the question he had raised. He gave himself as a priest and a religious and a student to much prayer and penance and study, and into his intellect, one of the mightiest of all times, God poured an abundance of light. He saw much of the greatness and perfection of God, and he wielded his doughty pen in telling men what he saw; his immortal volumes live still and they are placed in the hands of every student who seeks to know what God is.

Two years before his death, their author had a vision of God, and now all his wonderful "Summa," containing such lucid expositions of the perfections of God, seemed to him as a thing of "so much straw," and he never finished it. Divine light, prayer, study, penance, a keen intellect and a heart burning with seraphic love, had combined in producing to the boyhood question of Thomas Aquinas an answer that is the admiration of all who read it.

None the less, compared with that flashing glimpse of the reality, it seemed to him now as nothing more than so much straw. His luminous mind and inflamed heart were, after all, only finite and crude instruments when employed to express the ineffable perfections of Him Who is infinite. Can any offence, even venial, be considered lightly in view of such transcendent sanctity?

You are confused if your six-year-old child says something *outré* to your visitor, even though he does not intend to be rude nor understand why he may not ask that question. You are full of apologies if you bang a door in your employer's face, even unintentionally. A man may pride himself on his courage, but he may still tremble before a judge, a mere fellow-man, when he knows in his heart that he is guilty of the charge.

Who then shall find words to express the magnitude of an offence against the all-holy and all-powerful God—not an unintentional offence either, but a deliberate and cold-blooded act of arrogance and refusal to obey?

"What is God?" Go over the world and count up the thousands who walk our streets at night, and add to these the teeming millions who cover the face of the globe. Let your mind go back to the millions who have preceded the present generation, and forward to embrace the countless millions yet unborn. God knows every single one of all these, and every single idea that ever crossed or will cross, those human minds. "God knows me so thoroughly," writes Bishop Vaughan, "so thoroughly through and through, that it would be absolutely impossible for Him to know me, and all my thoughts, feelings, and desires, more perfectly and more exhaustively, even were He to withdraw His attention from all other beings in order to rivet the whole of His attention on me alone." Who dare assert that venials aren't serious?

Every thought in the mind of every student is like a tiny drop drawn from the infinite well of divine knowledge. The surgeon's most delicate instrument, devised with such skill to perform the most complicated operation, is just a shred of evidence manifesting the might of God's power. The machine built with so much labor, reflecting so much glory on him who invented it, is the merest indication of the limitless expanses of His infinite strength. In a mighty earthquake you know how great cities collapse at one quiver; did God choose, for a single moment, to take away His supporting hands, the entire universe must fall to pieces in the same way. Venial sin not serious? Not serious to display arrogance and wanton disobedience to Him Whom even the winds and the seas obey?

We hear often enough about man's insignificance and daily experience proves it further. Man prides himself if he makes a new discovery in some small corner of God's universe—a new drug, or gas, or new property in some one plant. But there is still an immense uncharted sea about which he knows nothing.

Thus there is his ignorance. There is also his weakness, his utter dependence on his fellow-men for even his existence, his constant illnesses which are a foreshadowing of his passing hence and of his final corruption.

What of his greatness, his real greatness, not greatness as dreamed of by the dupes of sin, and the votaries of the world and worldly ambition? In what does man's real greatness consist? We have seen it already. Man is great, because he has an immortal soul which is actually capable of possessing God here and hereafter.

The soul has been described as a capacity for containing divine life. God created man's immortal soul in order that He might pour into it a share of His own very life. By sanctifying grace man is elevated to a new life, God designing, so to say, to saturate the very texture of the soul so that it becomes "drenched with His divinity." All St. Paul's epistles are full of this noble concept—that we share with Christ His own very life, that in some marvelous manner He takes the human soul and sows in it the seed of His own life, and that man must develop that tiny seed, so as to ensure its continued progress, till finally it attain that measure of growth destined for it by Him Who deigned to plant the seed.

Thus God has planned an intimacy with man far closer than that which exists in the most sacred human relationships. Because of this intimacy, this "oneness" with Himself, He demands love from His creature, a love greater than any human love. "He that loves father or mother more than Me, is not worthy of Me. . . . He that loves son or daughter, husband or wife, more than Me, is not worthy of Me. . . ." Now perhaps we begin to see into the malice of venial sin, and to understand something of its insolence. For the man who sins deliberately, even though his offence be only venial, stifles the growth in his soul of this divine life. He willingly tolerates in his soul a barrier which hinders the perfecting of God's plan. He is far too careful of himself to run the risk of committing mortal sin, for he is selfish enough to want security hereafter as well as here. But, to a God desiring and wishing to give Himself to him in this holiest intimacy, to a God longing to possess entirely this immortal soul, the man cries out: "Thus far shall You come, and no farther."

There are certain sins and sinful attachments from which he refuses to be divorced, and he prefers these to the fullness of divine life. There are certain nooks and corners in the temple of his soul which he has reserved for little idols. He cannot have these and the full friendship of God, so he blandly lets that friendship go and tells you venial sins aren't serious!

Once more try, though the attempt must ever remain a failure, to span the infinite abyss between God's sanctity and man's sinfulness, between the omnipotence of God and the weakness and instability of man, between the depths of His knowledge and wisdom and man's ignorance. Think of these, compare the two carefully in prayer, and you will understand what an affront is venial sin, which, at least in a measure, spurns God's offer of friendship, forbids Him free access to the soul, ties the hands of God when He approaches the soul laden with graces, and compels Him to withhold them. All this, because the soul deliberately prefers to cling to an irregular attachment. All this, because the soul, having never clearly thought out the malice of a venial sin in this light, dismisses it with a shrug of the shoulders.

This is the viewpoint of the divine expert as He examines into the nature of venial sin and reveals to us what He finds.

3. Slippery Ground

Venial sin is black ingratitude to a most loving God and arrogance and insolence to a most powerful and most holy God. But if you are inclined to say that these motives leave you cold, because they assume that you possess a measure of unselfishness to which you lay no claim, let me appeal to yet another argument which touches more closely our own personal interests.

A man who had spent the greater part of his life in India came home to England at the end, to finish in the midst of the pleasant scenes of his boyhood. Among other curios he brought back with him was a little tiger's cub. The tiny creature was perfectly tame and went about the place, a friend of everybody, not unlike a little cat. One sunny day the owner was sitting in a deck chair in his garden. His right hand held the book he was reading, and with his left, flung carelessly over the side of the chair, he was toying and playing with the tiger's cub.

Now in the center of the man's left palm there was a small cut which had been bleeding half an hour earlier. As the tiger's cub licked the hand, presently the tongue came in contact with the fresh wound and for the first time tasted human blood. At once there was a notable change in the animal's attitude; a craving for more human blood had been awakened. From that day, the tiger's cub became a menace, and the owner, fearing lest the craving would prove a danger to his own life, took his gun and shot the little creature.

In every human heart there is a tiger's cub, and the offhand way we dismiss smaller sins as being in no way serious argues to an insanity and recklessness which would make us blush in matters which we consider to be of greater importance. That man took no risk with the life of his body and we applaud his prompt action in dealing with danger. But the man who settles down complacently to a habit of venial sin is jeopardizing the life and eternal salvation of his soul. Let a man go on consistently making light of venial sin and there is God's word for it that he will go farther. "He that despiseth little things shall fall by little and little."

A boy or girl does not become a great sinner overnight. The devil is far too astute to suggest full-blooded crime to a person hitherto careful to guard against all sin. But indulge in a small lie here and there, just to get out of an awkward corner, and if that fearful habit be allowed to grow a day may easily come when it will lead the soul right into mortal sin and to the very mouth of hell. It is the story of the tiger's cub again.

You may find yourself in the witness-box and you take an oath which you know to be false. You call upon the most high God to support your solemn statement that your words are true. How did your conscience ever reach such a condition of utter callousness? Just as the mason builds his wall brick by brick, so you, by making light of small lies have built up a habit of sin. With the laying of each new brick the wall becomes higher and firmer, and with each new lie, too, the evil habit is developed until you hardly discriminate between a statement made under oath and one made in everyday parlance. As you pick your steps down from that witness-box you might well think of yourself as being surrounded by the flames of hell. God is not mocked. Your false oath is a mockery of His divine majesty, an outrage on His truth. You have deceived a human judge and a human court, but your soul, reeking with crime, is visible in all it foulness to Him Who neither can deceive nor be deceived. To this pass have you come, largely by your indulgent attitude towards venial sin in the past.

God's Law, as interpreted by the mouth of His infallible Church, is, says your modern world, altogether too strict in matters of sex. We are human after all, and God is full of mercy; we are not all intended by Him to be priests and nuns, and we need a little moral holiday now and then. So, with a thousand specious reasonings, we try to let ourselves down lightly. But if ever you hear of a poor boy or girl whose life is in shreds as a result of immoral practices, you may take it for certain that the depths were reached by a pandering to the lenient doctrine of the world concerning these "minor" offences. It is always a question of the tiger's cub being allowed to get the first taste. Little by little the soul, once God's temple by sanctifying grace, begins at first to totter till one day it collapses in a heap of smoking ruins.

Let a parent condone petty thefts in a small child—only a penny off the shelf or an occasional dime from a purse—and once again a most vicious habit, fraught with dangers to the soul of possibly gigantic proportions, may well be the ultimate result.

The man who is up for embezzlement of perhaps thousands of dollars will admit that his sleight-of-hand trickeries are the outcome of small acts of theft begun at home in early childhood, continued in school where he got into the habit of stealing other boy's books or pencils or money, and escaping detection. He will tell you how a search was instituted in the college to catch the thief, how traps were laid for him, but your budding criminal was too slick and too cunning. He reveled in evading the justice of the law and gloried in outwitting those who suspected him but could secure no proof.

The tiger's cub has been aroused, and as the years go on, the young man discovers ingenious ways and means of growing rich quickly. His mind is always running on these lines—how he can live on his wits, how he can taste the sense of victory by carrying off his prize with impunity. God's Law, it need not be said, causes him little anxiety at this stage. Mortal sin has long ago ceased to have any fears for him; still less does the thought of the holiness and love of God affect his attitude towards life. He is a confirmed sinner. He has the orientation of mind toward sin that regards it as part and parcel of life. His sense of sin is entirely destroyed. And why? Because his evil instincts in childhood were allowed to grow uncontrolled; possibly even they were developed by the parents whose duty it was to teach him how to curb them.

Look around you and observe any other types of noted sinners. You will find that their vicious lives, in nearly every case, are the logical outcome of a habit of venial sin that is condoned. It is true that no number of venial sins added together can ever reach the malice of a single mortal sin. It is true that no number of deliberate venial sins can inflict upon the soul the fearful death that results from one mortal sin. But it is none the less true that he who walks in habitual carelessness concerning venial sin is traveling by a very slippery road. Let him stumble continually and the chances are that in the end he will have a very bad fall. It is easier to sail with the wind than pull against a strong current. But let the little skiff have her way, let her run along pleasantly with the breeze, and there is no knowing if she ever again will touch land. There is no knowing what reefs are out there at sea against which she may be dashed to pieces, no knowing what strong currents may drive her completely out of her course. The way of many a soul is strewn with wreckage because of sins which began as mere venial sins. "He that despiseth small things shall fall by little and little."

This free and easy attitude towards venial sin has its evil effects also on one's associates. Let me exemplify. A young man takes up a position for the first time in your office and settles down to work by your side. Hitherto he has been scrupulously honest but now he discovers that you, his senior, make nothing of petty thefts. You help yourself to the firm's notepaper and stamps for your own letters. You loaf whenever you get the chance and suffer no qualms if you waste time for which you are paid to work. Until now, that boy beside you has always preserved a clean tongue, but your easy habit of swearing, or retailing an occasional "hot" story, though at first it displeases him, gradually begins to seem the manly thing to do.

Don't you see what the result is going to be—that soon he will be as bad as yourself, or worse? That he, too, will condone venial sins, waste his time, take what does not belong to him, slacken in his vigilance against impure thoughts and desires? In his case, too, the story of the tiger's cub is very likely to be repeated. Whose responsibility is this?

You smile indulgently at the scruples or uneasiness of that new apprentice and you tell her that after she wears off the convent school training she will cherish no misgivings about what she reads or what companions she associates with. It is not so easy for a person younger than yourself to stand up to cynicism; human respect will get her down, as it has often done before. Your attitude towards venial sin has injected its poison and leaves that girl more susceptible to the intrusion of the more venomous microbe.

All of which means that you are like a soldier who hands out secret information to the other camp, or one who supplies the enemy with food and clothing. You are a traitor to Christ and you try to pass off your treachery as not being serious! In another place we have seen something about the ineffable beauty of an immortal soul. But your own venial sins mar that beauty, and your example, leading others to imitate you, brings about a like ugliness in their souls. Venial sin is like a blot of ink on an otherwise spotless page, or like a running sore on a face otherwise healthy and good to look upon.

You feel embarrassed in select company with such a mark on

your face. You try to remove it or cover it up, and, until it has healed, you keep as much as you can out of the public eye. But how can you live and move and have your being under the all-seeing eye of the infinitely-holy God and experience no embarrassment when He looks upon those loathsome offences which you treat so lightly? How can you so readily absolve yourself from the truly appalling guilt of spreading the virus abroad in the souls of others? "If any one of the angels or saints were marked with this stain (venial sin), he would instantly be removed from the presence of the infinite sanctity of God. And the same would be true of even the immaculate queen of heaven, the Blessed Virgin herself."

We might add, with St. Catherine of Genoa, that if, to suppose the impossible, a soul could enter heaven in the state of venial sin, it would of its own accord rush thence into the cleansing flames of purgatory. To endure the holiness of God without being free of every stain would be a more terrible torture for the soul than to suffer the agony of purgatory.

4. Purgatory

Mention of purgatory brings to mind another argument for the gravity of sins which are only venial. It is often our way to persuade ourselves that the punishment of that place is not too terrible. We are lopsided in our view here, too, because here once more we are using the wrong background. We are comparing purgatory with hell, and because we know it is less than hell, we therefore imagine that we can treat it leniently. But, says St. Augustine, the fire of purgatory is more terrible than anything in the way of pain that can be seen, felt, or imagined in this life. It is a temporary hell, a mitigated hell, from out of which no soul may be delivered until it has paid the last farthing.

You know how a man chafes under a prolonged illness. He falls off a high ladder and breaks several bones, and for six or eight months he must lie in bed, perfectly still. The doctor assures him that the cure is certain but he can offer no speedier remedy. He does his best to keep the patient cheerful, telling him that everything is shaping well, and that if he continues to improve he may be able to sit up in another week or two. But, even with the certainty that he is on the mend and that the complete cure is only a question of time, still the long hours all day and all night, while he lies there motionless on his back, drag by wearily enough.

Now the soul in purgatory has this same assurance. The punishment is only temporary, and the soul has the certain promise that ultimately it will be freed from this prison house to leap up into the arms of God and enjoy forever the unveiled beauty of the Godhead. Beyond all question that glad expectancy is a source of super-abundant joy to the soul. But the cure is dreadfully slow, and the soul is absolutely helpless to hasten, by a single minute, the hour of deliverance. Is all this a light sentence? This is the atonement which a just God owes to Himself, because He is just, for those venial sins which the soul in life regarded as mere trivialities.

It is to be recalled here too, as we did when considering mortal sin, that God, in assigning this punishment in purgatory, is not moved by caprice or by passion. When the soul leaves this world with the guilt upon it of even one unrepented venial sin, the judge places it in the balance and weighs out with nicest accuracy the penalty which it deserves. There is no desire of vindictiveness, no impulse of passion. Such things are unthinkable in an infinitely-holy God. The sentence pronounced by such a judge on a single unrepented venial sin differs from His sentence on a mortal sin only in this—that for venial sins the punishment is temporary, whereas hell is eternal.

Venials aren't serious? There have been times when God punished venial sin even in this life, in order to instil into our souls a salutary hatred of it. King Oza stretched forth his hand to prevent the ark of God from falling. His intentions were indeed the very best, but still to touch the ark was not permitted him. God's indignation was enkindled, though at most the offence was only venial, and He struck the king for his rashness and he died on the spot.

Venials aren't serious? The divine expert thinks they are.

We have to beware of rushing to the conclusion that God is hard or cruel in punishing venial sins so drastically. The truth is, rather, that such sins must be frightful indeed to demand such a penalty from such a judge. We have insisted that the judge is impartial, all-knowing, objective, a judge never influenced by passion, above all corruption and impervious to any bribe. Such is the judge who takes the scales into His hands to apportion the punishment due to even a single venial sin.

Before going on to the next section of our book, it may be worth while to sum up briefly our findings so far. The attitude of many Catholics towards venial sin betrays a lack of faith. For it is generally felt that such sins are no great harm. This very dangerous view, we saw, is accounted for in large measure by the fact that we estimate the gravity of venial sin by comparing it with mortal instead of regarding it as an offence by a mere creature against an all-loving, all-powerful, all-knowing God. Viewed in this light it must be clear that, to commit a deliberate venial sin, even to gain an immense temporal blessing like a permanent peace, can never be permissible.

Looked at from the more selfish angle, unrepented venial sin often leads on to mortal sin, and even if it does not, it merits a truly terrifying punishment in purgatory. Its evil influence spreads and infects the souls of others, who, in their turn may be led on to grievous sin.

The severity of purgatory argues, not to a God Who is cruel, but to the terrifying nature of venial sin the evil of which such a God assesses thus. If all this be true, and it is true, then to defend the thesis that venials aren't serious is to be guilty of the insanity of flagrantly contradicting the divine expert when He expounds the only sound philosophy of life.

5. The Right Ideal

A man who thinks seriously about venial sin and sees it from the point of view of Our Lord may easily find growing up in his soul an abhorrence of it. God grant it, for, after mortal sin, there is no more terrifyingly evil thing. The man's hatred may next translate itself into a very definite resolution. Since venial sin is so dreadful in itself, such ingratitude, such insolence, so fraught with risks of even more dire consequences, he may make up his mind to eradicate from his life all venial sin forevermore. But, however estimable those intentions of his may be, he has to be warned that in making such a resolution he is purusing a Utopian ideal. Despite the fact that deliberate venial sin is all that we have been taught in the school of the divine expert, it is none the less true that, without a special grace from God to which we can lay no claim, it is impossible for us to avoid it completely.

So deepseated is our corruption as a result of the fall, that sin, at least semi-delibrate venial sin, is a necessary evil. Even the most earnest, fervent soul will sometimes succumb to its attacks. Even at the height of their fervor some of the saints would suddenly show signs of impaticnce, or give way to petty pride or vainglory, or allow some uncharitable conversation to escape them. "People do not become automatically perfect," writes Mr. Walsh in his *Saint Teresa of Avila,** "on entering a religious order, they have only begun a lifetime of conflict against weaknesses which must be conquered one by one. Even saints, far from being bodyless abstractions, selfless and sexless, have faults that can be very irritating to those about them." The knowledge that this is so may surely be a source of encouragement. "Saints," somebody has written, "like all masterpieces, are made slowly."

What is to be our attitude then, towards venial sin, if it cannot be altogether avoided even by the saints? What may we reasonably hope to attain to in the matter of ridding ourselves of it, if we are faithful to God's graces? To begin with, an immense amount *can* be eradicated; practically all deliberate venial sin can be avoided by people of goodwill. If we find ourselves constantly falling and apparently unable to rise or at least incapable of keeping on our feet, the ideal then to strive after is—never to make peace with that sin, never to settle down with a fatalistic air to a deliber-

* Walsh, William Thomas, *St. Teresa of Avila*. Milwaukee, Bruce Publishing Company, 1943.

ate habit of sin, even in venial matters. Perhaps illustration may help.

You are constantly confessing breaches of charity, talking about your neighbor's faults, or telling small lies, or loss of temper, or stealing little things. Last week you told that sin, and again the week before. Indeed, if you look back over a period of six or seven years your tale has all been of a piece, and if the Lord spares you for six or seven more you see no reason why you should change! Doesn't it look very like as if you are not really in earnest about getting rid of that temper or other sinful habit? "If every year," says à Kempis, "we rooted out one vice we should soon become perfect men."

If you set the ideal before you which we have been suggesting —never to make peace with a given sin—you are not going to let yourself "get away" with your offence. You resolved firmly in confession to watch over one fault in particular, your harsh conversation, for instance. But you slipped up at the very next opportunity. Very well. The broken resolution is now going to be followed up by a penance. You are not going to that show tonight although you have a ticket, although you have been told it is a fine show, although you have been looking forward to it all the week. Why not? Because you broke your promise about that harsh speech of yours. Or you deprive yourself of a little treat you had promised yourself, or you go without reading that interesting book—all for the same reason. Do something like that every time and your habits of venial sin will disappear like mists before the rising sun.

But it is imperative that you do not let yourself off! Persevere, and after a while the result will be that when you are tempted to talk uncharitably, or to fall into whatever fault you are watching, the memory of the penance which will certainly follow will come to your mind. So you decide: better not!

A blind old man was in the habit of receiving a visit each evening from one of the boys of the town. The visitor would fill the old man's pipe and then read for him for half an hour or so.

One evening, just as the pipe was drawing nicely and the old man was settling down to listen to the reading, he suddenly pulled the pipe out of his mouth, laid it on the table, and apostrophized himself thus: "No pipe this evening, because you lost your temper this morning!"

No doubt a general purpose of amendment is sufficient in a confession where the penitent has only venial sins to tell. Still, to tackle one of these energetically and methodically in the manner shown will secure much more lasting results for the soul. The saints recommend this way of dealing with our venial sins, for "if every year we rooted out one vice we should soon become perfect men."

Another very effective habit to acquire if we want to lessen our venial sins is saying *no* to ourselves, when *yes* is much easier to say, and is not a sin. You refuse to look in that shop window where the crowd is gathered; you make yourself walk up the stairs one step at a time when naturally you want to rush; you refrain from tearing open that envelope to read your letter immediately, instead you leave it on the table while you go upstairs to change your coat; you do not permit yourself to ask that unnecessary question, to look and read the name on that dangling label, to mail that letter which will not be delivered any sooner in any case. To give in in such cases is not a sin, but the effort required to restrain oneself here is going to be an enormous advantage when you have to check habits that are indeed sinful, whether venially or mortally so. Having said *no* frequently where there was no question of sin, you are now in a much stronger position to say it when sin intrudes itself ingratiatingly into your path.

Such methods of combating venial sin are salutary indeed. Still there is another which may prove even more effective. We know that Our Divine Lord walked the highways and byways of life, not only to open heaven for us, but also to provide us with a perfect model of what our conduct ought to be. Just as the artist tries to produce on his canvas as perfect a likeness as possible of the person sitting before him, so does every true Christian strive each day to reproduce in himself a more exact likeness of Jesus Christ. The artist studies every detail of the model—the folds of the garments, the color of the eyes, the position of the hands—all with a view to reproducing the same on his canvas.

This, too, is the inspiring task that lies to our hand as followers of Christ. It is a high ideal, of course, and even the saints fall far short of it. Still, man's free co-operation is an essential element in the work. And part of his co-operation consists in this—that he keeps his eyes continually fixed upon the model, and never gives up the effort to behave in all places and in all times as he sincerely believes Jesus Christ would behave in the same or similar circumstances.

How would He answer if He was questioned in that rough manner which instinctively annoys you? What stand would He take if this particular question came up for discussion while He was present? Would He speak here, or would He keep silence? Would He show just anger, or would He bear this insult or thoughtlessness or ingratitude without any sign of indignation? What sort of reception would Jesus give to this intruder? What reply would He give to this letter? If He had to endure this lingering illness how would He comport Himself? If He were victimized as you consider yourself to be, what would His reaction be? If that proud domineering person were to address Him as you have just been addressed, what would Jesus say, and how would He treat that person at their next meeting? If that sacrifice was asked of Him—to wait on some difficult patient, to rise at night to attend that sick parent, to give up that promised treat in order to be present at the meeting of a special Church activity—what would He do, in these circumstances, Jesus Christ, the perfect Model of men?

We remind ourselves of this grand ideal of reproducing in ourselves the mind and heart of Christ because, as is clear, it automatically cuts the ground from under our venial sins. We can, to be sure, attack our venial sins one by one, as already suggested, but, by "looking upon Jesus" and aiming at as perfect an imitation of Him as is consistent with human frailty we have a method that is more direct and more inspiring. It is one that is recommended many times by Our Lord Himself. "Learn of Me," He says; and again, "I have given you an example, that as I have done, you do also." The man with this aim constantly before his eyes is not likely to retain for long a deliberate affection for venial sins or try to extenuate their malice.

Let me suppose you have to carry a picture of great value from one end of the city to the other. You entrust it to a messenger boy who has only the dimmest notion of the worth of what he holds in his hands. Accordingly, when you are well out of sight, he gets rid of the weight at the first opportunity, by throwing your picture into the back of a passing truck, and leaping in himself after it. On the journey the car jolts badly and the frame of your picture loses some of its gilding. The rising dust falls upon it, and when the rain comes drops penetrate into the canvas. By the time your picture is restored to you, it has lost much of its beauty and you are rightly indignant with the youngster, and you berate him soundly for his carelessness.

Now "my soul," says the psalmist, "is always in my hands," and the Apostle adds that we bear our treasure in earthen vessels. Treasure in earthen vessels is easily lost, and the soul entrusted to our frail keeping can very soon become besmirched with stains. It is possible to assume a condoning attitude towards those stains—like the boy carrying your valuable painting—and tell ourselves that things are well enough. It is possible for us, too, to place our treasure securely, and shield it from much of the dust and protect it from most of the joltings. Better still, we have even the power to hand back the treasure to its owner, when we reach the end of the journey, not in a state of preservation merely, but with its beauty actually enhanced a hundredfold, with the divine image more sharply defined than the day that image was first impressed upon the soul in baptism.

What man who thinks is going to allow that noble image to be distorted and disfigured by saying, with a tolerant shrug of the shoulders, that venial sins aren't serious? If you, who understand the value of your picture, are rightly angry with the boy for his want of care, can you not understand the concern of the divine expert who sees so clearly the damage wrought on His masterpiece by deliberate venial sin?

V. Music While You Work

"If a plan is to be fruitful, it must be positive. Not to give way is merely negative. The plan of a brave and vigorous army is a positive one—to worry the enemy, to pursue him, harass him, force him to surrender."—Père Plus, S.J., *in* Facing Life, p. 33.

1. Walking the Plank

Some of us, I suppose, have made the pilgrimage to Lough Derg.* After that long fast of seventy-two hours, it is no matter for surprise if we feel ravenously hungry. When recounting our experiences afterwards, we will tell our friends, perhaps, that we did not find the fast as severe as we had anticipated. But the point we will stress is, not that we felt hungry—that is taken for granted—but that, all things considered, the pangs were not as painful as we expected.

The hunger does not cause any surprise because in every man there is a natural tendency to eat and drink. He cannot live without food and at all costs he tries to obtain it. This is everyday experience.

In this section of our book, the divine expert looking at life would wish to put before us His eminently comforting and encouraging teaching about temptation. Having shown us the purpose of our lives, and the monster that tries to block our road—sin, mortal and venial—Our Divine Lord now bids us, while working earnestly at the one task enjoined upon us, the will of the Father, to cheer ourselves on the road by tackling our temptations with an optimism which He will show to be most reasonable. Music while you work? Yes, certainly, music in our hearts while we work our way through life, cheerfulness in our souls notwithstanding the trials and pitfalls that beset our path.

What is the solid foundation for this optimism, so characteristic

* An island in the lake of the same name in the county of Donegal, is Lough Derg, popularly known as St. Patrick's Purgatory. It was a favorite place of retreat for the Saint, and is still venerated by thousands of pilgrims every year.

of every true follower of Our Lord? First of all, it is consoling to remember that it is as natural for a man to be tempted as to feel hungry if he abstains from taking food, or cold if he travels in the Arctic zone. He possesses within him passions which all the time clamor for satisfaction, while outside of him there is the devil, and there is the world, waiting to allure him into sinful ways. All three conspire to tempt the man, to rob him of his peace of mind, and ultimately to lead him into grievous sin. (It is well to insert a parenthesis here and say that our passions, in themselves, are good. But, as we shall see presently, they must be made to fulfil the role of servants. Hence the imperative need, not of crushing them entirely, but of controlling them. Without this control the servants become despots.)

So no man goes through life without temptations. That is the state of affairs and there is no use on earth in working oneself into a condition of misery about it. To think that all is lost merely because one feels tempted, and tempted even very violently, is to imagine oneself an angel and not a human being. Temptation is not sin. A man may be bombarded with fierce attacks of temptation, and these may be launched against him at the most sacred moments—when he is kneeling at the Communion rail, for instance—and there need not necessarily be attaching to them the smallest breath of sin or imperfection.

We have only to turn over the pages of the saints' lives to see how true this is. We find St. Paul groaning under the attacks of some temptation. He speaks about "the sting of the flesh," and "the angel of satan sent to buffet him." In his distress he cried out three times to beg God to deliver him, but he begged to no purpose. God refused to take away the temptation, but what He promised was grace sufficient to endure its attacks unscathed. "My grace is sufficient for thee." What a source of deep consolation! As soon as he realizes it, all his despondency drops from him like a cloak. "Gladly therefore will I *glory* in my infirmities that the virtue of Christ may dwell in me." No more pessimism, but actual rejoicing in his very weakness.

Much nearer our own day we have St. Alphonsus Rodriguez,

the Jesuit brother. He describes how he, too, when an old man who had served God with heroic fidelity for nearly fifty years, was subjected to almost incessant temptations against the virtue of purity. Remember that at this time Alphonsus was canonizable, and he has since been raised to the altars. So we, who are not saints at all, may well take courage.

The same is true of every friend of God. Time was when a saint of today, the Little Flower of Jesus, was surrounded by a group of sentimentally pious biographers. They would have St. Thérèse the pampered darling who was shielded all through her short life from temptation, and who, when she entered Carmel was treated there as a simple little child and allowed more or less to have her own way in everything. It is well that such travesty of the truth has been dynamited. Thérèse's own autobiography, and much that has since come to light, make it abundantly clear that if she became a saint, she paid for her sanctity by the practice of heroic fidelity in face of fierce attacks of the evil one.

So the divine expert begins by impressing this truth upon us. Never imagine, He would say, that any of the saints escaped the scorching fires of temptation. The truth is that they were probably more persistently and more violently tempted than we ourselves. Saints, for the most part, were men and women who, had they not become great in sanctity, would probably have become great in sin. They would never stop short at half-measures. They had hard battles, and they realized well that if they were beaten in the fight they would sink very deep indeed in the wrong direction.

Most of our difficulties in the matter of temptation arise from the trouble we experience in controlling our imagination. The wise man compares the imagination to the wheel of a cart, always whirling, and St. Teresa calls it "the fool of the house," always looking for something with which to amuse itself. One might almost be inclined to say: Get control of your thoughts and your imagination, and acts and words will look after themselves. "The thoughts that absorb you," says an American writer, "are the thoughts that mold you." So it will be useful to set down a few practical hints about the management of this imagination of ours.

We often cross the border-line between temptation and sin because we allow the imagination to deceive us. This it does in two ways especially. First of all, the imagination is very prone to augment, out of all proportion, the *difficulty* to be encountered by those who resist temptation.

Suppose you put a ten-foot plank on the ground and ask your friend to walk along it. That's simple, and he goes from one end to the other without the slightest difficulty. This is his first test. Now take your plank and place it securely on two stands, each of them seven feet high. Ask your friend to get up and walk the plank now. He tries, and possibly he succeeds, but it is with much more difficulty than when the plank was lying on the ground. But why should this be? He has just as much space to walk on, really, as in the first case. Yes, but *his imagination* pictures the risk of falling a distance of seven feet to the ground. He *feels* he *might* fall, and so he has more difficulty in passing your second test.

There is a third trial. This time you bring your friend away to a wild country place and put your ten-foot plank across a chasm with a drop below it, on each side, of a thousand feet. Will he walk the plank this time? Not he! He *might* fall. In vain will you use your powers of persuasion and expostulate as volubly as you wish, that, in point of fact, he has just as much space to walk upon as when the plank was lying on the ground. No use. His imagination will not allow him.

But make another supposition now. While you are still arguing with him you both of you hear a wild shout, and, on turning round, you see a man rushing madly towards you brandishing a knife that glistens in the sun. A raving lunatic! What is to be done? There is one hope of escape, only one. If once you were at the other side of that chasm you were beyond the man's reach. The chances are that now, almost without reflection, you and your friend will race for your lives across that plank and pull it up after you on the other side. Safety! But, before the insane man appeared, you stood there trembling in front of that drop of a thousand feet. You were quite certain you never could muster up the courage to run across. Yet you have done it now. Why? Once again because your imagination worked the moment you realized that here is even a greater danger. The man is clearly determined to run both of you through unless you get away immediately, so you seize upon the only means left you of escape.

All of this goes to show how much we depend on our imagination. Now the devil's business is to get control of this faculty and fill us with fears and terrors that are really exaggerated out of all proportion. He will paint in very lurid colors the difficulty of avoiding that person or place which offers a dangerous attraction, or of keeping away from that person who has been already, perhaps, a source of sin. He stresses the fact that the fight is going to be long-drawn-out, that never once may we yield, that it is foolish to think we can keep to such a stern program, that we are young and foresee a lifelong struggle, that it is useless to fancy we can possibly manage to resist all the time, constantly contradicting in ourselves tendencies that seem to be irresistible.

So this is his first way of exciting the imagination, by summoning up all sorts of difficulties which fill the poor soul with alarm. Now nobody wants to maintain that there is no grain of truth in these suggestions of the evil one. We have just seen how the saints themselves had to fight, and fight hard, and in their teaching they are emphatic that the way to heaven can be reached only by those determined to permit no parley with the enemy. "The kingdom of heaven suffereth violence," says Our Lord, "and the violent bear it away." Our only point here, for the moment, is that when we allow our imagination to run away with us, it quite often succeeds in *augmenting* very much these very real difficulties.

The second way the imagination plays us false is by overstating the pleasures to be got from sin. It is true, of course, that vice has a strong attraction for our sinful nature. "I am delighted with the law of God," says St. Paul, "according to the interior man, but I see another law in my members, fighting against the law of my mind, and captivating me. . . . Unhappy man that I am, who will deliver me from the body of this death?" Passion when gratified does, indeed, bring with it a spasm of great pleasure. On this pleasure the evil one trades, exaggerating the satisfaction that will accrue to the man he is tempting. But the sinner himself is the first to admit, if the gratification be sinful, that the pleasure is too dearly bought. It may happen that a sinner will deny that he has any remorse or sense of shame after his sin, but this only argues to an unnatural perversion. He has so stultified his mind and so degraded all his nobler instincts, that they do not register. "Man, when he was in honor, did not understand; he has compared himself to the brute beasts and is become as one of them." For a time the sinner may deaden the reproaches of his conscience, but the awakening will be all the more terrible afterwards.

Normally, however, the sinner will confess that there is no real happiness to be got from sin. Before the sin, when the poor sinner is being assailed by temptation, the evil satisfaction is made to appear so sweet. He says, if he yields, in so many words: "I'm going to have this, at all costs; come what may afterwards." But, no sooner is the damage done than regret and shame and remorse demand their toll. Even in the actual act of committing the sin, the thought will sometimes come to the sinner: "Is this all there is in it? Is sin worth the price after all?" The joy promised by sin turns to gall and wormwood at the touch. Let the tempted person give way and this is the inevitable result—inevitable, because mortal sin drives God's grace out of his soul, and happiness without God is a contradiction in terms. Let the tempted man only stand his ground for a while and soon he begins to taste the sweetness of victory, a sweetness without admixture of any bitterness, because it comes from the testimony of a good conscience.

"One thing life has taught me," said an old man, "is that there is no happiness in sin." Very true. But the imagination, troublesome faculty that it is, persists in decking out sin and passion in a most alluring garb. Has the divine expert any practical helps to offer us to help control our imagination and unmask the deceits by which it tries to exaggerate the pleasures of sin and the difficulties of virtue? Yes, He has.

2. Two Practical Hints

A first hint about managing this faculty might be expressed by citing the proverb: Let sleeping dogs lie! In every human heart there is the surge of passion, so, whether we will or no, passion has to be reckoned with. In another place we have compared this passion to the tiger's cub. You know how you can goad such a beast to fury if you want to be perverse. He is safe behind his bars in the zoo and you come along and dangle food before him which he cannot reach. It is maddening, especially if he is hungry, to see quite close to him what he longs for, and to be unable to get at it. He will howl with disappointment and rage. If he were asleep in his corner and you failed to rouse him, you would walk away, but, in your present malicious mood, you enjoy seeing his anger and listening to his cries. It is unfair to the unfortunate animal, but you will have it so.

Now in the matter of temptation the trouble with us is very like the trouble with the animal in the cage. Passion will not arise within us, ordinarily, unless it receives some stimulus from outside. Leave the wild beast alone and you find he will keep quiet enough. But place before his eyes the object he craves for, and at once you evoke an immediate response. At once he is all out to get it. Every obstacle he would sweep aside in the insatiable longing to reach the thing he wants.

It is the sort of thing that happens every other day. Your friend pulls out a packet of cigarettes and offers you one. You were not feeling the need of a smoke nor even wishing for one, but when the object is put before you, there is an instinctive response. Out goes your hand as you thank him for his offer. You are passing along the sea front on a beautiful summer day. The sight of the waters awakens a picture in your imagination. How you would delight in having a dip on a day like this! The response is immediate again, and in five minutes you are plunging in the waves.

Or you are placidly reading your paper in your back garden on a summer evening, when suddenly you hear the excited cry: Fire, fire! Your imagination responds immediately. At once you think of your child in the crib, of your home, of that valuable picture, of your radio-set—all you treasure rushes confusedly into your mind, and in a flash you see the possibility of serious loss. The paper and the armchair are all forgotten and you hasten at once to the scene of danger.

Hence do not play with the imagination. Realize in time that it augments both the difficulty of avoiding sin, and the pleasures to be secured from sinful gratification. Then resolutely make up your mind not to give the imagination the stimulus of a deliberate bad thought or wicked suggestion, and you are on the high road to victory.

This is the reason why the saints warn us so insistently about shunning to the best of our power occasions of sin, for these provide that stimulus to the imagination that often leads to disaster. St. Alphonsus Liguori has written well that the devil cares little about a vague general purpose of amendment in confession. He smiles contentedly when the penitent promises to "do his best," or to "change his life," or to "make a new start." All these formulae will probably lead nowhere, because they do not face the issue in a practical way.

But let the sinner promise from his heart: "I am not going to meet that companion again. It is not in any way necessary for me to meet him or her, and I know if I do there is imminent danger of serious sin. Therefore I am not going to take that risk." Or: "I will not read that type of book again." That is a practical resolution to refuse point blank to give the wild animal the first stimulus, and if the penitent but perseveres, the rest of his troubles will gradually die a natural death. It is a resolution of this kind that makes the evil one gnash his teeth in impotent rage.

The devil is a skilled psychologist and he has centuries of experience behind him. So he knows exactly how to work on the imagination in order to effect his foul purpose. He tried his tactics, with notable success, as far back as the garden of Eden on the fateful day when he stirred up the imagination of our mother Eve. "*Why* did God command you? . . ." And she looked at the tree and she saw that the fruit was fair to behold. Had she not stood and listened to the tempter, had she not gone over and looked at the tree, her imagination would not have been taken captive, and there would have been good reason to hope that she would never have sinned. But the sight of the fair fruit dangling there, and the ingratiating manner of the tempter, proved too strong when once she yielded an inch, with the disastrous results which to this day her sons and daughters are experiencing.

Hence, says the divine expert, treat this matter of temptation in the business-like way you would deal with any other important affair in your life. If you are in charge of money and you foresee danger, you will place your money in a safe and lock the door. If you are going out for a walk and you suspect that there will be heavy showers, your excellent wife will warn you to take your umbrella, though many men hate umbrellas. In the same way, if you see that you are going to be troubled with temptation, and you may take it for certain that at least sometimes you will run into stormy weather, it is reasonable to recognize the root of the trouble and get hold of it. Keep your imagination under control by letting sleeping dogs lie. "The thoughts that absorb you are the thoughts that mold you."

But I cannot put my imagination into the safe. It is part of myself, and at times, in spite of all the good will in the world, the temptation haunts me, clings to me, keeps me agitated and troubled until finally I begin to think that surrender is the only way to peace. It is all very well to tell me not to start the trouble myself by dangling a bad thought before my imagination, but what if such thoughts come along unbidden and uninvited? I cannot put up my umbrella and take shelter from them.

This question brings us to the second hint with which the divine expert would help us. He reminds us at this stage that when we were children and, not having much sense, wanted to play with some dangerous object—a knife or a rusty key—our mother very deliberately took away from our childish hands what she knew would injure us. She removed the occasion, and we have just expatiated on that hint as number one to help us in our temptations. But mother did more. She gave us something else instead of what she took—a toy which could do us no harm. Why did she do so? Simply to occupy our attention and imagination. The child's thoughts were focused on that unlawful object. There was no use trying to explain to him that he could not have it, unless at the same time she substituted something which he might have. The toy took away his attention from the first object and gave him something else on which to exercise his imagination.

The application to ourselves when assailed by temptation is easy to make. The imagination again wants to play with danger. "The fool of the house" is always restless, always wanting to fidget with whatever presents itself. Hence, when temptation comes, it is of primary importance that we do not begin by working ourselves into a state of panic about it. There are earnest souls who, the moment they have a stray thought, will at once begin to resist by screwing themselves up into all sorts of shapes in order to get rid of it. They will invoke Our Lord or our Lady with fierce energy, they will call upon their favorite saints, all the time affirming to themselves and the world in general that they do *not* want to consent, that their will is to *reject* this unlawful thing, that it is there *in spite of them.* This method is not to be commended. All it does is to show very clearly that such good people are very far from committing any sin in face of the temptation.

Have you ever had the experience, when on a bicycle, of trying to avoid running over a stone? You see it a few yards ahead of you and you say to yourself: "Now I must not go over that stone. I have just got a new tire and paid dearly for it, so I do not want to run over that stone." If you keep on saying and thinking like this, the chances are that you will go right over the stone. The fact that you kept dwelling on it seemed, somehow, only to impress the more deeply on your mind the very idea you wanted to shun.

With temptation, if you keep violently repelling the evil suggestion, protesting that you do not want it, you *may* at times be only injuring yourself because you are driving in by such tactics the very thing you want to drive out. Of course we are taught to pray, and very earnestly, in time of temptation, but our prayer should not be inspired by terror or panic, but by confidence and love. Having said a short fervent prayer, perhaps a favorite ejaculation to our Lady, I now take my troublesome imagination and wrench from its hands the dangerous object, and give it a harmless toy instead. How can this be done?

Instead of saying that I am *not* going to think of *this,* let me fall back on the simple device of saying that I *am* going to think of *this other*. Let me have up my sleeve a few easy methods ready for the time of emergency. When the day's work is over, a person is assailed, for example, with troublesome thoughts. He quietly and calmly says his little prayer to Mary, and then he begins at once to recall all that happened him since he got up this morning —morning prayers, and (we hope Mass and possibly Holy Communion) what his daughter said at breakfast, what a scene there was when little Jackie spilt the hot tea on his thumb; then there was the day's work—the people he met, the bargain he struck, the plan that was suggested to him to break out that wall at the back and give himself more room for storage; the line in which he stood waiting for the bus, the accident he witnessed, the exciting item on the evening paper. What has become of the bad thought? The chances are that it has gone; it has been banished much more effectively than if the man was to keep on "resisting" all this time.

Or a riddle, a problem, is sometimes useful. There is the problem of the four elephants setting out for holidays. I see them all traveling along—father, mother, and two children. Father and mother weigh, each, a ton, and each of the two children weigh, each, half a ton. Presently the four of them come to a wide expanse of water which they want to cross. There is a raft at hand, but it will carry only a ton at a time. So the problem is how to ship the entire family over.

We may safely leave the solution to you. If you haven't fallen asleep or forgotten your bad thought by the time you have shipped the whole four over, then bring them all back again, and keep bringing them backwards and forwards as long as the imagination clamors for its harmless toy. In nine cases out of ten the troublesome thought will die a natural death.

One might sometimes summon up in the imagination a situation bordering on the ridiculous. It does not matter if it be silly, provided it be innocuous. This time, then, I find myself climbing a high tree, when the heel of my right shoe gets caught in a small hole in the trunk. Try as I will, I cannot extricate it. In fact, my efforts have only served to jam the shoe more firmly. So I have to manage an extremely difficult operation. In a most precarious position, I have to balance myself as well as I can. With my left hand I have to cling to a bough of the tree, and with my right I have to open my shoe-lace so as to free my foot. If I am blessed with a vivid imagination I can fill in details. The picture will have served its purpose if it helps to banish the bad thought.

Most effective of all is some spiritual device—in addition to the prayer already recommended. It is often an immense help to look at a crucifix or at a statue of our Lady; to take hold of one's rosary beads; to summon vividly before the mind one of the scenes from the Stations of the Cross. Such a reaction indicates a lively spirit of trust in God and our Lady, and a recognition that while I fear all things from my weakness, I hope all things from the strength of divine grace.

If temptations come during the day, the same or similar methods of warfare must be employed. Having said a short and fervent prayer, let me, very deliberately, refuse to dawdle with the daydream. Take up a good book, at once; mend that puncture now; oil that machine; dig in the garden; polish those brasses; bake that cake; have a useful hobby and get busy with it. Lest we be misinterpreted, it is well to state that only one of these wholesome occupations is here recommended at a time. I shudder to think of what might happen if you were to try to oil the machine, and polish the brasses, and bake the cake, all at once! In fact, the possibilities of such a course might easily supply matter for another "harmless toy" when temptation comes. Anyhow, the point is, of course, that any harmless pursuit if taken up resolutely and calmly and promptly will occupy your imagination, and nine-tenths of the work is done.

This is all very well on paper. The theory is fine, but what of the practice? I find it desperately hard to put away that dangerous thought; all that is in me seems to crave for it, and I have not the slightest inclination to try to look for a harmless toy to play with. This is quite true, perhaps. But does it follow that because one experiences difficulty, therefore there is sin, or that therefore you must show the white feather? Of course not. Merely that temptation is difficult to overcome need not, therefore, worry the tempted person unduly. Before we finish, we hope to hear from the divine expert a doctrine that will be full of encouragement for us if we are inclined to grow despondent about our chances of overcoming our temptations.

Our two practical hints, then, are to let sleeping dogs lie, and lay in a good store of harmless toys against the day or the night of temptation.

3. Temptation and Sin

One of the reasons for music while we work, for deep joyousness in God's service, is the assurance we have that temptation is not sin. It becomes sin only when the tempted person gives to the temptation *the consent of his will.* Once he deliberately accepts the evil suggestion, even in his mind, and allows his thoughts deliberately to dwell upon it, then, but not until then, has temptation passed over into the region of sin.

There will be times when it is not so easy to know how far the consent of the will has gone. That evil picture in my imagination was so alluring and I looked at it for a while, and now I do not know whether I consented or not. I am now preparing for confession, and I do not know whether I ought to tell this thing or not. What am I to do?

The simplest course, if you are not scrupulous, is to tell it to the priest just as you see it. "I had a bad thought and I do not know whether I consented or not. I accuse myself of dallying with the temptation." A simple question from the priest may be needed and after that I can dismiss the subject forever from my mind. Bad thoughts are rather elusive entities, and often it is impossible to determine whether consent has been given or not, or to what extent.

Still, there are one or two useful principles to direct the tempted person. St. Alphonsus Liguori takes the case of a person who, after the temptation, is doubtful as to whether or not he consented. There was a storm of impure suggestions in the mind, and now the man or woman is ill at ease, doubtful about the consent of the will. The saint would put a question. "Does the tempted person remember that, when the storm was raging, he called upon Mary? Can he recall that he invoked her name at the time of the temptation? If that is so, and *now he is in doubt* as to whether or not he consented, he can certainly assume that there was no sin because no consent."

We have italicized the words "now he is in doubt," because clearly, if there is no doubt at all that there was full consent, then there was certainly sin. It will not serve to say that, although I *know* I consented, still I did call on Mary and therefore did not sin. It would be an impious distortion of the saint's teaching to try to flatter myself that all is well *merely* because I called on our Lady. No amount of calling on her will exonerate me from blame, if in my heart and soul I am certain that I gave the consent of my will to sin. But if there is a clear case of doubt after the attack is over, and now I remember that I turned to her for help at the time when it was being launched, I am, in such case, quite safe in assuming that all is well. "Nobody ever called upon Mary and was not graciously heard by her." So teaches her great and devoted client.

A second principle when a man is in doubt is to form his judgement by the standard of his normal life as a Catholic. He has had a serious temptation but cannot decide about the consent of his will. He may ask himself what sort of Catholic is he? Is he one who ordinarily avoids as best he can the occasions of sin—persons, places, things which attract him to sin? Does he go regularly to the sacraments and to Mass, does he pray with at least a fair measure of regularity and sincerity? Is he straight and honest in his dealings? In a word, is he making a consistent effort to be what he knows a decent Catholic is expected to be? If he is, and now he tells you he is doubtful about the consent to a sinful suggestion, you can assure him that there is no sin. The whole orientation of his mind shows that it is set against sin. Had he sinned indeed, especially mortally, such a man would not have a doubt at all. The mere fact that one who normally tries sincerely to be a decent Catholic has a doubt, justifies him in assuming that there was not full consent.

The case is quite other with a Catholic who is habitually lax. This time you have to deal with a man who ordinarily is free and easy in the practice of his religion. If he misses Mass through his own fault or comes in very late, he will not worry too much. He has no great appreciation of the heinousness of sin, and he feels no sense of compunction even when he is sure that he has offended God grievously. In a word, he is slipshod in the service of God. And he comes now in a state of doubt? Did he really consent to that evil suggestion? I greatly fear that in such a case the dice is loaded against him. The whole tenor of his life leads one to judge that in this case the consent of the will has been given.

Hence we find ourselves coming back again to the need of self-denial. "The kingdom of heaven suffereth violence, and the violent bear it away." Even in little things, the habit of self-denial is an excellent antidote to consent to temptation. You want to lounge back comfortably in that armchair; make yourself sit up quite straight, at least for five or ten minutes. You want to cross one foot over the other; once in a while refuse to do so. You are offered a cigarette; sometimes, at least, force yourself to go without. The thought comes into your mind to go off and have a delightful evening at the seaside; sometimes make yourself instead peel off your coat to a good evening's work, or force yourself to go and visit that poor sick person and bring him tobacco or fruit or the book you promised him three weeks ago. He may be old, uninteresting, and without friends—all the better.

It is wonderful what joy this sort of thing brings when it is done for a high supernatural motive. But more than that, the habit of saying *no* in matters where there is no sin stiffens the will all around. No wonder a man succumbs to temptation if he never asserts his will. If he lives habitually a flabby, self-indulgent life, always or nearly always giving into his whims whenever that is possible, provided they are not actually sinful, it must not be matter for surprise that he has no grit, no self-restraint when temptation dangles before his eyes a gratification that is definitely sinful.

Parents have much to do here. It is lamentable to watch the ease with which many of them yield to every whim of the growing child. Anything for peace! Anything for a quiet life! Soon the child makes the discovery that he has only to cry loud enough and long enough to get anything he wants. He is never taught self-denial. Parents will cajole and coax with a penny, when they are bound to assert the God-given authority that He has entrusted to them, and for the use or misuse of which they must render a strict account. The result is that selfishness develops at a rapid rate in the child, and when he comes to boyhood or young manhood, he finds himself enormously handicapped. This is the time when ordinarily temptation begins to grow serious for him. He has never been trained to self-denial and self-control. The result is that often, in his case, temptation leads to sin, possibly to sinful habits that may take long years to break.

4. The Victory Is Certain

As we said, it is all very well in theory to lay down principles about governing ourselves, but this nature of ours is partly animal as well as partly spiritual. And that animal is such a stubborn mount! He fights hard to have his way. He will rear and snort fiercely if he be opposed, and it is no simple matter to keep astride of him at all and avoid the disgrace of a fall.

There is a fund of solid comfort in the recognition of our weakness. It is an immense consolation to keep in mind the truth that the avoidance of sin and the salvation of the soul is a task utterly and entirely beyond the power of unaided human nature to accomplish. "Without Me," says Our Lord, "you can do nothing," least of all the divine work of saving your soul. We cannot even think a good thought without God. We cannot even desire to love God unless He inspire that desire. Clearly then, we cannot possibly resist the fascination of sin and the violent and persistent attacks of temptation without God either. And that is precisely why we have boundless confidence. The great Apostle cried out that when he was weak, then he was strong—weak when left to himself, but strong with the very strength of God Himself when upheld by divine grace. If we had to depend merely on ourselves for victory we might well despair. If we had only the natural though most useful helps already suggested, we might hand in our gun, for, since our struggling is not with flesh and blood but against principalities and powers, our weapons must be supernatural. God sees to it that they are, that supernatural arms are supplied to us sufficient to conquer every serious temptation. "God is faithful, and will not permit you to be tempted beyond that which you are able, but will make also with the temptation issue that you may bear it."

"I can do all things in Him that strengtheneth me." "God is able to make all grace to abound in you . . . ," ". . . that, where sin did abound, grace may the more abound." "If God be with us who shall be against us?" All these consoling texts have the same message of encouragement and that is why the true Christian, though he may be assailed by attacks, is never despondent. There is music while he works, for he knows in Whom he puts his trust. As often as he recalls that God has pledged His word to give grace sufficient to ward off every serious onslaught of the enemy, then indeed he can face the long road with a song on his lips and gladness in his heart.

The victory is *certain*. Let that truth be stressed again and again. There is the divine assurance that if the tempted person cooperates, grace will infallibly be given to withstand every serious attack. Whatever the past may have been, whatever crimes may have blackened the stainless robe given in baptism, it is *certain* that, from this day and hour, until he dies, that tempted person will be granted grace sufficient to go right through the rest of life, right up to the deathbed and thence into eternity, without ever again sullying that robe with a mortal sin. Let that person, if he wills, bemoan his past mistakes, let him lament his abuse of grace in the years behind and his many lost opportunities, let him grieve for the souls he has led away by the frightful sin of scandal. He may have done all this and more, but, no matter what his past, no matter how deep-seated his habits of sin, the statement holds that he can begin from this moment a new life, and that God's word is there to guarantee him grace sufficient to avoid the commission of another mortal sin for the rest of his life.

Some of the Fathers of the Church compare the devil to a mad dog who is chained. You have no fear of such an animal, provided you keep your distance. He may snarl and bark, he may whine, he may wag his tail and show signs of making friends with you. But, sensible you, you have been warned that he is mad and therefore untrustworthy, so, whatever attitude he assumes, your course is to keep clear. Provided you do so, he is powerless to injure you; he can only go the length of his chain.

The devil can tempt a soul, violently and persistently. He can keep nagging at that poor harassed soul, sometimes for years, in his effort to win consent to sin. But this he can do only by God's permission, and only to the extent for which that permission is given. When he is allowed to tempt a soul, God, Who loves the soul, defines exactly the terms according to which the evil one may tempt, and then He apportions for that soul grace sufficient to guarantee complete victory over all serious sin. All the soul has to do is to co-operate, and even in the very act of co-operating, it needs grace, grace which will be offered by a generous God.

The divine expert has already shown us part of what is required on our side by way of co-operation. We have to shun occasions when possible, and we have to try to get control of our imagination. But there is also the much more effective and much more important part which consists in keeping in contact with

Christ. He is the source of all our supernatural strength, so, like the branch which draws sap from the parent stem, the soul must draw grace from Jesus Christ. Sin is a form of blindness. It darkens the eyes of the soul and makes the sinner hard, coarse, sometimes even repulsive to look upon. The reason is that his soul is dead. But when sin is conquered and he begins to feel the immense sources of strength he has in Jesus and Mary, then everything changes. He knows indeed his utter weakness; sin has schooled him well in that. But, what is perhaps even more useful, he now knows also his strength. Boundless confidence must necessarily follow.

Mr. Walsh, in the work quoted above, gives a most moving and graphic account of the struggles of St. Teresa—her torture of conscience lest she might be deceived by the devil, the troubles brought upon her by well-meaning friends, her dread lest she be burned as a witch by the Inquisition! "There came a time," he writes, "when it seemed as if she could not endure one more suspicious word or look. For twenty days of unutterable loneliness and desolation she had gone without the Bread of Life at her confessor's command. Even God seemed to have deserted her as she knelt all alone, trying to pray; and instead of the divine comfort there descended upon her a terrifying and paralyzing helplessness which left her unable to form words or to read them, unable to think any thought except the foul and heavy one that she was the dupe of the devil and might be lost forever. Tired and sick and tormented, still she rejected this perilous idea. Dimly but tenaciously, in the deepest sanctuary of her struggling soul, she clung to some tenuous thread of hope in this darkest of spiritual nights, and thus she remained kneeling like a statue of agony for four or five hours.

" 'There was no consolation for me, either of heaven or of earth, but the Lord left me fearing a thousand perils, to suffer.'

"Finally, as she stood her ground with the last desperate ounce of strength, the tide of battle turned, the familiar Presence stood beside her, and the Voice spoke with delightful clarity through the parched and empty places of her soul some of the very words that Moses had heard from the burning bush: 'Have no fear, daughter, for I am, and I will not forsake you. Have no fear.'

"All her anxieties seemed to vanish in that moment, and the devils with them. 'All the fears I used to have are gone, even to this day . . . rather it seemed to me that they (the devils) were afraid of me. There remained to me a domination over them, given me by the Lord of all, so that I trouble myself about them no more than about flies. They seem to me so cowardly that when they see that little notice is taken of them they have no strength left. *These enemies know how to make a real fight only against someone that they see surrender to them,* or when God permits that they tempt and torment His servants for their greater good.'

"Taking her cross in her hand, she faced the hosts of evil, crying: 'Now come, all of you, for, being the servant of God I wish to see what you can do to me!' "

The history of this great woman is a striking illustration of the truth we are trying to emphasize—that the devil is a chained dog and not, therefore, to be unduly dreaded, and secondly, that God's sufficient grace is guaranteed against every attack made by the evil one in matters of mortal sin.

Let the natural helps unite with the supernatural; let the struggling soul labor to get control, but also, and especially, make good use of prayer and the sacraments—the two great means of keeping in contact with Christ—and the soul is entrenched in an impregnable position. When the Apostles were out on Lake Genesareth a great storm arose and they were in imminent danger of being drowned. They tugged might and main at the oars but made no progress. After that they awakened Our Lord Who was lying asleep in the stern. He stood up erect there on the boat, and raising both hands majestically over the waters, He said to the raging waves: "Peace! Be still!" Instantly there came a great calm.

That is a figure of what the soul must do when out on the ocean of life it runs into squalls of temptation. The Apostles used the natural means—they tugged at the oars. But they also prayed. They made contact with Christ. A true Christian, thank God, can do both these things, too, and the same happy result is guaranteed by a promise that is divine.

5. The Reason Why

We have insisted all through on the deep and personal love of God for every individual soul He has created. "Wit it well; love was His meaning." A little consideration will prove that temptation, too, is permitted to befall simply because God loves. We are at times inclined to argue the other way round and affirm that if He did indeed love, He would shield our souls from the blasts of temptation. This is not so.

Temptation is a school and in it the first most useful lesson that is mastered is that fundamental virture of all holiness, solid humility. "What doth he know that hath not been tried?" Novices in virtue may flatter themselves that they are making progress, that they have acquired much patience, or charity, or firmness of purpose against grosser sins. But it is only when the atmosphere changes and they find themselves in surroundings where sin and laxity are easy and virtue difficult, that the acid test is applied. Serious temptation destroys the proud man's belief in his own superiority. It teaches in a deadly practical way what no amount of theorizing could accomplish, that there is no depth of depravity so deep but the soul is capable of sinking into it.

In the walks of life a man may come across sinners who have fallen low indeed into the mire; they have covered their baptismal robe with the mud of many vices. Let him envisage the greatest sinner on earth, a man who has lost all realization of the noble purpose of his existence and who long ago has abandoned all struggle to lead a life worthy of a human being. When a man who has himself been tempted comes to know him he is not going to raise his eyebrows in surprise or pious horror. In his own heart there is the deep conviction that he himself is quite capable of sinking as low, and lower, and that he owes his escape to one thing only—the infinite mercy and grace of Jesus Christ. "Without Me you can do nothing."

Moreover, if he is to persevere, if he is to continue to stand clear of the terrible pitfalls which have made such havoc of the other's life, he must lean, from one day to the next, from one moment to the next, on the same saving and strengthening grace. This frightful attraction which vice has for our fallen nature can be made one of the most solid props of our spiritual lives, and the realization that this attraction is so strong is taught and enforced most of all in the school of temptation. "There goes Philip Neri," said the saint to his companion, on meeting a notorious sinner, "only for the grace of God." Such a deep and heartfelt conviction is another name for humility, the foundation of the edifice of true sanctity.

The humble man is glad to be tolerated. He has no time for discussing the shortcomings of his neighbor, or even thinking about them, for he is too vividly conscious of his own frailty and his own need of watchfulness over self. It does not occur to him to compare himself with others, to think himself in any way their superior. The foolishness of such comparisons he knows too well, for he has experience of his own weakness and instability, and realizes he has quite sufficient work to do in steering clear of sin himself. An invaluable lesson, this, and there is no place better for conning it than the school of temptation.

This happy result is seen in the case of St. Peter. At the table of the Last Supper, Our Lord warned His twelve disciples that one of them would betray Him and the rest would all be scandalized in Him that very night. At once Peter is on his toes to defend himself against the imputation. Whatever the others might do, Peter would never be disloyal; of that he was certain. The Master insisted that this very night Peter would deny Him three times, and again Peter is loud in his remonstrances. There you have him before he enters the school of temptation—self-assertive, independent, priding himself that he is stronger than the others. "Even though all should be scandalized in Thee, *I* will never be scandalized!"

We know what followed. Temptation came and Peter failed badly. He was filled with fear and three times he denied, with an oath, that he even knew the Master to Whom he had pledged such loyalty. What was the result? "Peter, going out, wept bitterly." Next time we find him after the Resurrection, kneeling in early morning on the seashore. Jesus is standing before him, and there is the triple question: "Simon, son of John, lovest thou Me?" This time Peter answers with all the earnestness of his great heart: "Lord, Thou knowest all things; Thou knowest that I love Thee." But no one can fail to detect the note of deep humility now. No self-assertiveness this time, no odious comparison with the others, only the sincere avowal that, sinner though he is, he is deeply aware that in his soul there is an unalterable love of Jesus of Nazareth. Humility is learned well in the school of temptation.

In that school, too, a man learns gratitude to God. Suppose that in the past he succumbed to sin. The divine expert has shown us already what should have been his sentence in strict justice. Remembrance of what he owes must make his heart swell with gratitude till it nearly break. And when another fresh struggle comes along and he comes forth victorious, again through God's grace, there is now a new reason why he should make music in his heart as he realizes his fresh indebtedness. He used his weapons —he tugged at the oar, he prayed, he did not play with the danger, he did not let his imagination run riot—and when he did these things Jesus stepped right into the midst of the storm and commanded the winds and the sea, and there came a great calm.

Suppose you are out swimming and you get into difficulties. A passer-by leaps in, takes you on his strong shoulders, fights the current for you, and brings you into the bank, breathless and exhausted, but safe. You would consider yourself a very poor specimen of manhood if you were not grateful. Jesus Christ has saved your life, too, the life of your soul, not once but perhaps hundreds of times. Count up your falls and your chances; make out a list of your serious temptations; the total will bring you somewhere near the entirety of your debt to Christ.

It is well worth remembering, too, that temptation increases enormously the merit of a soul—if the tempted person wins through. Take a case of a man who has made a good confession after years of separation from God. Drunkenness, perhaps, was his besetting sin, or impurity, but now, with the help of Jesus and Mary, he comes out from that confession determined to live a new life and shun the dangers. For a while all goes well, but sure enough one day, perhaps without warning, a strong temptation seizes upon him. The struggle may be long and violent, and often he will be near despair. On top of his temptation there comes, perhaps, a reverse in his business, a good deal he missed, an opportunity of securing some rare commodity he stupidly overlooked. Or his wife is in a cross mood, or the weather is miserably cold or overpoweringly warm, and he feels the urge to be done with resistance and let things rip.

He is not alarmed by the temptation which he had been taught to expect. He gets down to it according to the instructions of the divine expert and he comes out of the struggle, let us suppose, with the proverbial flag still flying. What is the net result to his soul of all he has gone through? When the struggle commenced that man had a certain amount of sanctifying grace in his soul; now that the fight is over—at least for a while—he has increased his stock of grace in a manner and measure that would amaze him if he could look into his own soul and see the difference.

Consider now another man who has never known the taste of drink. For him it is no struggle to refuse the offer of a drink. He can pass by that saloon twenty times in the day and never experience even the beginnings of a desire to enter. For all this he gets no merit, or very little. No doubt he, too, will have his own peculiar temptations, but drinking to excess is not one of them. The other man's wrong desire, which he successfully combated, has beautified his soul marvelously and added much to the right side of his account for heaven. He is immeasurably better off, spiritually, because he was tempted.

But even in this life there is a reward, too. The fact that he has been tempted and won through will make the next struggle easier. There may indeed be many another fight before complete victory is won, but each time he overcomes he is in a stronger position for the next attack. It is not so difficult, he learns, to stand his ground. He has done it before—ten, twenty, or thirty times. Why not do it again? The good habit is strengthened. The temptation begins to lose its force. St. Teresa has told us that the devil is a coward who knows how to make a real fight only against those who surrender to him. "If then this Lord is powerful as I see He is, and I know He is, and the devils are His slaves—and of this it is not to be doubted since it is of faith—what hurt can they do to me, being as I am the handmaiden of this Lord and King? Why shouldn't I have strength to fight with all hell?" What a sense of relief and courage this brings the poor sufferer! And once again it comes through his experience of temptation. "What doth he know that hath not been tried?"

One often comes across people who serve God well, but are conspicuous for their sense of self-righteousness. You cannot accuse them, nor can they accuse themselves, of any serious sin in God's sight. They go regularly to the sacraments, they are faithful to their times of prayer, they pay their debts, and they feel they can look the whole world in the face. Yet, with all this, there is something in the type of person we have in mind that repels one somewhat. They are so cock-sure of themselves! Let them hear of a scandal and you will be treated to a merciless castigation of the offender. Let a genuine case calling for charity be brought to their door, and they will launch forth against beggars and idlers. In a word, what seems to be wrong with them is that they are sadly lacking in the gift of sympathy. They are always ready to speak the "hard word."

What a change temptation can make in them! Having now learned their own weakness, they are much more ready to compassionate others. They know the mercy with which God has treated themselves, and they begin at last to understand that they must treat others similarly. They see a new depth of meaning in the Lord's saying to love others "as I have loved you." They understand the implications of the Lord's prayer when they beg to be forgiven their trespasses even as they forgive those who trespass against them. Harshness towards those who fall through weakness is never a mark of zeal. Our Divine Lord hated sin with all the intensity of His immaculate heart and soul, and against sin He inveighed in a language that admitted of no ambiguity or compromise. But when it was question of dealing with a sinner, there never was a mother whose tenderness and understanding could bear comparison with His.

These are some of the reasons why a loving God permits the soul He loves to be lashed with the storms of temptation. With good reason then does the Apostle tell us: "My brethren, count it all joy when you fall into divers temptations."

We propose to end with a little parable calculated to dispel an idea that sometimes discourages an earnest soul. Many of us lose heart in the fight with temptation because we do not keep sufficiently before us the correct meaning of perseverance. The man who perseveres is not necessarily he who does not sometimes fall on the road, but he who, after he has fallen, rises again, and keeps rising until he reaches his destination. But our parable will attempt to explain.

A man takes out his car from his garage in Dublin and proceeds to drive with his family in the direction of Cork. For a while all goes well, and they all enjoy speeding along on this beautiful sunny evening. But presently, about three miles outside Dublin, his peace of mind is suddenly disturbed. An ominous pull on the steering wheel tells him only too plainly what has happened. A puncture, and our good friend explodes on the fourth letter of the alphabet, or, if he remembers in time that the children are behind, he says "Bother!"

However neither explosive will refill his flat tire. The whole lot have to get out. Dad has to peel off his coat, turn up his shirt sleeves, look very important as he removes the punctured tire and puts on the spare. Once more all are smiling. All file in again and away speeds the car at forty-five or fifty miles an hour.

But we are living in troubled times, and when the car gets into a half-way town, it is halted by a trooper who demands the driver's license. No trouble there, and our man dives into the breast pocket of his coat. Gone! Another explosive, but it has no effect on the masklike face of the policeman. No proceeding further without that license!

What has happened? He had that paper when he left Dublin, of that he is quite sure. He gets a brain wave. When he took off his coat and threw it on the hedge before mending that puncture, there is a chance that it might have fallen out. So there is nothing for it except to turn the car right about and go back to the spot. There follows consultation with mother and the youngsters and some difference of opinion as to where that exact spot is, but finally all are agreed that it was *here*. And here, too, is the missing document, lying on the grass. The owner retrieves it, charges once more in the direction of Cork and the trooper, and this time safely passes beyond the custodian of the law.

Suppose that later still the man has an accident and the windshield is smashed and his hand badly cut. But he bandages the hand with a handkerchief and insists on driving on, windshield or no windshield, till finally, after many tribulations, he steers in triumph into Cork.

Has that man been lacking in perseverance? Of course not. He has proved his mettle by the very fact that though so many difficulties did get him down, he refused to remain down. You would say he did not persevere only if, after that puncture he flew into a rage, left the car there by the side of the road and packed himself and his family in the bus back to Dublin. Or if when accosted by the policeman he tried to argue with him and browbeat him, and, when this proved ineffectual, he had sat there in the car and refused to go back for the license. Or finally you would say he did not persevere if, after that accident he had gone into a house to have his hand washed and dressed, and then had declared that he was not in a fit condition to drive any farther.

But merely because he had these various mishaps does not justify anybody in saying he did not persevere. He set out to get to Cork, and he got there, and the difficulties he overcame are only proof of his grit and determination.

On the road to eternity, too, we may have a breakdown. Temptation is so strong that sometimes we may give up the struggle and sin—even grievously—and notwithstanding all the encouraging teaching of our divine expert. The devil's next step is now to persuade the soul that the case is hopeless. If he succeeds, we have ceased to persevere. But after even a very serious accident, to get up and start again, and to keep getting up—that is to persevere. That attitude towards our temptations, that proper understanding of what perseverance means, will do much to give us immense courage in the days when the struggle seems hopeless. It is a policy that must lead the soul ultimately to the destination planned for it by the divine expert.

And that brings us to a final thought about temptation—the joy of the reward. There is always a sense of satisfaction when one achieves something for which one had to make a fight. You can remember in your schooldays, your keenness about the exams; how after the ordeal, on the way up the street from the examination hall, you compared notes and answers together and leaped delightedly into the air when you discovered you had done well. Then came the results, and there was the added joy of knowing authoritatively that your efforts were rewarded. You worked hard during term and now here is the result achieved. No wonder you were smiling on the world.

Or you can recall the satisfaction which your achievement gave you if you made good use of your hands at home. That cabinet your own hands have put together, that picture your own hands have painted and framed, that successful dinner you cooked, that cake you baked, that frock so much admired which you made yourself—all these are instances illustrating the truth that there is quite a peculiar feeling of gratification in surmounting an obstacle, in exercising a faculty, in finally achieving the result you had in view.

But who can express the joy of the soul that discovers it has "passed" in the great final examination of all? When the soul's handiwork is praised and approved by Jesus Christ? "Well done, good and faithful servant!" Here is sense of achievement indeed. It will be an examination on love. And love is shown, not by fine words or pious feelings, but by deeds. He does most who loves most. He loves most who conquers most, who pulls against the current, who is brave in the storm, who refuses to be beaten, though blinded by the rain and famished with hunger. He loves most who in time of temptation keeps his eyes fixed on the shore, and on the immovable Figure of Christ standing there.

true words or pious fictions, but by deeds. He does most who loves most. He loves most who conquers most: who pulls against the current, who is brave in the storm, who refuses to be beaten, though blinded by the rain and lamed with hunger. He loves most who in time of temptation keeps his eyes fixed on the shore, and on the immovable Figure of Christ standing there.

PART II

AN EXPERT SHOWS HOW

I. Learning Christ

"All of us, when we pray, are beggars of God. We stand before the gate of our great Father; indeed we prostrate ourselves and we sigh and supplicate Him, for we want to get something from Him. And that something is nothing less than God Himself.

"What does a beggar ask for? He asks for bread. And you, what do you ask for from God except the Christ Who says: 'I am the living bread'?"—St. Augustine.

1. Personal Contact

There is a whole world of difference between knowing Christ and knowing about Him. If a man is interested, let us say, in some branch of science, he may know much about an eminent scientist who lives at the antipodes. He can give you all the details of his career—the place and the year of his birth, what studies he has pursued, the books he has written, the theories and views defended in those books or rejected, the arguments for and against, the different countries in which this scientist has lived, and the chain of circumstances which led him to settle down in a distant land.

All these facts he knows at his fingers' ends. But one day the two of these men meet. They are introduced by a mutual acquaintance, and little by little the knowledge of each other ripens into friendship. The student now knows the man, himself. He has come to admire him for his personal charm. It is pleasant to drop in at evening time for a chat about the subject in which they are both so keenly interested. It is stimulating to listen to this man expound a theory or expose a fallacy or answer an attack. The sound of his voice, the ring of earnest conviction, the facial expression, the apt gestures he uses to emphasize his views—all these add enormously to the fund of information already collected about the man from his own writings and the accounts of others. It is one thing to read about him in books, or even peruse his written word; it is quite another to knock at his front door, to receive a warm handshake of welcome, to sit in an armchair by his fireside and discuss at one's leisure whatever question one wishes to raise.

Now we know about Our Lord from the Gospels in much the same way as the student knows about the scientist from books. But if we are to know Him we must meet Him and make personal contact, and the meeting-place is prayer. The Gospels hold up before our eyes, to look upon, the exquisitely beautiful picture of Jesus of Nazareth, but in prayer He steps out of the frame and lives again, and we know Him. He is "Jesus Christ, yesterday, today, and the same forever." The kindness mirrored forth in His every action shines indeed across the streets of Nazareth or Capharnaum, or into the death chamber where the daughter of Jairus is lying, but prayer shows us the love of a living Christ sending its comforting rays in a steady stream down through twenty centuries.

The Gospel depicts a Christ looking with tenderness upon every form of human suffering; prayer gives us admission into a secret place apart, where we find that same look of sympathy, but with this huge difference, that now those eyes of Christ are fixed upon ourselves. We read in the Gospel about the infinitely merciful treatment meted out to Mary Magdalene, the woman who was a sinner, or Our Lord's divine wisdom rescuing from the clutches of her enemies the poor woman taken in adultery. But in prayer we draw near to Him with our own load of sin and sinfulness; we kneel down before Him, and over us bends the same Jesus to lift from our shoulders the burden that is pressing upon them, and raise us to our feet. It is indeed touching to watch Him weeping at the grave of Lazarus or mingling His tears with those of the widow of Naim. But to know and understand very clearly that that same heart of Christ goes out in sympathy towards ourselves when the hand of death is laid upon those we love, this is heartening beyond words, and it is one of the truths that dawns upon the soul that is perseveringly faithful in prayer.

Perhaps there is no trait in Our Lord's character more stressed than the eagerness He shows to make men know Him. Shortly before the end of His life He rode into Jerusalem upon an ass. It was a day of triumph. The streets rang with cheering. Adults and little children alike formed themselves into a procession and shouted themselves hoarse: "Hosanna! Hosanna to the son of David! Blessed is He that cometh in the name of the Lord!" Fathers and mothers lined the roads, too, or thronged close about the Prophet, or spread their garments on the ground for Him to walk upon. His enemies are filled with impotent rage. "Do you see that *we* prevail nothing? The whole world is gone after *Him*."

The hearts of His disciples are bounding with joy. So at last it is coming—the realization of all their cherished hopes, the long-awaited establishment of Christ's kingdom on earth. So slow had He been about making a beginning that they had chafed at the delay. He had preached a doctrine that accorded ill with their own ideas and ideals. He had warned them that if they were to enter into His kingdom they must become as little children. He had scared them badly by foretelling that He Himself would have to endure frightful torments which He expatiated upon in careful detail—scourging, and mockery, and finally a disgraceful death by crucifixion. Further He promised that they themselves would be hated by all men, that they would lament and mourn while the world around them would rejoice. He showed a disconcerting lack of interest in money, in the insignia of kingship, in scepter or crown or royal attire. So they were rather at a loss to understand.

But today marks a welcome change. Today the crowds surge about Him, on all sides acclaiming Him king, and He does nothing to hinder them or silence their cheering. On the contrary, He declares that if they did not speak, the very stones would call out. Yes, it is a happy change. Today, it would seem, He sets Himself at the head of His people to lead them to victory. Soon hated Rome shall lie in the dust before His victorious advance. Soon Jerusalem will once again be able to raise her head high and take her place proudly before the nations of the world as capital of Christ's new kingdom. Wherefore, "Hosanna, blessed is He that cometh in the name of the Lord!"

Thus pleasingly did they muse as they walked along. I take my position at the corner of the street to watch the procession go by. As Jesus comes directly into my line of vision I drop on my knees for I know Him to be my God. Somewhere down the street there is a jam in the procession and this is most fortunate for me, for He halts just there right in front of me, seated on the ass's colt. I lift up my eyes to look upon His face and I am suddenly surprised, suddenly apprehensive. For what I see there is, that while every countenance round Him is radiant with joy and alight with excitement, tears dim the eyes of Jesus Christ! And Jesus wept, the central figure of all these celebrations. Why? Because, in spite of this enthusiasm and waving of branches, in spite of their loud proclamations of His kingship, they still do not know Him. "And seeing the city, He wept over it saying: 'Jerusalem . . . if thou hadst *known*. . . . Thy enemies will not leave in thee a stone upon a stone . . . because thou hast not *known* the day of thy visitation.' " Their dreamings and fancies about an earthly kingdom were all astray. They had missed completely the pivotal point of His teaching that His kingdom was not of this world. Jesus wept because they did not know Him after all.

But it was not only of the thoughtless mob that this was true. On the following Thursday night He has His own twelve disciples all about Him at the supper table. Though it is a festive gathering, the same sad complaint is wrung from His heart. These twelve have been His closest friends. For three years they have been with Him. They have shared their joys and their disappointments with His. Side by side they have worked and prayed and slept and eaten and drunk and spoken together. These are the men whom He has chosen to be His own in quite an especial manner. He has taken exceptional care to train them, to unfold before them His truth. They are His friends and from them He has kept nothing secret. And now, after all this, even these do not know Him. "So long a time have I been with you, and you have not known Me?" Not yet do they understand His answer to the riddle of life.

2. Trying to Teach

All through these three years of His public life He had been trying to make men know Him. He gave it as a trait of the sheep that belong to Him, that "He goeth before them, and the sheep follow because they know His voice . . . 'I am the good shepherd,'" He adds, "'and I know Mine and Mine know Me.'" Outside of that fold He is not known; "He was in the world and the world was made by Him, and the world knew Him not." The Baptist at the Jordan had told the same to the crowds assembled there. "There hath stood One in the midst of you whom you know not."

In an effort to remove the scales from their eyes and communicate to their minds at least a ray of this knowledge, Our Lord had repeatedly shown a patience truly divine in bearing with their heckling and petty exactions. He had multiplied miracles for them to see, going finally to the length of raising from the tomb Lazarus who had been four days dead. But they remained obdurate still, obstinately refusing to recognize Him for Who He was.

In dealing with the friends He loves and by whom He knows Himself to be well loved, there is evidence of this same anxiety. This eagerness is most noticeable, perhaps, during the forty days after His resurrection. He takes a special joy in coming to these friends of His and springing on them the glad surprise that it is really He, risen again and conqueror of sin and death. He appeared in the garden to Magdalene and at first she did not know Him. This must be the gardener, she surmises, and she proceeds to tell Him about her sorrow and disappointment on finding only an empty tomb. Then He says the single word "Mary." Instantly the light of recognition flashes into her eyes. "Rabboni, my Master!" And with a heart bursting with joy she falls down on her knees and takes her accustomed place at His feet.

That same day two other friends of Jesus were walking dejectedly out from Jerusalem to a little house of theirs in the country. They had such high hopes of this prophet who was mighty in word and work. They had even been led to believe that possibly He might be the long-promised Messias who was to redeem Israel. But three days ago He had been crucified, and with His death the sun had fallen out of their heaven. True, He had said something to the effect that He would rise again the third day. But then, this *is* the third day, and see, nothing at all has happened. They are disillusioned. To be sure, some women had gone to visit the grave early that morning and had come back with a story that His body was not there and that angels had spoken to them. But women, you know, are like that, always ready to accept fantastic tales, and these two, sensible men, had dismissed their report with indulgent tolerance.

The depressing atmosphere of the upper room began to pall on them after a while, and so, while yet a prey to these gloomy thoughts, they had gone for a walk in the direction of this house of theirs in Emmaus. It was here that Jesus joined them, but "their eyes were held, and they knew not that it was Jesus." He shows them how groundless are their fears. He explains to them, —and would that the explanation had been preserved!—the prophecies about the Messias, and He points out how perfectly these are fulfilled in the very Man whom they are lamenting. Arrived at the house in the country they are loath to let Him go farther. He goes in, at their earnest invitation, and sits down at their table. At last their eyes are opened. At last they recognize Him. There is something strangely familiar in His way of breaking that piece of bread. It is Jesus indeed.

Instantly everything is changed. Their hearts are burning within them. They rise from the table, their meal scarcely touched, and with light step they hasten back to the city to spread the good news among the other Apostles. But on their arrival in the upper room, they find the others all eagerness to tell their own story. For they have seen Him, too. He stood in the midst of them, the doors being shut, and saluted them in the old, lovingly familiar way: "Peace be to you!" They were frightened and incredulous. They clutched nervously at each other as they stood up and stared wide-eyed at the apparition. But He finally convinced them. It was not mere appearance, no ghost, no hallucination. It was really He, risen from the dead and dying now no more. They knew Him at last; there was no possible room for any more doubts.

In all these appearances during the days of Our Lord's triumph, one notices the glad expectancy with which He stands back and awaits the moment when His friends will recognize Him, and the eagerness with which He listens for the cry of welcome to leap from their hearts the moment they know that it is He indeed.

3. Lost Opportunities?

Still, side by side with this great desire of His to be known and His repeated attempts to make men recognize Him, and His sad complaints when they fail to do so, it is also an undeniable fact that He seems to go out of His way to remain hidden and unknown. He stole into His world on Christmas night in the darkness, and practically nobody knew. For the greater part of His life He buried Himself in despised Nazareth, a back-water place, where all the time He is unnoticed and unknown. He passed for the son of Mary and Joseph, no more—a quiet, unassuming woman, and her husband, the carpenter of the little place. It is only after thirty years spent like this in Nazareth that Jesus emerges and begins to mix with men in the highways of life. But only for three years does He associate with them, and even during that brief period you find Him very frequently slipping away from them into His beloved solitude. He has a predilection for desert places, and in a desert He hides Himself for full forty days at the outset of His already too brief public life. He loves to climb the slope of the hills, often in the stillness of evening time, and give Himself up to long hours of prayer far away from all contact with the multitudes of men. Is this what we should expect from a man who ardently desires to be known?

Then He allowed so many golden opportunities to be lost. Had He not a unique chance, for instance, on that memorable day when He multiplied the loaves and fishes? The crowds were wild with enthusiasm and wanted nothing so much as to seize Him and make Him their king on the spot. And what happened? "He fled!" In the most unaccountable manner He disappeared from their midst. He hurried again to the mountain He loved, "Himself alone. And when it was evening, He was there alone."

Another day Satan suggested to Him to throw Himself down from the pinnacle of the temple, pointing out with much show of sense that the angels would hold Him up and the miracle would set the whole countryside talking about Him. Another splendid opportunity if He wants to be known! But He will have none of it. "Begone, Satan, thou shalt not tempt the Lord thy God." Even when He does work a miracle He is at pains to keep it hidden. "See that you tell it to no one," is the injunction He frequently lays on the recipients of His favors.

So we have an apparent anomaly in the behavior of our Saviour. But it is apparent only, for the truth is that He does not will to obtrude Himself. He would have the soul come, of itself, to seek Him earnestly and perseveringly. He does indeed urge men to come to Him. He pleads with them to knock and assures them that they will find. He urges. He pleads. He uses gentle persuasions. But force Himself on us He never does, for love ceases to be love when it is constrained. The strong tendency of nature is to permit itself to become absorbed in something, anything almost, outside of Him. To resist this inclination and seek Him by deliberate preference entails much self-denial. But this is the spirit to which Jesus reveals Himself. Self-denial wins the reward of an intimate knowledge of Jesus.

To arrive at this, to know Our Lord with such holy familiarity, to taste and see for oneself that the Lord is sweet indeed, this is, instantly to yield up one's heart to Him without reserve. To know, to experience, that Jesus Christ is the one stable, abiding reality in the midst of a world of continually shifting shadows and make-believe; to understand, not out of books but from one's own personal relations with Him, that He is indeed a changeless friend, so eager to love and to multiply proofs of His love that He at once brushes aside all one's sins and meannesses at the first sign of true repentance; to know what it is to lay one's worries down before Him and pour into His ear, full of sympathy and understanding, the story of one's sorrow or shame or disappointment; to draw near to Him when harassed by temptation or torn with doubts and misgivings and scruples, and ask for His solution; to have acquired a facility in talking to Him about all one's concerns, great and small; to know Him in the Blessed Sacrament and in Holy Communion in such a vivid manner that in that sacred mystery He has become the center and core of one's life; to lift the veil, be it ever so little, that hangs over the face of the hidden God and allow its light to shed its rays into the very commonplace details of one's very commonplace day—how could anybody come to knowledge like this and fail to be caught up in the flames of love for Him? "Was not our heart burning within us, while He spoke to us on the way?" Such a knowledge of Jesus is the key to life's riddle.

So what we plead for here is not mere information about the facts of Our Lord's life. It is not even, or at least not merely, the science culled from the pages of Catholic theology. There are many souls who have attained to this intimate, quasi-experimental knowledge of Him which is here envisaged, and they have never opened a volume of St. Thomas Aquinas or Suarez. The facts of His life, the detailed and accurate information of the theologian, are like the dry faggots. But if they are to blaze out into this holy and intimate familiarity with Jesus, they must be set on fire, and only personal attachment to Jesus can supply the flame.

On at least two occasions His Apostles mistook Jesus for a ghost, a "phantasma," something unreal. One was when He came to them walking on the waters and they supposed that they saw a spirit. The other was in the upper room after the Resurrection. Both times Our Lord was at pains to disabuse them and prove to them that He was no mere spirit but a living person. "Feel My hands and be not afraid. See that it is I Myself. . . . It is I, fear not."

Now there are many whose external obedience to Christ's counsels and commandments leaves little to be desired. They have their code of religious observances which they adhere to with commendable regularity. They are careful to avoid sin, at least all sin that is mortal. They are punctual at their various duties and they discharge them conscientiously, and to everybody's satisfaction, including their own. They are efficient. Their opinion is listened to with respect and they expect their verdict to be accepted and their advice to be followed. They resemble faithful stewards, with a high concept of duty and responsibility. God is supreme Master and Lord and they are ever mindful that to Him one day an exact account must be rendered.

4. What Is Wanting?

Admirable, all this, but none the less does not one instinctively sense a want? What is lacking in such a spiritual life except just that personal knowledge of Our Lord which would infuse into all those duties the motive of personal love? St. Ignatius urges St. Francis Borgia to beg the divine Master for "His most holy gifts; the gift of tears . . . of joy, of spiritual repose, of intimate consolation, and for all the spiritual sentiments peculiar to these gifts, such as humility. For, without these gifts all our thoughts, words, and works, are *cold, imperfect, and confused.*" Throughout his *Spiritual Exercises* the same saint would have his exercitant pray constantly *ut intime cognoscam*—for an intimate knowledge of Jesus Christ.

It is good to find God-fearing, conscientious men and women who render to God the service of trustworthy stewards. But one loving friend is of more value than a hundred servants, how capable soever they may be, and loving friendship between Jesus and the soul is generated, under the transforming influence of divine grace, in the contact made and strengthened by a life of prayer. Remove this, and you have efficiency without enthusiasm, duty without zeal, the letter that kills divorced from the spirit that giveth life.

The same absence of devotedness to the person of Jesus is responsible for much that is merely sentimental and almost mawkish in the external practice of religion. There are souls for whom religion has come to resemble a sort of drug. They feed on their feelings. They devour spiritual books of the type that nourish a certain saccharine pietism but do not fill the soul or answer to its real needs. They listen to one sermon after another and they have a mania for following novenas and missions and retreats in endless succession.

God forbid that we should even remotely discourage them, but once again what is wanting to these pious souls? It is this—that they never take time or trouble to think out what they have listened to and shape their daily lives by its principles. They are very satisfied with themselves as long as they feel that they are holy, and they consider that the Lord has every good reason to be satisfied with them, too. But if their feelings change, if they no longer experience sweetness in their prayer, then immediately their whole spiritual life goes topsy-turvy. Or, if the preacher touches on any subjects that prick their conscience, they will assure you that his sermon does not appeal to them. Or if their director insist that they lay the ax to some pet imperfection and get down to business in the work of combating their faults, then they will confide to you that they are going to seek direction elsewhere, for clearly this priest, though without doubt excellent in his way, yet does not understand their special type of spirituality!

Mention is made of such souls here only to insist that, once again, what is the fundamental flaw in their spiritual life is that they have never really grown to know Jesus Christ. They have a code of petty devotions; they load themselves with medals and objects of piety. But their hearts crave for more solid fare. They resemble a starving man who turns away from his well-supplied table and tries to satisfy his hunger by walking out into his garden and inhaling the fresh air. "What then is the escapism in religion against which we have to guard? It is the turning of religion completely into a search for emotional or sensuous indulgence, using the pleasure which religion's outward appurtenances may give, simply to forget its inner reality, and so failing to face the problems of every day in the light and with the strength which religion should afford." (*Morals Makyth Man,* by Gerald Vann, O.P., page 195.)*

"If any man thirst," says Our Lord, "let him come to Me and drink." If the doctor makes a correct diagnosis of your disease, he will be keenly disappointed if you refuse to apply his remedy. He knows just exactly what the trouble is, and he realizes the immense benefit that would accrue to you from an operation or a course of treament. But you refuse obstinately. You prefer to drag on a sickly existence for twenty years, when he knows quite well that he could restore you to perfect health in less than six months. But you tie his hands. In some such way does the divine physician regard these ailing souls. What they need is "to comprehend, with all the saints, what is the breadth and length, and height and depth; to know also the charity of Christ which surpasses all knowledge, that (they) may be filled unto all the fullness of God."

For souls that reach the state of intimate knowledge, work is not duty merely; it is labor begun and carried through because the laborer yearns to give in this way an outlet to his love. Prayer is not a number of reflections and resolutions; it is personal, intimate, loving contact and converse with a friend who is loved and by whom the soul understands that it itself is loved. Kind deeds, acts of patience with those who try us, self-restraint under annoyances, control of tongue, discipline of mind—these are no longer merely acts of virtue to which we submit ourselves in order to develop our character, they are not even done, primarily, with a view to our own advance in holiness. These—and the same is true of all the trivialities that crowd one's day—are shot through

* Vann, O.P., Gerald, *Morals Makyth Man.* New York, Longmans Publishing Company.

with the motive of finding in them expressions of personal love, of personal attachment to Him whose cause is so worthy that it absorbs one's all—all one's time, all one's energy, all one's talents and interests. "To those who love God all things work together unto good." There is nothing else left except to make life one connected whole, a single unit, an edifice every department of which is lighted up with the same motive, the same driving power—experimental knowledge of the love and lovableness of Jesus Christ. "The love of Christ constrains us, and the heart of Christ sustains us."

This art of reducing one's whole life to an act of personal devotedness in constantly stressed in the Holy Scripture and in the saints. "Whether you eat or drink, or whatsoever else you do, do all to the glory of God." "Let all endeavor," says St. Ignatius, "to have a right intention, not only in their state of life but also in all details, seeking in them sincerely to serve and please the divine goodness for itself—casting off, as much as may be, all love of creatures in order to transfer their whole affection to the Creator, loving Him in all creatures, and all them in Him." "Such souls," writes Père Saudreau, "avail themselves far more freely of occasions for renunciation than persons of ordinary piety, and they know intuitively what will please or displease their divine and infinitely holy friend. They have all the delicacy of true love."

5. Hence It Follows

Knowing Christ in this way themselves, and understanding what others are missing who have failed to come to this intimate knowledge, it is not to be surprised at that this knowledge leads them on to a consuming zeal for souls. Like the doctor who has discovered what is wrong with his patient, the loving friend of Jesus sees with a clarity that baffles his powers of expression that souls are made to know God thus, to love Him and Him alone and all else in Him, to unify their whole lives in one consistent act of devoted personal service. But these same souls are groping and stumbling. Many of them are even buried in the darkness of lives given over completely and unrestrainedly to vice. Even among the pious and the good, how many there are who serve this loving Master almost as if He were merely an exacting judge; how many content themselves with a veneer of sentimental piety, and sadly and falsely delude themselves into believing that it is He whom they are loving!

When grace illumines a man to see into these deceptions, you have inflamed at once the fire of a zeal that breaks down all opposition in its efforts to share with others the knowledge it has found. Works of zeal undertaken in this spirit, which are the overflow of the soul's knowledge and love of Jesus Christ, will never impede the soul's own progress, never will injure the life of prayer and personal attachment to Christ. More than that. Such zeal does but feed the flame of divine love, and divine love in its turn speeds the soul from the sanctuary into the harvest field, there to labor amid the heat of the day, and return at evening time, after having brought to others the knowledge and love of Him by whom it has been captivated.

This same knowledge of Jesus engenders too, the fundamental virtue of all holiness—deep and sincere humility. We can see the light of recognition shining in the eyes of St. Peter, when, with his companions, he dragged into the shore the miraculous draft of fishes. What was his instinctive reaction? "Which when Simon Peter saw, he fell down at Jesus' feet, saying: 'Depart from me for I am a sinful man, O Lord.' " So too, the soul that is admitted to the holy familiarity with Jesus we are discussing is overpowered and overawed by a sense of its own utter unworthiness. Such a soul no longer needs lengthy considerations and motives to cultivate its humility. "A single ray of divine light," writes St. Teresa, "humbles us more before God than all the other reasons for humility which we may consider. In the penetrating light that comes from above we suddenly perceive the sublimity of God, His purity and sanctity, and, side by side with this, our own indescribable misery." The close union He deigns to effect between our own sinfulness and His ineffable holiness, the vivid and ever-present consciousness of the contrast between us, is indeed a sure foundation for humility, and who builds thereon does not need to fear when the winds beat heavily and the storms howl and the rains fall. His house rests upon the solid rock.

These are some of the effects that flow from this personal knowledge of Jesus Christ. That is why He evinces so great an anxiety that all men should attain to do as close a degree of this knowledge as is possible, for it vivifies their whole existence, it gives impetus to their zeal, it develops a sure and an abiding humility. And we, can we, too, hope to arrive at this intimate knowledge, "to know also the charity of Christ which surpasseth all knowledge?" And if so, how? How can we make Our Lord the living reality He ought to be? If hitherto He has been, wholly or in part, a vague "phantasma," how are we to set about the task of ensuring that henceforth knowledge of Him and personal devotedness to Him will become the driving-force of our whole lives?

As has been said already, such intimacy is generated only through the grace granted to those who seek perseveringly. We seek by meditating much on the things Jesus did and said, and such deep meditation leads on to knowledge *about* Him. But, in order to know Himself, we must crave for the gift of His grace. Our preparation of heart and our co-operation are indeed essential, but, despite all our efforts, our eyes will remain held until grace from on high comes to us and removes the scales.

The purpose of the chapters that follow is to allow Jesus Christ to move before us as He moved before the men and women of His time, so that, in St. Paul's phrase, we may "learn Christ." It is hoped that in this way we may be helped, even a little, to know more *about* Him. But if we are to come to grips with the reality, if knowledge of Him is to be the transforming, vivifying, illuminating force that it was and is to the fervent soul, then we shall have to go on our knees and beg for grace, like the blind man who implored that Jesus would grant him his sight. We shall have to knock and refuse to cease knocking until the door swings wide open—and we see!

II. The Attractiveness of Christ

"Hold Him, and keep Him for thy friend, who, when all others forsake thee, will not abandon thee, nor suffer thee to perish in the end."—Imitation of Christ.

1. It Can't Be Denied

It requires no deep study of the life and character of Our Divine Lord to see that there was in Him a wonderful attractiveness. By that we mean that He possessed a power to draw people to Him in quite an unprecedented manner. This fact holds out much encouragement for the aspirant to holiness, because it sometimes happens that we associate with sanctity an aloofness, a rigid sternness, that repels us and makes us inclined to avow that if sanctity implies the adoption of such an angular and strained attitude towards life, then we shall certainly take good care to steer clear of it. Men and women who are holy and sincere in their efforts to yield themselves entirely to God, are none the less always necessarily imperfect, and that is why in them there are often unpleasant traits which frighten us off.

Genuinely holy people sometimes retain all their lives a violent temper, or an imperious manner, or a lack of power to sympathize with those who suffer, or a harshness in dealing with sinners and an inability to understand or make allowances for another's repeated lapses. You will meet holy people who seem to be quite conscious of the heights to which they themselves have reached in the spiritual ascent. They impress you as being, apparently, not a little proud of their achievement, and you find yourself wondering if they forget that they have nothing except what they received. Or they are adepts at the art of pointing out the contrast, only by an *innuendo* perhaps, between themselves and others, and always with the honors on their own side. They almost seem to echo the pharisee's prayer, thanking God that they are not as the rest of men. Traits like these are a clear proof of the depths of our fund of pride. They are also sometimes permitted by God to cling to the sincere aspirant to sanctity in order to convince him of his innate weakness and inability to rise above it unless he be lifted up and sustained all the time by divine grace.

But there is a marked difference when we approach Our Lord, the perfect model of all holiness. In Him there is no angularity, no single characteristic that might alarm us or deter us from the effort to become like Him. On the contrary, everybody felt His attractiveness. All men of good will who came in contact with Him experienced at once a magnetism in His personality which made them overjoyed to have met Him, which compelled them to listen to Him when He spoke, which caused them to part from Him with obvious regret and to watch eagerly for the next favorable opportunity to come back to Him again. This attractiveness of Jesus we propose to study, and one reason for doing so is that it cannot but encourage us in our own feeble efforts after holiness, if we understand that holiness and happiness must necessarily go hand in hand. True sanctity, such as we are going to see in Jesus, its source and fountainhead, sets the feet of the earnest seeker securely on the road to happiness. "A saint who is sad," writes St. Francis de Sales, "is a sad sort of saint." "In a heart united with God," says St. Jean Vianney, "it is always springtime."

Let us begin then, by taking into our hands the Gospel story and turning over the pages almost at random. Our attention can scarcely fail to be arrested by the many examples we come upon of the actual fact of the attractiveness of Jesus. One morning, early in His public life, Our Lord joined the crowd that had gathered around the Baptist at the river Jordan. As John stood there by the bank with the listening multitudes hanging on his words, he presently stopped short. His eyes have fallen upon a stranger who is standing over there, on the fringe of his audience. A rumor had been circulating that John was, perhaps, the long-promised Messias. "No," he declared. "I am not. But look at yonder man. There is He whom you all seek. Behold the Lamb of God. Behold Him that taketh away the sin of the world—the latchet of whose shoe I am not worthy to loosen."

But Jesus walked down along by the edge of the river, in His quiet unobtrusive way, and, it would seem, He was soon forgotten by the majority of the crowd. There were two, however, who separated themselves from the rest, in order to follow after Jesus. When they had proceeded some distance and were now quite alone, He turned His head round and saw them walking behind. So He put them the most natural question in the world: "Whom seek ye?" His directness of manner disconcerts them somewhat. They are a little abashed and awkward, for the truth is that they want to go wherever He is going. It is not an easy admission to make though, so after a minute's silence they answer His question by blurting out another. "Master," they say, "where dwellest Thou?"

And Jesus said: "Come and see." "They came, therefore," adds the evangelist, "and they saw the place where He abode, and they stayed with Him all that day," wanting just this, just to be with Him, this and nothing more. It is the very first time they have come in contact with Him, but they experience the presence in this stranger of an attractiveness that draws them, almost irresistibly you would say, to Himself. They cannot explain it, but there it is. The hours of the day pass by unheeded. Whatever plans they may have made do not seem to matter now. Nothing indeed matters, except to remain here as long as He is willing to have them with Him. "They stayed with Him all that day."

A little later we find Our Lord seated at the well of Jacob. His disciples have gone into the neighboring town to buy food, and Jesus, weary of His journey and the heat of the scorching summer sun, is resting here and awaiting their return. "Jesus, therefore, being weary of His journey, sat thus on the well."

Presently a poor outcast woman comes over from the town to draw water. She is alone and it is the middle of the day, and both these facts are an indication of the woman's character. For the custom of the women was to walk out together in the cool of the evening and wait for each other till all had filled their pitchers, and then go back home again. But she comes by herself, and in the daytime, for with her no self-respecting woman would associate. Jesus knows all about her. But this sinless Christ, who loved sinners while He hated sin, engages her in a wonderful conversation, with the result that she rushes back breathless to the city and spreads the news everywhere that she has discovered the Messias out at the well of Jacob.

Now it is to be carefully noted that the Samaritans were hostile to the Jews, so ordinarily Jesus might expect but scant courtesy at their hands. His reception in their city, is, therefore, all the more significant. First they come out themselves to see Him as He sits on the wall of the well. Then and there the spell of this man captivates them and they press Him to accompany them back into the town. He yields to their earnest entreaties, and after He has come with them, it is only with the most evident reluctance that they permit Him to depart at all. They wanted to keep Him for themselves, you see. So He has to explain that others need Him, too. He must preach to other men also, and tell them the message entrusted to Him by His heavenly Father. However, He stays with these Samaritans two full days. He remains thus with a people to whom the very mention of the Jews was an abomination and lo, these hostile people are enthusiastic about Jesus of Nazareth.

Merely to have seen Him and heard Him speak is sufficient to attract them in this unprecedented manner. "We have heard Him ourselves now," they tell the woman who first introduced Him, "and we know that this is indeed the Saviour of the world." Such a reception and from such a people! This was all they wanted, these Samaritans, this and nothing more—to be with Him, to forget all the commonplace details of their daily lives, and upset any arrangements that might keep them from being with Him. The attractiveness of Jesus!

On at least two occasions vast multitudes followed Him for whole days on end. So fascinated were they by Jesus of Nazareth that they grew quite careless about even their most pressing needs. In their hunger for the words of power and wisdom which dropped from His lips, they forget all about food for their bodies. On both occasions He had to work a miracle for them in order to feed them in the desert.

Another day, at Lake Genesareth, they thronged about Him so closely that there was danger that He would be pushed into the water. So He signed to Peter and asked his permission to use a boat of his which was lying near by. There, seated a little distance from the shore, He addressed them from the boat and once again they are spellbound as they listen and watch Him.

We have it that "the whole country was stirred" when the news went forth that Jesus of Nazareth was passing by. The people were instantly possessed by one only desire and longing—to see Him and hear Him, cost what this may. Farmers out in the fields at once threw the reins across their plows and came to Him, just as they were, with the clay caked on their hands. Nets were dropped by the fishermen at the shore and they hurried, so as to make sure not to miss Him. Women who were bent over the fireplace preparing the evening meal heard the news and the meal was forgotten, and they ran out of their hamlets to gather around Him. The sound of His very name was a delight to little children, and no game or sport, how entertaining soever, could detain them a moment when once they had learned that Jesus of Nazareth was passing by. They loved Him, this man, as they never loved anyone else. Why, they could not tell you, but beyond all doubt there was something in Him that drew them and filled them with contentment when they were with Him. This was all they wanted, just to be with Him and bother about nothing else. Once more it is the attractiveness of Jesus. "The whole country was stirred."

We shall have to be satisfied with one more example only of this trait in His character. The examples seem to multiply as one scans the pages of the great story. This time it is His deadly enemies who come forward, all unwittingly, to give evidence in His favor. They had sent the soldiers after Him with instructions to seize Him and bring Him back a prisoner. Tough men and well used to tasks of this kind, they set out to do as they were bid. But they returned without their man. "And why?" exclaimed the infuriated scribes and pharisees. "Why have you not brought Him?" "Why indeed?" came the answer. "Never did man speak as this man." Even the coarse soldiers whose finer instincts had long since been blunted by the rough life they led, even they could not fail to recognize the attractiveness of Christ. They were perfectly conscious that they were dealing with no ordinary man. There was something in this Jesus which elevated Him to a position that was unique. "Never did man speak as this man!" And later still, even their masters themselves were unconsciously to endorse this judgment. It was Palm Sunday, and the grand procession had just passed round the corner. Pharisees and scribes were huddled here together, mad with jealousy. They looked into each other's eyes, green with envy, and whispered: "Do you see that we prevail nothing? *We* are out of the picture. The whole world is gone after *Him*."

Sanctity forbidding or repulsive? Look well upon Jesus, the perfect model of all holiness. See how His lovable ways draw all sorts and conditions of people—little children, rough soldiers, farmers, fishermen, saints and sinners—and then understand something at least of the attractiveness of Christ, and by necessary consequence of the attractiveness of holiness.

2. He Hasn't Changed

That same attractiveness of Jesus persists in our own day, for Jesus does not change with the march of years. "Jesus Christ," says St. Paul, "yesterday, today, and the same forever." St. Teresa meant us to understand her quite literally when she wrote: "Jesus Christ is my all; without Him all is nothing to me." Her great heart burned within her because she had been drawn into this furnace of divine love. And, on the scrolls of history the ink is never dry, nor the hand of the scribe ever idle, as he places on record the life-stories of men and women, thousands of them, who bear eloquent and indubitable testimony to the truth proclaimed by the great saint of Avila. You will find those words stamped on the heart of many a young girl, who, like Teresa herself, turns smilingly away from the glitter of the world's tinsel, because the warmth of love of Jesus burning within her urges her to a life of immolation. They are written in large characters, those words, across the silent cell of many a recluse who has fled far from the make-believe of the world and buried himself in solitude because there is a hunger in his heart for reality. And he understands that that reality is to know Jesus of Nazareth, to love Him intensely, to break down every obstacle which might impede the flow of the grace of Christ into his soul.

"Jesus Christ is my all; without Him all is nothing to me"—the words have sped men and women to the ends of the earth in a mighty campaign for Christ, devoured with an insatiable longing to bring the light of the world to nations sitting in darkness and the shadow of death. They are emblazoned, those same words, upon the banner followed by a whole army of martyrs and confessors in every age, who went to death with a smile on their faces, who braved exquisite tortures, who were hungry, and cold, and naked, or prostrate under exhausting heat, who were flung to wild beasts in the arena, or roasted over slow fires, or scourged, or jeered at, or, like the great Model, done to death by crucifixion. On these the world casts a commiserating glance of pity, and with a shrug of the shoulders, calls them fools. And the world is right. They *are* fools, "fools for Christ's sake."

They suffered and died and sweated and toiled, because within their breasts they carried a furnace of enthusiasm for Jesus Christ and His cause. Love of Him is the mightiest force, the weightiest motive, which in past ages has driven men and women to scale heights of self-sacrifice which no other motive or force could reach. Love of Him today is the secret of many a hidden life of silent endurance. Love of Him today surges up in many a generous heart, awakening a craving for opportunity to suffer for Him, to toil for Him, to be a "fool" for His sake, to be walked on, trampled upon and despised for love of Him, and for the love of Him that fills one's heart to give love's supreme proof—to pour out one's blood for Him. "Fools" they are indeed, but "the world will know their wisdom when the drums of doom are heard."

High-sounding words, empty pharseology, the cynic will say. But no cynic is expected to read these pages. They are written for those who know, by the testimony of their own lives and by their dealings with other faithful friends of Jesus, that the attractiveness of Christ is a fact, throbbing with life, quivering with energy, today, in the midst of the materialism of our twentieth century. Christ endures. Love of Christ persists, though it may be surrounded with a sin and perversity, unequalled, said Pius XI, since the days of Sodom. "Jesus Christ, yesterday, today, and the same forever."

3. What's the Secret?

Having thus established the fact of Our Divine Lord's attractiveness, we have now to try to discover its explanation. What marvelous power is this, wielded by Him in His lifetime? What is there in His character which, still today, makes men's hearts leap up with zeal for Him, a man who lived and died twenty hundred years ago? This is no new question. Down through the centuries whole libraries have been built in the attempt to provide the answer, and the attempt is, admittedly, a failure. The pens of saintly men and learned men in every age have covered page after page, and piled volume upon volume in the effort to delineate the perfect character of Jesus of Nazareth. And, after all this, the writers have laid their pens down, and with a sigh of despair have confessed that what they have written falls as far short of the reality, as does the small child's crude essay fall short of the polished diction of a Newman or a Macaulay.

The beauty and perfection of that character are quite beyond the power of pen to write, be the scribe an Aquinas or a Bernard of Clairvaux, or a Goodier or a Marmion in modern times. As for the spoken word it, too, is a feeble medium by which to translate into language the splendors shining in this man, this Jesus of Nazareth, even if the preacher comes to his task equipped with weapons like the golden eloquence of a Chrysostom or the burning conviction ringing in the rugged sentences of a Xavier or a Curé of Ars. Christ's panegyric will never be adequately preached. The story of Christ will never be compressed between the narrow pages of a book, be that book so spacious that the whole world itself could not contain it.

So all we can try to do in a little sketch of this kind is to single out a few of the salient traits in this perfect character of Jesus Christ. These, it is hoped, may throw at least some tiny glimmer of light on the secret of His attractiveness, and encourage us in our struggles to be like Him. What, then, do they find in Him, those crowds who follow Him everywhere He goes? More than once He has almost to use force to free Himself from their importunities, when the need for rest or food becomes imperative or when He retires in order to pray—so as to teach them, that, though for Him such withdrawal was not necessary, it would be imperative for those who would come after Him in the apostolate. What then is there in Jesus that seems almost to obsess men like this? Why does Christ attract?

The first and most obvious answer leaps to our lips when we recall that in the soul of every man there is a hunger for God. Man's own experience bears him witness that there is a void in his heart, and that he cannot rest satisfied as long as it remains unfilled. He reaches continually for something outside of himself, something which he knows and feels to be essential to his happiness and well-being. Often he is sadly mistaken in thinking that the object of his quest is sin and sinful gratification.

The fact is, that that vague something is the knowledge and the love and the possession of God. Give him perfect health, and every facility for travel, for study, for sport, for sightseeing. Give him money, and friends, and congenial surroundings. To be sure, he will play with these things for a while, and for a while, like the child amusing himself with toys in the nursery, he will extract from them a measure, perhaps even a large measure, of enjoyment. But the child will cast aside its playthings at last, and rich men will have to confess that their accumulation of wealth leaves them unsatisfied, and the poet will assure you that to sport is as tedious as to work when a man has nothing else to do except to seek sport and amusement. Where then is he to find this happiness for which he is aching, if not in wealth, or health, or travel, or sport, or learning? Is the desire to be eased at all? Ask Augustine of Hippo, who hungered as we do, and thought to stave off the pangs by plunging headlong into the wildest excesses. Taught by his own experience, he took up his pen and wrote the sentence that has been quoted till it is threadbare: "Thou hast created us, O Lord, for Thyself, and our heart is restless until it rests in Thee."

It is easy to see, then, the first reason for the attractiveness of Jesus. These men and women crowd about Him in this fashion, for the fact is that God has stepped into their midst. In Him, therefore, they find a contentment that completely satisfies their yearning for happiness. So all they want and desire is to be with Him thus, this and nothing more. It is quite true that never did man speak like Him, because Jesus of Nazareth is not man only, but God also. Knowledge of God is the quest of man's mind, and love of God the longing of man's heart, and here in Jesus he finds both. Jesus is the "power of God and the wisdom of God"; small wonder then that they cannot tear themselves away from Him.

Sinners, many of them, long habituated to the gutter; blinded worldings beginning at last to be disillusioned about the baubles they have pursued with such eagerness; generous souls, too, who are stirred by a high ideal—all these flock to Jesus of Nazareth, for all share in common this hunger and this thirst for God. And Jesus of Nazareth *is* God.

But, even as man, even as a member of the human family like ourselves, Our Lord's character has certain most lovable elements that are quite sufficient to account for man's sweeping enthusiasm for Him. We find in Him, first of all, as man, an astonishing self-forgetfulness. In His dealings with others He is always so approachable, ready at a moment's notice to upset His plans in order to be of service to others. Indeed, people came to take this for granted, so you find them making demands upon Him at most unreasonable hours, and for most unreasonable reasons.

Open St. John's third chapter for confirmation of this. All day long Our Lord has been at the beck and call of everybody and anybody who wanted Him. Without a thought of His own needs, He had bent down to listen to their tales of sorrow, and to pour into hearts, that were crushed under a load of anxiety, the balm of His words of comfort. He had gone around doing good, wherever opportunity offered. And now it is night, and He has retired at last into the house where He is lodging in Jerusalem. Nothing could be more reasonable than that a man who has toiled ceaselessly since early morning should now be permitted to have these few hours for repose, or, perhaps, for prayer with the Father in secret. But what happens actually? Nicodemus, a ruler of the Jews, chooses this most inconvenient hour to call. And for what purpose? Perhaps he wants only a word or two with Jesus? Not at all. He wants to invite himself in. He wants to sit down and speak without restraint. He wants to ask a great many questions which are vexing his mind.

No, he has not made any appointment. He does not seem even to consider the possibility that Jesus would not receive him. Why could he not come at some other time? Why, for instance, not hold over these questions until tomorrow, until after Jesus has taken His well-earned night's rest? Or why did not Nicodemus come forward today while Jesus was abroad and at the disposal of anybody who wanted to address Him? Well, you must remember, that Nicodemus was one of the great men of Jerusalem, and what would people say or think if they saw him conversing with the poor carpenter of Galilee? So he slips out under cover of night, for the simple reason that he is consulting at his own convenience.

It was all so inconsiderate, so very unreasonable, to obtrude himself in this way upon an exhausted man, and with so flimsy an excuse for the disturbance. Who could have blamed Our Lord if He had sent out word to the visitor to say that He was engaged, or in need of rest, or that He would see Nicodemus on the morrow? But that is not His way at all. Nicodemus is admitted—as he took for granted he would be—and it is no grudging reception. He is made to sit at his ease and bring forward all his questions one by one. There is no bustling him out, no suggestion of impatience or irritation, no fidgety vexation to let him understand clearly that the sooner he goes the better, no obvious indication that the Master has other occupations demanding immediate attention.

On the contrary Our Lord at once lays aside all his own arrangements. His weariness is forgotten. His prayer or His rest is postponed. Here is a man who wants him, and, without a single thought for Himself, Jesus puts Himself absolutely at the man's disposal. Such is the affability of Jesus; such is His approachableness. He is not subject to "humors." No one need be afraid of a rebuff. There is no necessity to watch out for a favorable opportunity of drawing near with your request or suggestion when it is to Him you are coming, for every opportunity is a favorable one. Much more even than His faithful Apostle, Jesus is "all things to all men," ready to receive them just whenever they happen to want Him, to listen to whatever they have to say, though another might think it silly or confused; eager to solve their doubts, to advise, to cure, to console anybody and at any time. He has no special "hours." His invitation is to *all* men. No wonder He won their hearts. No wonder a man so utterly selfless exercised over them an attractiveness without precedent or parallel or equal. No wonder the whole country was stirred when Jesus of Nazareth was passing by.

4. House Full

St. Mark in his second chapter gives us another example of this same readiness on the part of Our Lord to receive unreasonable people. He was preaching in a house at Capharnaum. As usual, no sooner did the word go out that He was there, than the crowds began to collect around Him from every side. "It was heard that He was in the house and many came together, so that there was no room—no, not even at the door. And He spoke to them the word." It is very easy to fill in the details of the picture. Our Lord sitting or standing there, in the center of the room; the men and women and children around Him, all with eyes riveted upon Him. He has their undivided attention, and it is well, for He has much of importance to say to them today. Here is a grand chance for the preacher to drive home, with all the forcefulness of His divine eloquence, the lessons He wants to teach.

But presently everything is disordered. The attention of everyone wanders. Outside the house four men have brought between them on a stretcher a poor invalid, trembling with palsy. "And when they could not offer him unto Him for the multitude, they uncovered the roof where He was. And opening it, they let down the bed, wherein the man sick of the palsy lay." Here, indeed, is an interruption that is quite inexcusable. Such a place to bring in a sick man, and his bed as well! Why, already there was not a square inch to spare! What a commotion there must have been among the densely-packed audience, all trying to move back and make room, and avoid colliding with the man and his bed! And as for Our Lord's grand sermon, it is thrown into confusion. A moment ago He had caught the ears of all, but now the thoughtless mob have quite forgotten. A most ill-timed and annoying interruption, and everyone is completely upset.

Everyone? No, not everyone. Not He who, more than any others, would seem to have most justification for showing displeasure. It looks as if Our Lord takes the whole thing for granted. It was all prearranged, you would say. He turns from His sermon and gives Himself to the poor sufferer who wants Him. This sick man was in sin, so Jesus forgave him his sins. He was in need of bodily healing, so Jesus cured him, lifted him from his bed, and sent him home happy. This is what the man wanted, so Jesus did it for him.

Jesus is always ready to help anybody, at any time, quite regardless of His own convenience or arrangements. There is no necessity to watch out for a favorable opportunity if it is to Jesus you are coming to make your request, for every opportunity is a favorable one. His unfailing readiness to be all things to all men and at all times—this is written in large characters throughout the gospel story, and it goes a long way towards explaining the wonderful attractiveness of Jesus Christ.

Again and again, as we continue to peruse the story of His life, we come upon further illustrations of this approachableness. Before we pass on to another trait of His character, we cannot refrain from delaying a moment at St. Matthew's eighth chapter. Here you find Him delivering the long discourse which we know as the Sermon on the Mount. He might reasonably have said that He is tired after such a sustained effort, and He might have dismissed the people and told them to think over what He had just been saying to them. But once more, see how approachable He is. And again we note the circumstances.

"Great multitudes followed Him," on His way down the mountain. Then a leper draws near with his petition: "Lord, if Thou wilt, Thou canst make me clean." The leper wanted Jesus to cure him, so Jesus cleansed the leper. Immediately after this, the centurion runs to Him to beseech a favor for his servant who is lying sick at home. The centurion's servant wanted Jesus, so Jesus cured the centurion's servant. "I will come and heal him." Next He goes into Peter's house, and there He finds Peter's wife's mother lying ill of a fever. This poor woman wanted Jesus, so Jesus "touched her hand and the fever left her." Evening closes in, and "they brought to Him many that were possessed with devils and he cast out the spirits with His word; and *all* that were sick He healed." These sick folk wanted Jesus, so Jesus went to the sick folk and cured them all, laying His hands upon each one of them in turn.

It is the same story every time. Never a thought for Himself; no consideration for His weariness after that lengthy sermon to the multitudes; on all sides He finds people who want Him, so He comes to them. He does not seem to know what it is to spare Himself. Is it to be wondered at that such a selfless man drew all sorts and conditions of men and won their hearts?

5. No Compromise

But with all this approachableness Our Lord is never merely one of the crowd. Side by side with His unfailing readiness to help others and accommodate Himself to their plans or even their whims, He always preserves a quiet dignity of bearing and a care never to compromise Himself. Men are forced to respect Him even when they hate Him, for the marvelous self-possession of this man marks Him at once as their superior. With everybody Jesus is easy and free, but with nobody is He free and easy. This quiet reserve, balancing to a nicety His approachableness, is a second element in the human character of Our Lord which goes to account for His attractiveness.

His enemies are lynx-eyed. Not a movement of the man do they allow to escape them. They lay themselves out to ensnare Him in His speech, to beat Him in argument and confound Him before the people. They dub Him friend of sinners, a winebibber, a man possessed of an evil spirit, through whose power it was that He worked His miracles. And Jesus, knowing the men He has to deal with, can yet, in His compliant, easy way, walk into the inns and sit down to meals with publicans and sinners. He can invite Himself to dinner with Zachaeus, the despised publican. He can permit Magdalene, the woman who was a sinner in the city, to come near to Him while He reclines at table in the house of the pharisee. He can allow her to kneel here at His feet, to kiss them, to pour her precious ointment upon them.

These things Jesus can do, and in the sight of such enemies can He do them, and then, in face of all that, he can turn upon them and throw down a challenge such as none other than He dare utter. "Which of you," He demands fearlessly, "can convince Me of sin?" Open out wide the book of My life. Read every chapter with minute care. Scrutinize every line and every sentence and discover, if you can, one single instance of sin. They did not accept the challenge. They did not dare to, for they knew well His life was without blame. Gentle He was, always. Ready to help anyone at any time, yes. But the lovableness in Him never degenerates into mere sentiment. He is Son of God as well as son of man, and His quiet reserve, His sinless life, His care to maintain in all places and at all times the dignity proper to His position, makes Him the most attractive of men. His approachableness wins their love; His dignity commands their esteem.

There is nothing remotely suggestive of over-familiarity in His love. There is never a trace of subservience in His submission. With friends and with foes there is always the consciousness that this man is perfect master of Himself. This marvelous proportioning between kindness and firmness it is that captivates people's hearts when they come to know this man, this perfect man, Jesus Christ, yesterday, today, and the same forever.

6. Sincerity

There is yet a third characteristic of Our Lord that is a contributory cause to His attractiveness. This is His limpid sincerity. He is sincere, in the first place, with Himself. He gathered around Him a school of disciples and He taught them a new philosophy of life, one that demanded a spirit of entire self-sacrifice. So sublime was His teaching that many of them considered it was beyond the reach of human frailty and they turned their backs upon Him. But Jesus asks nothing from His pupil in the school of sanctity that He does not practise Himself. He is always consistent. It is this sincerity, this transparent honesty which gives Him so strong an influence over the people.

They could not but mark the contrast between this new teacher and their scribes and pharisees, and the contrast was all in Christ's favor. "He taught as one having authority" and what helped this authority enormously was that they saw Him living what He preached to them. "Jesus began to *do* and to teach." His sermons were not culled from dusty folios, they were read from the book of experience. Men heard from His lips not merely the letter of the law that killeth, but the word of God "living and efficacious." There was, of course, in His words a divine power because He was God, but for the moment we are considering His doctrine emanating from Him merely in so far as He is man. Conviction rang in His tone of voice because He had reduced His lofty ideals to practice in His own daily life, and they knew it. There was unction in what He said, and pathos, and forcefulness, and courage, all according to what the occasion called for. It was clear that His heart burned with a consuming desire to convince, as they saw Him to be Himself convinced. It was this obvious sincerity, proven by this consistency between theory and practice, that so readily struck a responsive chord in the hearts of His hearers.

Jesus taught that man is placed by God in this world. From God he comes and to God he returns at death. Therefore man is God's property, and therefore, too, man's one and only business in this world is to find out what God wants him to do, and, having found it out, to bend all his energies to the doing of it. This was the theory of life as propounded by Our Lord. In His very first public discourse He warned the multitudes: "Not everyone that saith to Me: 'Lord, Lord,' shall enter into the kingdom of heaven, but he that doth the will of my Father who is in heaven, he shall enter into the kingdom of heaven." The unique privilege even of being His mother avails nothing unless this honor be accepted in a spirit of obedience to God's will. It was thus that Mary accepted it, when she bowed her head to the divine decree, saying: "Be it done unto me according to thy word!" That is the reason why, as He was preaching one day, and a woman, moved by the unction of His words, exclaimed that the mother of such a son was surely blessed, she received an answer that must have startled her. "Yea, rather, blessed are they who hear the word of God and keep it." Mary was indeed blessed, blessed among all women, for she had been chosen out of all of them to be in truth God's mother. Her real title to blessedness was indeed this magnificent privilege, but this privilege precisely and only because it was God's will for Mary.

This, then, is Our Lord's theory of life, and with it the conduct of His daily life is in perfect harmony. A few times He summed up His life's work, and each time He showed clearly what gave it value and significance in His sight. It was not His miracles, nor His success in swaying the minds and wills of the people, nor his popularity, nor His power to attract men capable of appreciating the beauty and nobility of His character. Life had one purpose only, the doing of the Father's will. "I came down from heaven, not to do My own will, but the will of Him that sent Me." This is His standard of values. This will of the Father governs His every choice, prompts His every action and word, whether He lives or dies is to be determined by whatever the will of the Father ordains Jesus is consistent in theory and in practice. Jesus is sincere, and sincerity invariably attracts.

Our Lord never tires of impressing upon men that if they do God's will they will save their souls. The light of eternity shone continually across His path like a beacon and it influenced all His teaching. Witness His vivid parable of Dives and Lazarus—Lazarus, the penniless beggarman, starved to death at the gate of the rich man's palace, and the terrifying contrast in eternity. For Lazarus was borne by angels to paradise, but the rich man, when he died, was buried in hell. Lazarus remembered eternity; Dives, preoccupied as he was with having a good time, forgot all except this present life.

Or there is the story about the farmer who sowed good grain in his field. But in the darkness of night his enemy came and sowed tares. Both grew up together, but the farmer decided to wait till the harvest before trying to uproot the weeds lest, in digging them out, the good crop he might also injure. So do good men and evil men rub shoulders in this life, but eternity is hastening and with it the inevitable apportionment of merit or everlasting punishment.

Another day He describes the wealthy farmer whose yield at harvest was so fine that his barns were too small to contain it. What would he do? He would knock down those little barns, and build instead fine roomy ones; he would stuff them full of good grain, and then sit back and enjoy comfort and plenty. A wise man, says the world. Sensible fellow to make provision for the future, commented his next-door neighbor. Good man of business, thought his servants. But God—what was God's verdict? God regarded this wise man, this man of sound business capacity, this far-seeing fellow, as—a fool! "Thou fool! This night do they demand thy soul of thee, and whose shall these things be for which thou hast labored?" His soul! Eternity! The idea never entered his sensible head.

This is the strain in which Jesus speaks to the people. Is it necessary to point out that here, too, His conduct is consistent? Every page of the Gospel record is there to testify that, in the practical working out of His life, Jesus valued time only as it was fraught with opportunities of preparing for eternity.

He inculcates humility. Let no disciple of His seek first place when invited to a banquet; let him always keep in mind that if he wishes to enter heaven he must become like a little child. Let the followers of Christ do indeed all the good they are capable of, but let them beware of all ostentation, all desire to be seen by men and lauded by them for their deeds. If they seek men's applause they will lose the reward promised by their Father in heaven. Even when they pray, let them seek, by preference, the secrecy of their own room. When they give alms, let not their left hand know what their right hand does.

Is He consistent and sincere here, too? Does He not point to Himself as a model? "Learn of Me that I am meek and humble of heart." In another this might be arrogance. In Jesus it was the simple statement of literal truth, and they knew it. Jesus taught humility, and Jesus is the very first to put His teaching into practice.

So with what He says about poverty. "Blessed are the poor in spirit. . . ." "It is easier for a camel to go through the eye of a needle, than for a rich man to enter into the kingdom of heaven." Once more He Himself is the first to lead the way in reducing theory to practice. He was born in the poverty of Bethlehem, and at Nazareth He passed for the son of a poor artisan. In His public life He had to work a miracle to secure the money needed to pay a tax. He can proclaim to the world: "The foxes have their lairs, and the birds of the air their nests, but the son of man hath not where to lay his head." Jesus is sincere. Jesus is consistent.

Prayer was His constant occupation, even in the midst of engrossing work. He prayed always, and that was why, when He spoke about prayer, He was merely telling the people about His own experience. Before all else Jesus is a man of prayer.

Jesus never rejected a truly repentant sinner, no matter how black his past record. Magdalene, Peter, the thief on the cross, even Judas, even His executioners, were all in turn to be the recipients of His offer of merciful forgiveness. Who, then, is better qualified than He to denounce bitterness and wrangling and refusal to forgive? The men and women who stood listening to these denunciations knew well how much He had forgiven, and with what readiness. He asks from them nothing that He is not doing Himself.

Finally, Jesus taught that self-sacrifice was absolutely necessary for anyone who wanted to save his soul. "If any man will come after Me, let him deny himself, take up his cross daily, and follow Me." Was he sincere here? Was He consistent? A glance at the hill of Calvary and all that preceded it, and the answer is plain for the whole world to see.

7. The Manliness of Christ

Of a piece with this sincerity with Himself is the sincerity of Our Lord in dealing with His enemies. Their lies and deceits He held in execration. They were hypocrites. They knew it, and He knew it, and they knew that He did. Without a semblance of fear or hesitancy this sincere man proceeds ruthlessly to tear away the mask and show them to the world for what they are. "Generation of vipers, how can you speak good things whereas you are evil? . . . I know you, that you have not the love of God in you. . . . You will not come to Me that you may have life. . . . Blind guides who strain out a gnat and swallow a camel! . . . Woe to you, scribes and pharisees, because you make clean the outside of the cup and of the dish, but within you are full of rapine and uncleanness. Thou blind pharisee, first make clean the inside of the cup, that the outside may become clean. Woe to you, scribes and pharisees, because you are like to whited sepulchers which outwardly appear to men beautiful but within are full of dead men's bones. So you outwardly appear to men just, but inwardly you are full of hypocrisy and iniquity. . . . You serpents, generation of vipers, how will you flee from the judgment of hell?" Language like this from a mere workingman, and a workingman from Nazareth at that! The carpenter's son has the insolence and temerity to address in this aggressive and insulting manner, the highly respectable citizens of Jerusalem! But the charges He makes they dare not deny, for well they know that here, as always, He is speaking the truth.

It is not to be tolerated, so they resolve on His death. But strong men and sincere men loved Him more than ever because they were filled with admiration for His manliness. Jesus was gentle and patient—this they had seen many times already. But now they learn that His is a gentleness that would never quail in presence of vice nor observe an obsequious silence whenever sin had to be called by its right name. He is sincere with His enemies, as witness these scathing denunciations, as witness a scorn that loathes their detestable hypocrisy and tells them so. They are speechless, for His withering accusations are unanswerable.

Jesus is sincere with Himself; He is sincere with His enemies. But Jesus is sincere, too, as no one else ever was sincere, in His loyalty to his friends. This trait will form the subject-matter of another section of this book, so it is mentioned here only *en passant,* and only to round off what is being set forth. Merely human affection is built on sentiment and that is why it is so fickle. But as Jesus walked through this world, in every human being upon whom His eyes rested He saw an immortal soul. That is why He loved. That vision which He had of the stupendous value, and beauty, and destiny of an immortal soul, that possibility for wondrous growth in grace which He saw in such a soul, lies at the root of His sincerity. It is the explanation of His affability, of His patience, His gentleness, His readiness to forgive. It is the motive which actuates His fearful warnings, His strong denunciations. If the soul be lost, all is lost. If the soul be in danger no words can be too vehement to bring home to it the imminence of its irrevocable disaster.

The love of the saints for men is like this. "They have guessed the blinding value of a soul." Hence their impassioned appeals to sinners. Hence their ceaseless labors, their journeys, their hunger and thirst, their readiness to be separated from home and friends. Hence their penitential lives. Hence their readiness to brush aside an insult over which another will keep brooding, and for which he will finally demand a formal apology. The man who is wrapped up in the interest and zeal he has for souls has no time to be nursing grievances, for there is an immense harvest and the time allotted for gathering it in is rushing past at an incredible speed. In a man or woman of this type you find a love for the neighbor as broad as the Atlantic and as deep, for, like the Master, their look penetrates into the interior where they recognize an immortal soul. The vision eclipses all else. "They have glimpsed the blinding value of a soul."

8. Counter Attractions

Christ attracts, but why, I wonder, are there so many whose eyes seem to be held? To these He is not a personal, intimate friend at all, and what they hear about His lovableness leaves them cold and unmoved. They experience, perhaps, a vague wish to realize, they would like to share the enthusiasm of others, but they cannot, or they think they cannot. Can this be accounted for—that Christ so unselfish, so patient, so sincere, should leave them indifferent? That the writer of a novel can arouse their interest in and love for an imaginary hero, and that the very Son of God, made man for love of them, evokes no response, or only a very feeble response, from their hearts? Why is this?

Christ attracts, it is true, but there is a counter attraction. Sin and the world also have wares to sell, and it is beyond question that these wares are decked out in a most attractive garb. The hunger for happiness in man's heart reaches for what sin and the world have to offer, under the delusion that herein contentment can be found. Sin and the world promise this satisfaction, and it is to be admitted that they certainly do afford a measure of enjoyment to their votaries. But a spasm of violent excitement, or a thrill that leaves a hunger for more, is not happiness. What the soul craves for is more lasting fare.

Pope Pius XI complained of a spirit of restlessness that is abroad today, an apparent inability on the part of many to settle down steadily to any serious occupation. Natural pleasure, indeed, has its place in man's life, a place assigned it by the Creator. But what the Pope deplores, and what every right-minded man and woman must deplore with him, is the growing tendency to set pleasure on a pedestal it never was meant by God to occupy. As long as pleasure, which should be a servant, is permitted to be a usurper, so long will the attractiveness of Christ remain a hidden treasure, outside the realm of personal experience.

Our Lord is inexorable in teaching that friendship with Him can be purchased only at the price of sacrifice. Many are quite prepared to give a quiescent assent of the mind to this "hard saying," and then go their way and forget all about it in practice. That is why the attractiveness of Christ remains a sealed book.

If the counter attraction is to be resisted we have to come back again to the Baptist at the Jordan. "Do penance!" It is a note that jars, but it is the secret key that opens the way to intimacy with Jesus. Wherever the stern lesson is learned and put into practice, and in the measure in which it is learned and put into practice, there the attractiveness of Christ is realized, not merely believed in.

Many men yield to the counter attraction and miss Him. True gold is not easily discerned when the eyes have long been dazzled by the glitter of tinsel. But who that has once understood the value of the gold would be prepared to throw it away and take the tinsel instead? And who that has once sat down at a banquet in his Father's house would ever again dream of trying to satisfy himself with the husks of swine?

III. A Day with Christ

"Fear not, for I have redeemed thee, and called thee by thy name. Thou art Mine."—ISAIAS, xliii.1.

1. THE RENDEZVOUS

IT IS MOST fortunate that we are able, from the different accounts given us by the inspired writers, to reconstruct the series of events which occupied one entire day in the public life of Our Lord.

Early that morning He is alone. We can easily enough envisage Him walking along a country road that winds its way through the fertile uplands of Galilee. Hills green with pasture rise up on His right hand and on His left, and the valley lying between teems with golden corn. Over there on one side He can just get a glimpse of the waters at the southern end of Lake Genesareth where they narrow and flow down between the banks of the river Jordan. There is no sound of human voice to be heard for the farmers have not yet come out of their hamlets to begin the day's work in the fields. Only the bleating of the sheep or the lowing of cattle sends its echo into the valley, or high above His head the song of birds breaks out, filling the air with a rain of melody.

As He walks, there is a look of gladsome expectancy on the face of the Lord. He has appointed this morning for the reassembling of His twelve Apostles. A few weeks ago He had dispersed them, two by two, round the various towns and villages, and had given them minute instructions concerning the methods to be employed in the work of spreading His Gospel, the good news He had brought to men. And now they are to be back this morning. Soon they will be here, telling Him how everything has fared. He is first at the spot agreed upon for them to meet, and He sits down here on a mound of grass by the side of the road to await their arrival.

From this point of vantage where He is sitting, Jesus has a

full view of the valley that stretches out at His feet. Presently His attention is attracted by a movement in the trees below. He watches and sees two men push their way out into the open space and at once their eyes turn instinctively in His direction. Their pace quickens as they recognize Him and you might have seen them point Him out to each other assuringly. They are coming down from the north, from Tiberias perhaps, or Magdala, the city of pleasure. Two others are approaching from behind where the Master is seated. Their mission has been to Naim, or, it may be, to Nazareth where Mary His Mother will have made sure to meet them and ask all about her divine son. Others are over from Cana or down from Capharnaum. Indeed, they are closing in about Him from every direction, six pairs of them in all, all eager to meet Him and each other once again and to recount the labors and the successes and the failures of the past few weeks. What will have impressed itself most deeply of all on their minds is the tragic death of the Baptist. They want to talk much about this, the price he had to pay for his fearless and outspoken denunciation of Herod's sin. Our Lord will not fail to point out that everyone who would be His disciple and take his stand against the world must be ready to pay the same price.

So now He is alone no longer. Two by two they have come to Him and knelt there before Him for His blessing. It is good to feel the pressure of His hands resting on their bowed heads, good to receive His smile of welcome. They press in around Him, Peter and Andrew, Philip and James, and the rest of His twelve. There is so much to talk about. Full as they are of the news of their missions, they can scarcely allow each other time to tell it. Their preaching has worked marvels everywhere. Multitudes followed them from all sides. They went into the homes of the sick and healed them with the touch of their hands. The whole countryside is stirred by the wonders they had wrought. Why, even the evil spirits themselves were subject to them, and at their command had gone out of the unfortunate persons possessed. Everything is looking most hopeful, in spite of the death of John the Baptist. Judas himself is jubilant and enthusiastic today.

Throughout all this, Jesus sits and listens, asking here and there just an occasional question, looking in His deep searching way straight into the eyes of each man as he tells his story, an intense interest showing itself in the expression of His face, and a wealth of affection for each of them, even for Judas—perhaps especially for Judas—which He makes no attempt to conceal.

All this enthusiasm may be a little childish. Running through it there may be at least a narrow vein of self-complacency and self-love, but in the main it is the outcome of their love for Him and for souls, and His human heart appreciates it. Later, He will train them to detachment from this success and popularity, but He is infinitely patient in waiting for His opportunity to enforce a lesson. They are only His novices as yet. For the present, then, He will be satisfied to shield them from another danger which He sees well enough is threatening, though from them it is hidden. Active labor, even of a sacred character, must not engross them. They have to learn the value, and indeed the vital necessity, of prayer and withdrawal from the turmoil of exterior things.

Their preaching has been blessed with great success, and He wishes, as they do, to make sure that the success is going to be permanent. On another occasion He will tell them: "In this is My Father glorified, that you bring forth fruit, and *that your fruit should remain.*" They have brought forth abundant fruit, it is true, and His heart rejoices to hear all about it. What is wanting now, in order to secure that that fruit will *remain?*

For this it is absolutely necessary to be filled with the spirit of prayer. Their work is supernatural, the end they have in view is supernatural—the salvation and sanctification of souls. But a supernatural aim requires that the means employed be supernatural also, and foremost among these means is a steady, constant stream of prayer, vivifying and purifying all their exterior labors. They cannot possibly enkindle the fire of His love in the hearts of men if they be not themselves aflame, and prayer is the fuel that must feed that flame.

Every period spent in prayer is like an armful of dry brushwood placed upon the fire. When it is thus constantly replenished a time comes when the fire can no longer contain itself within the strait barriers of the apostle's heart. It must needs break out and communicate itself to others. Hence the apostle's influence for good will be in direct proportion to the union he maintains with God by his life of prayer. The more close and constant this union, the more freely will divine grace flow into his soul, as the sap flows unimpeded from the parent stem into the branch. It is only through the grace of God that souls can be won; therefore the apostle's task is to be a bearer of that grace. His supplies he must draw from the Heart of Jesus, the inexhaustible storehouse, and it is especially by prayer that access is gained to this treasure. "Without Me," Our Lord proclaims, "you can do *nothing*."

2. Come Apart

So now that all about their work is at last told, it is Our Lord's turn to speak. He stands up and advances a pace or two, right into the center of the group. His comprehensive gesture includes them all. With both arms fully extended He looks from one of them to the other in that deliberate way of His, and He gives expression to an invitation that must have thrilled them to hear. "Come apart," he says, "into a desert place and rest a while." It is an invitation to lay aside their excitement, to forget for a while all their eager plannings about external things, and withdraw from the tumult. What does He want them to do in the desert place? They are to come face-to-face with God, using if necessary even a holy violence in the effort to do so. They are to pray. They are to kneel down and allow Him to look into the innermost places of their souls.

The object of the sojourn in the desert is to bring about between God and the soul this close contact. When thus "apart" with Himself, God often chooses to draw aside a little of the veil that generally hides from men's view the realities of life. The result is perspective, quite a new outlook on life and the affairs of earth. When immersed in work, even apostolic work, when tasting the pleasures, even the good and innocent pleasures, of life, there is always danger lest one's vision be jolted out of focus. The soul must step out of its everyday environment in order to be in a position to see life through the eyes of Christ. From this new angle all things are seen and their value judged by a different standard. The light of eternity is now recognized as the only true norm.

You will always find that those who listen to His invitation and give themselves much to prayer gradually lose interest in many of the things which hitherto used to absorb them. The tittle-tattle about your neighbor; the latest movie which everyone has seen; the details about that swell marriage—where they went for the honeymoon, what the bride wore, what gifts they received; the gossip reported in today's paper; even a grave subject, like war or rumors of war, can no longer grip the attention in quite the same way, when in the desert place there has once been vouchsafed the larger vision to the soul.

"Come apart into a desert place and rest a while." The prospect fascinates these friends of Jesus. Apart with Him, Jesus all to themselves for an entire day, and no troublesome crowds to bother them, or try to take Him away from them! It is rich reward indeed for their weeks of labor, just exactly what they would love to have suggested themselves. So, light-hearted as children, they retrace their steps down along the slope of the hill, but this time there is the huge difference that He is with them. Once more they cross the valley, and thence make for the lakeside. Everything they require is here, boat, rudder, oars, and a sail—all ready to hand beside the edge of the water. Peter leads the way and kneels on the sand to hold the bow steady while Jesus, in His sandalled feet, steps in and sits down in His place. The others follow after the Master, the last man remaining behind a moment after the others to give the boat a good push off from the shore. Then he leaps in. All oars are out together, they dip, and away speeds the little craft, heading straight for that "desert place" which they knew Our Lord to have in His mind.

3. Disappointed Hopes

They can scarcely realize it. It seems almost too good to be true that they are going to have Him like this, all to themselves. His thoughtful ways, His gentleness and patience and unfeigned love of them, combined with His firmness and fearlessness, have long since completely captivated their hearts. They knew full well the power of the words that fell from His lips. And now here they are, rowing all together to that lonely place, and He is going to be with them all the day long, and they are going to sit at His feet and listen to that voice, and be taught those sublime lessons of His in a language of which He alone holds the key. Truly a fascinating prospect.

But alas, for their grand expectations! As they pull in, in sight of the lonely spot they had in mind, the gladsome light that had been shining in their eyes gradually gives place to a scowl of anger and disappointment. The very worst has happened. Before them stretches out the northern shore of the lake—and it is black with people!

So here ends the fond dream of the twelve Apostles. Ruefully they have to admit it in their secret hearts, for by now they know well what manner of man is Jesus of Nazareth. He will never have the hardihood to tear Himself away from these multitudes, and come "apart" with his chosen few. "He received them," one of the twelve wrote afterwards, "and began to teach them many things. He spoke to them of the kingdom of God and healed them who had need of healing." One almost suspects him of wishing to add: "And in the midst of this, He forgot all about His twelve Apostles, and lost sight entirely of the invitation He gave them to spend the whole day apart with Himself alone!"

In this manner the hours passed by, Jesus teaching; Jesus answering questions—some of them foolish questions or tiresome questions enough; Jesus listening to stories of sorrow and knowing exactly the correct word to say by way of comfort and courage; Jesus healing their sick; Jesus giving Himself selflessly to anybody who happened to want Him. The pleasant program planned this morning for Himself and His Apostles seems to be all forgotten. Everything is working out so very differently. But how could He go away, with all these poor people needing Him so sorely? They have come seeking Him, like sheep gone astray, and is He, the shepherd, going to turn His back upon them? To Him they look to lift their burdens; He is able to give rest to their weary souls, and is He going to deprive them of it? He had said: "Come to Me and I will refresh you," and now that they have come, is He going to seek to evade them? Would He ever turn aside those who come to Him for guidance?

It is another instance of His readiness to lay aside, for the sake of others, His own plans and allow everything to be upset. It is only when we try to imitate Him in this, that we discover for ourselves how difficult it is. You are traveling in the bus and the driver takes you, by accident, a few hundred yards past your stopping-place. You are furious, or at least much irritated, especially if the rain is falling, and you tell him so in no measured terms. When you sit back and examine your motive, you must see it is selfishness. Your arrangements are upset, in a trifling way, and you object, like the still imperfect disciples, unlike the perfect Christ.

You are in a hurry and somebody intercepts you. He is a bore. You glance at your wrist watch impatiently. You answer him shortly and bustle him out of your way, and you make no sort of effort to hide your annoyance. It is not easy to be patient, or even civil, at a moment like this. When finally you do succeed in shaking him off, you turn the corner and run unexpectedly into a great friend of yours. Such a transformation now! At once you are all smiles and, despite your hurry, you are going to manage, somehow, to spare a few minutes for a chat. When you do part, it is with obvious reluctance and the comforting assurance that you may meet very soon again. You will probably be late for your first appointment. Too bad, but it was worth it, and you will frame some sort of an excuse.

All this, and much more of the same kind, when examined through the eyes of Christ, may well be recognized as evidence of a secret pride and selfishness. Like the disciples, it is very true that often we know not of what spirit we are.

Sanctity is very tolerant. Sanctity is self-effacing. Genuinely holy men and women have got into the habit of analyzing carefully the motives of their actions. They are inclined to let pass by them much about which others make a great fuss. They are not much concerned if by doing so they seem to be failing to stand up for their "rights." The fact is that they have so steeped themselves in the life of Christ, and have grown so accustomed to His manner of acting, that they try as a rule to let others have their way, unless by doing so they would compromise principle. Like Him, they prefer to keep silence when self-love would urge them to answer back. Like Him, they will only smile good-humoredly, when the rest of us flare up. Like Him, they will seem not to hear that unkind remark or notice that deliberate insult. Like Him, they will watch for an opportunity of repaying with kindness those who have told a story against them, or wounded their feelings with the sharp arrow of a sarcastic tongue. Like Him, on the occasion we have under consideration, they show wonderful patience when people are unreasonable and interfere with arrangements.

All this is sheer nonsense to those who have not learned Christ. The natural thing is to chafe and complain loudly, to sweep away all opposition and insist on having things one's own way. It seems as if the poor Apostles had still much of the natural man in them. Small blame to them if they were annoyed—so we incline to think—for here is the entire day being wasted and they are almost wholly out of the picture. At last evening begins to close in, and now they hope that there may be some chance that He will dismiss the multitudes, and permit themselves to have even an hour or two in quiet with Him. He had promised the full day after all.

4. In Praise of Trust

They must watch for their opportunity. They manage to push their way through the crowds and seize upon one of His few unoccupied moments to tell Him what they want. "Master, this is a desert place and it is late now. . . . Send them away that they may buy themselves victuals. . . ." Send them away! That would be scant courtesy, to dismiss in summary fashion the five thousand men, not to mention the women and children, who had shown such devotedness to Him all day. He has plans of His own to cope with the situation. He must provide for them, somehow, even here in this desolate spot.

"How many loaves have you?" He asks. Andrew moves about among the people and presently returns with the report that a little boy has brought along with him five loaves and two fishes. Nothing more? That is all—an utterly useless and inadequate ration, in any hands other than those of Jesus of Nazareth.

In the account of what follows it is very easy to detect traces of peculiar satisfaction in Our Lord, as He makes His detailed arrangements. He is going to allow Himself the joy of providing a feast for His friends, of working a miracle in order to supply their needs. First of all, they are ordered to sit down on the grass. They divide up into groups and obey, their eyes fixed all the time, curiously, questioningly, on the face of the Master. What can He have in His mind? Next, the little boy is brought forward and told to hand over the store that was probably intended as lunch for himself and his smaller brother. He does so, of course, because it is the command of the great prophet, though one might suggest it was not without a sorrowful glance at the departing satchel. Then Our Lord takes the five loaves and the two fishes into His hands and, standing, lifts up His eyes towards heaven in fervent prayer. He blesses the food and gives it back to the disciples, bidding them distribute it among the hungry, expectant crowds. Marvel of all marvels, it multiplies in their hands.

No sooner is one loaf given away, than another appears in its place; no sooner have the two fishes left the hands of the Apostles, than two more are discovered. There is sufficient for all, and this is indeed a great miracle, but still more wonderful is it that there is superabundance. "They did all eat and were filled . . . and they gathered up and filled twelve baskets with the fragments . . . which remained over to them that had eaten."

In view of this miracle it should not be difficult to understand and apply to our own lives, the lesson of boundless trust which Jesus is never tired of inculcating. In the very first sermon He preached He gave prominence to the importance of depending with child-like confidence upon God. In a passage of great beauty He endeavors to wean men from their excessive anxiety about what is merely temporal. Let them lift up their eyes to heaven and see those tiny birds flitting across the sky this evening. They are senseless little creatures, with no foresight to gather into barns against the winter. Let them look on those lovely flowers swaying there in this autumn breeze. His hearers have a Father in heaven who clothes these things with such splendor. They have a Father in heaven and not even one of those small birds drops to the ground but He knows all about it, and permits it to happen.

Now, He concludes, you are the *children* of that Father. Is it much that you should entrust to Him your needs, seeing what care He takes of even the flowers that wither and the birds that live for only a season?

As He continued His missionary career, Our Lord loved to come back again and again on this same theme. Wherever He found this trust He praised it; wherever trust was wanting He plainly showed disappointment and displeasure. The centurion fell down on his knees before Him to plead for his servant who was lying at home, ill of the palsy. "And Jesus said to him: 'I will come and heal him.' " The centurion's humility took alarm; he was not worthy that Jesus should enter under his roof and he said so. Let the prophet only pronounce the word from a distance and the servant will be all right. This deep trust won from Christ the cure that was sought. But He seemed unable to refrain from adding a word of commendation of the man's spirit of confidence, declaring that he had not found so great a faith in Israel.

A little later a poor woman with an issue of blood drew near to Him, trustingly. If only she could just touch the hem of His garment, she felt sure the cure would be effected. She, too, is rewarded in the same way; she, too, is praised by Jesus, and sent back home healed of her infirmity.

His disciples going out to preach were instructed to bring no scrip for the journey, nor two coats, nor shoes, nor a staff. The Lord for Whose sake they were about to work would provide whatever was necessary. Let them leave all to Him, trustingly. Indeed, if they did not waver in their trust, the mountains themselves would obey them and at their word betake themselves from one place to another!

So, from a great number of instances, do these few which are selected show how much He had it at heart that His disciples should be men and women of boundless trust. "Your Father knoweth that you have need of all these things."

When they failed Him, He was not slow in expressing His disappointment. One night out on the lake, a violent storm had arisen and His Apostles were panic-stricken. To be sure, Jesus was with them in the boat, but, exhausted from His toil, He had placed a pillow under His head and fallen fast asleep. "Lord," they cried, "save us or we perish." Save them indeed He did, commanding the seas and the waves, but not until He had first rebuked them for their lack of trust. "O ye of little faith, why did ye doubt?"

There are three reasons, among many others, why He expects us to have this trust in Him. The first is, that He, being the well-beloved Son of God, must necessarily find favor in the sight of His Father. We trust, therefore, that whatever He asks for us from the Father, the Father will grant. Secondly, He demands this trustful spirit because He is our own elder brother. By grace He has adopted us into His family, and He is immeasurably more solicitous about our true interests than we ourselves can ever possibly be. Lastly, as proof of this anxiety, He has placed at our disposal all the infinite treasures of the merits of His sacret Passion—what St. Paul loves to style "the unsearchable riches of Christ." We have only the dimmest concept of the immense spiritual wealth that is thus ours for the asking. We complain of our weakness, but He is strong to sustain us. We are crushed underneath a load of sin and sinfulness, but Jesus is sinless, Jesus is sanctity incarnate, and Jesus belongs to us—more even than that, by grace Jesus has identified Himself with us! "All things are yours, and you are Christ's, and Christ is God's." "In all things you are made rich in Him . . . so that nothing is wanting to you in any grace." "He Who spared not His only-begotten Son, but delivered Him up to death for us all, how hath He not, with Him, given us all things?"

Yet another illustration of His longing to make men trust Him is this act of feeding all these thousands with five loaves and two fishes in the desert place

5. Using Force

Enthusiasm waxes high at this miracle and the crowds want to take Him forthwith and make Him king by sheer force. But once again that is not His way; His kingdom is not of this world. We have it recorded that He *compelled* the Apostles to go again into the boat and row out to sea, while He Himself dismissed the people. It is a most significant word, that "*compelled.*" One thinks of the Apostles as being quite conscious of their own importance. After all, was it not in *their* hands that the food had multiplied? It is not a little gratifying to move in and out among all the people, and, with all due reserve and modesty, of course, and while disclaiming all credit for the miracle, at the same time to enjoy a secret complacency in listening to their laudations.

A new danger is beginning to raise its head, and Jesus is quick to see it and ward it off. Vainglory, love of men's applause, has a deadly fang. It might easily rob them of the merit, or much of the merit, of their good works. It might easily filch from God the glory due to Him alone. It might, and actually it has done so, many many times since those days. That is why Jesus *compelled* them to leave the admiring crowds severely alone. You can almost hear Him calling them by name. You can almost imagine Peter pretending not to hear! They would wish to stay on for a while, delighting in the sound of these canticles of praise. But Jesus was inexorable, and with His command ringing in their ears, they trudge down to the shore and put out to sea.

There was another reason, too, for their reluctance to go. We have to remember that their day had been spoiled, and it was only natural that now at last they would want to stay on with Him and have Him to themselves. But it would not by any means satisfy His standards for them that they should be *only natural*. Neither indeed are they to be *un*-natural. But the Apostles of Jesus must be, above all, *super*-natural. With their present affection for Him there was mingled the merely natural pleasure they experienced in being in the company of a man of such charm. The supernatural love which He wants from them will not indeed supplant the natural, but it will elevate and purify it. From what is merely natural in their love they must be detached. Their devotion to Him must rest, not on sentiment but on doing God's Will. So He *compelled* them to give up their natural love of what they would naturally like to do, in order to exercise them—even by a holy violence—in that spirit of detachment which sets the soul free to seek and love God alone, and for Himself alone.

So once more the boat's moorings were loosened, the oars were put out, and twelve disappointed men proceeded, reluctantly enough, to row across the lake.

Meantime Jesus Himself has sent the crowds back home, and now at last quite alone, He began to walk at a slow pace up along the slope of the hill. Twilight is gathering in, and all day long, since early this morning when He had welcomed back His Apostles, He has been in the midst of men, at the beck and call of anybody who happened to want Him.

Throughout the day's work there has been most vividly present to Him the awareness of the nearness of His heavenly Father. He always saw the face of that Father, for He enjoyed uninterruptedly the splendors of the Beatific Vision. After such a strenuous day as He has had, you might suggest that now a good night's rest is due to Him, and you would be right. But St. Luke has another story to tell. "He fled Himself again into the mountain," he writes, "in order to pray, Himself alone . . . and when it was evening He was there alone."

6. At Sea

Meantime, what has been happening to His twelve Apostles? Misfortunes have multiplied about them today, and night has brought the severest test of all. For they have run into one of those sudden storms that sweep down from the high cliffs surrounding the lake. It is to be very well noted that they encounter this great danger, notwithstanding the fact that it was in obedience to Christ that they undertook the voyage at all. Indeed, we have seen that they had to be *compelled* to go. It is often His way of testing His friends. When we are in the state of life for which He has destined us, we fancy He ought to shield us from grave temptations. Often He does not. Each walk of life has its own peculiar temptations, and love of Christ proves itself precisely by loyalty to Him in the midst of the storms which He Himself has foreseen and permitted.

This whole episode is in many ways very typical of human life. Like the Apostles every man is launched out on the sea of life. Like them we each have undertaken the journey because He has told us. There should be nothing whatever to surprise us, or alarm us unduly, if we run into many a squall of temptation, even persistent and fierce temptation, and even though that temptation comes to us because we are discharging the task He has imposed upon us to do. There may be many an anxious moment before we finally reach the shore and safety. That night, when the Apostles were in imminent danger, Jesus was praying for them as He knelt on the mountainside. He knew all about the panic that had seized them. He foresaw this danger when He compelled them to embark. He not only allowed them to run into the storm but He actually ordered them to face it. But their security lay in His protecting prayer.

And where does ours lie if not in that same prayer of Christ ascending for us from the altar and the tabernacle as faithfully as it arose from His Sacred Heart that night when the little boat was being made the plaything of the winds and the rain?

What commotion there must have been on board! The Gospel tells us they were filled with a great fear, and we are inclined to consider it excusable under the circumstances. For all that it was reprehensible, for it argued to a want of that trust in Him which He had always been at such pains to engender. It is true that the waves are rising mountains high, and the tiny craft is threatened every moment as she is pitched here and there by the violence of the storm. But why are they in such difficulties, except because He has put them here? The danger is not of their own seeking and when they have reached a higher degree of holiness they will understand that since He had ordered them to come out here, He would know how to deliver them. And what about it, if even He never came to their aid at all? Should not the prospect of dying in obedience to the divine will have been enough? Later, indeed, they will understand all this, for most of them will give this very proof of their love.

But at the moment they are filled with terror, and it is a consolation to us to witness it. For which of us does not quail before the storm at times, even when the storm breaks in upon us through no fault of our own? Even when it comes direct from His hand, just as it came to the Apostles tonight?

There was no sort of use, though, in lying down in the boat, and giving up the struggle, so they did all in their power to grapple with the elements. They tugged might and main at the oar, though they could neither make any headway nor get back to the starting-place. Even though with us, too, the night be pitch dark and the wind howls about us, even though there be no apparent result from all our efforts, there is only one mode of action to be adopted—at all costs, like them, to keep trying. "God," says St. Teresa, "withholds Himself from nobody who perseveres."

That is the happy experience of the sorely-tried Apostles. Their persevering efforts are rewarded abundantly, for Christ comes to them walking upon the waters. The elements that were a source of danger are now the very same that bear to them their merciful deliverer. The very trial that weighs so heavily upon you, that harassing temptation which seems impossible to shake off, that mental anguish, those torturing scruples, that good position which you lost through no fault of your own—whatsoever it be—if it clearly comes from God's hand, despite all appearances to the contrary, it is permitted by His love. Beyond all doubt, it is going to prove to be the very channel through which grace will flow into your soul, on condition that, like the Apostles, you do but persevere.

After they had struggled by their own efforts for a while, Jesus came and took complete control and brought them all safe to land. This is how His day finishes—still at its close do we find a Christ Who is all things to all men.

Yes, the whole scene vividly represents our sojourn here. For every follower of Christ there is necessarily the fight on the ocean wave. It is hard to be struggling always and we grow weary in well-doing. Times there are when the promised prize seems unreal and remote. But these are just the periods when Jesus asks for love's supreme proof, trust in Him and in His promises in spite of all. "Even though He should kill me, I will trust in Him." For we are certain that ultimately the storm will be quelled, and the night will pass away, and the darkness will be swallowed up in the glory and the radiance of the dawn, when Jesus at last guides the little barque and brings it safely to land. It will be the ending of a day with Christ, a happy ending after so many trials. But it will be the beginning, too, of a new day, a day the brightness of which will never wane, for it is now everlasting day, and this is a new land where there is no longer weeping nor sorrow, for the former things are passed away. The shore we have now reached is called the Beatific Vision.

IV. The Charity of Jesus Christ

"For this cause I bow my knees to the Father of our Lord Jesus Christ . . . that you may be able to comprehend, with all the saints, what is the breadth and length and height and depth; to know also the charity of Christ, which surpasseth all knowledge, that you may be filled unto all the fullness of God."—EPHESIANS iii. 14, 18, 19.

1. GOD IS LOVE

WHEN ST. JOHN wanted to sum up all God's attributes, His eternity, His awful sanctity, His all-embracing knowledge and infinite power; when he cast about for the attribute which, to our way of thinking, might be regarded as most characteristic, he chose the *love* that fills the heart of God. "God *is* love," he wrote, and in the life of the God-Man proofs of that love crowd into every chapter, one might almost say onto every page, of the Gospel story.

In that sacred narrative He holds up for us to look upon a heart that He assures us is on fire with love for all men. He is at pains to impress upon them that when He speaks thus He is not using the language of metaphor but stating a simple truth. So astonishingly genuine is this love; so solid and unshaken and unchanged does it stand in face of the assaults of treachery and falsehood; so completely does it efface all memory of the cowardice, the pettiness, the selfishness, the crimes even, of the sinner who falls on his knees and with sincere sorrow asks to be forgiven; so exultant is this love of Christ when men at last begin to show signs that they are getting at least a glimpse of its reality, and so keenly disappointed when they refuse to believe in it; so eager is it to make every allowance and discover every excuse; in a word, so immeasurably beyond the ambit of our small minds to fathom, or our halting speech to utter, is this wonderful thing, the love of Jesus for us men, that the saints—they who have most thoroughly "learned Christ"—have made language to yield up all its treasures of eloquence in the effort to tell us what it is and what are its qualities.

And with what result? Why, only to confess that that love of Christ is a luminary so bright that it stands out apart in the firmament, quite on its own, dwarfing all human love, or rather gathering into itself everything there is in human love of beauty and of truth, and excluding every trace of the selfishness by which human love is too often marred. The fact is that words are an inadequate medium by which to describe the treasures of love for men that are contained in this Sacred Heart. Prayer opens the door of this treasure-house when the earnest seeker knocks perseveringly. He is granted admission, and, as he looks around him in amazement, two truths gradually break in on his mind.

The first of these is the one already spoken of, that God is love. But the second is even more overpowering. For the soul soon discovers that all this wealth of the love of Christ is waiting for every man and every woman who gains access to it. "He loved *me,*" wrote St. Paul, "and He delivered Himself up *for me.*" The riches of the Sacred Heart are to be poured out unstintedly on each individual. "Yea, I have loved *thee* with an everlasting love."

We propose in this chapter to examine in some detail a few of the qualities which are found in this love of Christ. When the prophet was ordered to build a tabernacle, he received minute instructions regarding its size, its furnishings, the material to be used, and all the injunctions were summed up in a concluding sentence. "See that thou make it according to the pattern which was shown to thee on the mount." The words may be applied to Our Lord, for He is the perfect pattern for all mankind. Look at the love in the Heart of Christ; study well and in detail its qualities; then, under the action of grace, labor to reproduce it, in so far as that is possible. To do this is to "learn Christ."

That love that fills Christ's Heart possesses, first of all, the note of universality. Men are chary of giving their love to others for the reason that the supply they have is limited. Those we love we segregate from the multitude—father and mother, husband and wife, sons and daughters. These we enclose in a place apart which we call our home. On these we lavish our love, and, by the time we have given them their due, there is so much the less left for others.

But Christ's love is not circumscribed in this way. "Come to Me *all* you that labor and I will refresh you." "If *any* man thirst, let him come to Me and drink." Here is a promise that is a proof that He who promises must be God. There are such depths of love here, that Christ has no fear, need have no fear, that the supply would ever lessen, even if the entire world was to hearken to His invitation and draw near to drink at the fountains of its Saviour. On the contrary, His complaint is that men remain deaf to His call and vainly attempt to assuage their thirst at sources that are polluted. "My people have done Me two evils. They have forsaken Me, the fountain of living water, and they have dug to themselves cisterns, broken cisterns, which can hold no water." "You will not come to Me that you may have life."

"If *any* man thirst . . ." He stands on the dusty roadside in the full blaze of the summer sun, stands with both arms extended wide in a comprehensive gesture, to embrace and welcome, not Jews merely, not Gentiles merely, not Greeks or Romans or slaves or masters only, not only saints, not only sinners, not only the people of His own time, not only the people of any time. Knowing His love to be infinite, He is conscious that He can pour it without any limit into the hearts of all men, of all times, of every race and color and class and clime. He knows that He has the power to do this, and He begs one favor only—that men will draw near, of their own free-will, and permit Him!

And here, as in everything else, the conduct of Our Lord is in perfect consistency with His promise. Look and see Him stepping out of the boat at Lake Genesareth. His arrival is the signal for commotion on all sides. The people "running through the whole country, began to carry about in beds those that were sick, where they heard He was. And whithersoever He entered, into towns or into villages or into cities, they laid the sick in the streets and besought Him. . . . And as many as touched Him were made whole." There is a somewhat parallel instance in another place. "When evening was come they brought to Him many persons that were possessed with devils. . . . And he, laying His hands *on every one of them,* healed them all."

Individuals can come to Him, and come at an hour that is inconvenient for Him; they can be most unreasonable in the requests they put to Him—this we have seen. The crowds, too, can make their own of Him and He yields to them, makes Himself their servant, for He has come to minister, not to be ministered unto. The general multitude is welcome, but each individual, too, is made to feel that he is a personal friend, as if he alone mattered, as if his particular need was of such personal concern to Jesus that all the others were forgotten. It is the universality found thus in the perfect pattern.

The same trait is discovered in the love of those who imitate Him most closely. They have eyes to discern Christ underneath the rags of the beggar who stops them in the street They have vision to recognize Christ in the bore, in the bearer of gossip, in the casual acquaintance met in the course of a railway journey, in the sick man or woman lying in the hospital bed. They are not vindictive; as a rule they are the first to apologize, even though the other person is in fault. For the fact is that a huge arc-light seems to shine across their path wherever they go, and it reveals to them, Christ in His sinful members, Christ in His suffering members, Christ in those who are full of self-pity, Christ in the ungrateful and in the thoughtless and in the cynical members, as well as Christ in those who radiate kindness and love, Christ in the unselfish, Christ in the hardworking. They see Christ in those who pray, Christ in those who consecrate themselves to Him as priests and religious, Christ in those who fall and rise again, and Christ in those who fall, and, alas, remain fallen. "As long as you did it to one of these, My least brethren, you did it to Me."

This love of His is universal, not only in calling and desiring all sorts of *people*. It is universal also in this, that it is prepared to give any help that is possible to give. For Jesus cast out devils. He forgave sin. He raised the dead to life. He opened the eyes of the blind and gave hearing to the deaf. He fed the hungry. He visited the sick and left behind Him a ray of comfort. He defended His friends from attack, and often Himself supplied the answer which compelled His enemies to retire in silence and confusion. He showed unwearying patience with these same enemies, proving His claims, accepting their challenges, with a view to breaking down their blind opposition and winning them to His love. Let men set Him any test and He willingly submits to it, provided it be not derogatory to His position as Son of God.

2. With a Good Grace

Reluctantly we have to pass on to the second facet in the charity of Our Lord. Reluctantly, not because it is less attractive than the first, but because so much more remains to be said about the first. Side by side, then, with this universality of His love you find its willingness. Not only does Jesus do good to all and sundry, not only is He ready to perform acts of love the most diverse and varied, but all is done with a sweetness and a grace which enhances enormously the value of the deed. There is a glaring contrast, frequently, in our way of giving or doing. An alms is given, but with a diatribe against those who beg in the street. You post a letter for your friend, or you shut the window when requested to do so, or you move over in your pew in the church. Yes, but you take care to explain that, in order to post that letter you have to go by a street you had not intended and which you wanted particularly to avoid. You scowl at the man who asks you to move in your bench, and, if you do close the window it is with a bang that shatters the nerves of the person who asked you.

But when we turn our eyes upon Jesus Christ, we fail to find any such sign of irritation or impatience in His deeds of love. On the contrary when He is surrounded by those who need His help, that help is given with a graciousness and a spontaneity which embellishes it a hundredfold.

So true is this that those who know Him best understand that all they have to do, in order to enlist His sympathy, is to lay their difficulties or their wants quite simply before Him. Who knew Him better than His Mother, Mary? When the wine ran short at Cana of Galilee what did Mary do? She merely exposed the state of affairs. "They have no wine." She did not suggest what He should do, or how He should do it, or even if He should take any step at all. She merely pointed out the confusion and embarrassment that would happen to the newly-married couple, and after that, with confidence and peace of soul, she left the matter entirely in His hands. His love would arrange whatever was for the best. And her confidence was abundantly rewarded, for her divine Son came willingly to the rescue, working His first public miracle, even though His hour had not yet come.

Martha and Mary also knew Him well; they loved Him, and by Him they were especially loved. So when Lazarus their brother took ill, they sent Him a message. "He whom Thou lovest is sick." Once again there is here no direct petition, only a plain statement of the man's condition. Once they were sure that He knew, they trusted Him to take whatever action was for the best. Nor were they disappointed. Even when the brother was four days dead, and laid in the tomb—when Jesus finally came—even then the same implicit confidence is evident. "Now also [even now]," Martha declared, "I know that whatsoever Thou wilt ask of God, He will give it to thee."

And Jesus, drawing near to the tomb, lifted up His eyes in prayer and in a loud voice called the dead man forth—with what result we know. It is easy to imagine the transports of joy that must have been witnessed. Martha and Mary had done nothing more, let us remember, than merely to expose their sorrow, and here is the response from the Heart of Christ! Could a more striking instance be found of His willingness to give?

He sees the tears of the widow of Naim as she walks with bowed head behind the bier which contains the dead body of her only child. This time she does not even explain to Him the cause of her grief. But her tears are far more eloquent than any words could be. Jesus, being moved with compassion, draws near. He halts the procession, touches the coffin, and again in that authoritative voice of His, He calls out: "Young man, I say to thee: arise." And he that was dead sits up and begins to speak, and Jesus gives him back to his mother. Merely to witness her sorrow was quite enough. On His own initiative there follows this astonishing miracle. Such is the charity of Jesus Christ—familiar, easily condescending, doing good with a most winning sweetness wherever opportunity offers.

Today the world He still loves is lying amid the wreckage and the starvation and the diseases, physical and moral, which constitute the aftermath of a war of unprecedented magnitude and brutality. Are men even now prepared to turn to Him Who alone can heal and restore to life? To recognize that the only basis for a lasting peace is the Ten Commandments and the teaching of the Gospel? Are they ready, even now, to draw near to Him in humility and acknowledge that the chaos around them is of their own doing, the result of trying to drive God out of His world? Christ has not changed since the days of Naim and Cana. He still has that willingness to serve, to heal, to bless, to forgive, even to raise to life again. There is one salvation for our senseless world—to come back to Christ and expose its diseases to this heavenly Physician. Then, with the same willingness and eagerness as of old, will He bend over this crushed and bleeding wreckage and restore it to life vigor.

3. Unselfish

When Jesus went about doing good, He gave abundance of proof that He was actuated by no desire for self-advertisement. His charity, therefore, is selfless, and this is its third facet. As always, examples abound. Throughout the Gospel story I see Him doing good without any blare of trumpets, without calling attention to what He does, without seeking or wishing for any recognition from men. You remember how He reproached the pharisees and scribes because, although they performed many acts that might appear to be virtuous, all were vitiated by the motive. They sounded a trumpet before them so as to attract men's attention and make them look in their direction when they were giving an alms. They strutted proudly into the temple and gave generous offerings, but this they did merely to win the applause of those who were watching them. How He pitied their blindness! "Amen, I say to you; they have received their reward." And such a paltry reward—a few mumbled words of admiration from those who, the next moment, had forgotten that they were even said. And what a miserable exchange for the reward which these same deeds could have stored up in eternity, if only they had proceeded from the right motive! No wonder He called them "blind and leaders of the blind."

He will not have His followers deceived in this way. So He warns them, when they pray, to shut the door in upon themselves and their heavenly Father, and there, in secret, to speak with Him, confident that He Who sees in secret will repay them. When they give an alms, let not their right hand know what their left hand does. Let them give of their very best, not seeking men's approval, nor being discouraged by their disapproval. More than that. When they are persecuted by men, and hated, and held up to scorn, let them then rejoice exceedingly, provided all this happen through no culpable action of their own. Jesus, too, had this same kind of treatment to endure at men's hands, and the disciple is not above his Master. Men's hatred and opposition may very possibly turn out to be a source of immense blessing. If the friends of Jesus had been of the world, the world would love its own, would smile with favor on its own. But, precisely because they are not of the world and He has chosen them out of the world, therefore does the world revile them, and persecute them, and treat them with every mark of ignominy.

So this is the third facet in the charity of Our Lord—its unselfishness. He taught His disciples to shun men's applause, and in this, as always, His own example is the most cogent argument for the lesson He reads them. On Thabor He showed Himself in His glory, momentarily, to three of His Apostles, but as they came down from the mountain, He strictly charged them to tell the vision to no man. He gave sight to a blind man but so unobtrusively was the cure effected that even the recipient of it seems to know very little of his Benefactor. When He cleansed the leper He enjoined on him to "tell it to no one"; and a similar injunction He laid on the friends of the girl whom He raised to life.

Thus in vain does one look for any bustle, or elaborate ceremonial, in the charity of Jesus Christ. He does what He sees is right to do simply because He loves, and love is its own reward.

But all the same it would be a mistake to imagine that He was insensible to gratitude. A bitter complaint was wrung from Him when He cured ten lepers and only one came back to thank Him. And even that one was a Samaritan. "Were not ten made whole, and where are the nine? There is no one found to return and give glory to God except this stranger." Clearly, though He does not act in order to be praised by men, He is pained when the fitting word of gratitude is forgotten.

Unselfishness, then, shines bright in the example He gives us of perfect love. And so, if in the disciple this charity is to be reproduced, it will necessarily lay the ax to the roots of selfishness. And the roots are embedded deeply. Even in devout practices it is very possible to seek oneself. There are religious people who give much time to prayer but are nearly impossible to live with. There are very fervent souls who fast and do much penance, but they are intolerant of others, harsh in their criticisms, impatient of a word of advice or suggestion. But where the heart is aglow with true love, there is no room left for these ugly displays of selfishness, these unsightly roots which die so slow a death.

To yield to others wherever possible, especially to those who lord it over you, who are full of arrogance or blinded by ignorance—this demands a selflessness that often borders on the heroic. To lay oneself out to be exceptionally kind and thoughtful towards those who are boorish and inappreciative—this postulates a deep fund of understanding of the applications of the great commandment. To do much good to others and never to breathe a syllable about it to any man; to refuse to take complacence in even the thought that one has done it; to divert the conversation tactfully if men seem likely to refer to your good deeds and praise you for them; to leave men in their error when they mistakenly attribute to another the results of the efficient management for which you are the person responsible—to do this habitually, or even to keep trying to do it, is to drain the soul of selfishness and fill it with the desire and determination to seek for God's approval, and for it alone. It is to reproduce, in some measure, the perfect charity of Jesus Christ.

It is very easy to see how a contrary mode of procedure can mar an otherwise excellent act of charity. There are good people who give generously enough of their time and their talents, but whom all the same you would rather refrain from asking. And why? Well, on a former occasion you did summon up the courage to ask, and the person did what you wanted—but for a whole month afterwards never ceased to speak about it! Or he grew so excited and made, or appeared to make, such a vast compliment of your modest request, that you resolved firmly that this was the first and last time you would bother him. How very different this bustling manner from the calm we see in the charity of Jesus Christ—contented to do the kindly deed and then go His way quietly. He is ready to give, to help, to pardon, to cure, but all is done without any sign of making a compliment of doing it. You would say that it was the most natural thing in the world for people to ask and for Him to give.

The universality of His love—ready to help anybody and in any way; the willingness of His love, clearly manifesting that what He did was done with a good heart; the unselfishness of His love—seeking not to advertise itself, seeking no approval save that of the Father in heaven—here are three facets which will repay a careful study.

4. Four Types

Now you would say that a Man possessed of such lovable qualities must surely draw all men to Himself. In point of fact, as we have seen in another place, many were indeed so drawn. "The whole world is gone after Him." "The whole country was stirred" when the word was noised abroad that Jesus of Nazareth was passing by. But there is another side. There were others who refused to walk with Him, who would not allow themselves to be won or convinced, who remained violently and bitterly opposed to Him, notwithstanding the obvious sincerity of His love and the soundness of His claims. For it must be borne in mind that that love of His, while gentle and self-effacing and all-embracing, was uncompromising, too, wherever it encountered sin or hypocrisy. Consequently, when He saw clearly that men were shutting their hearts against the promptings of His grace, when He came upon obstinacy in sin, there He proceeded, in terrible and emphatic language, to warn the sinner of his responsibility and the fearful judgment that was overtaking him.

It was this fearlessness which goaded to fury those who persisted in their sins. Had He shown Himself ready to condone their vices, had He been willing to wink at their transgressions, had He allowed the impression to gain ground that He was ready to pretend that He considered them sincere whereas He and everyone else knew their duplicity, then those whom He offended would surely have been prepared to meet Him half-way. He would very probably have been admitted into their councils, for they would have been very glad, in this supposition, to make use of His influence with the people to further their own selfish ends.

But Jesus would have no favoritism purchased at such a price. His uncompromising attitude toward His enemies is yet another proof that the man who attacks vice, especially in high places, is not going to escape the vengeance of those whom he attacks. Though there never was a man loved as Jesus was loved, it is true at the same time that neither was there ever a man who was hated by men to the same degree.

In the Gospel story you find four types who opposed Jesus in this way. Each of the four had a different reason for his opposition; each had a vice from which they refused to be divorced. In each case it was a question of breaking down this particular barrier which was standing up against the appeal of His love. Either had to be sacrificed, either His love or the particular vice. In each of the four cases the dupe of sin elected to retain his sin and this entailed the rejection of Christ. It will be worth while commenting briefly on each of the four types.

The charity of Christ failed to win the pharisees and scribes. Why? Well, the souls of these unfortunate men were reeking with sin, though externally they were models of decorum and religious observances. It was true that they had the minutiae of the external practices of the law at their finger-tips, but their hearts were empty of divine love. Of what avail were their repeated washing of hands, all their parrot prayers, all their elaborate ceremonial in the temple, when devoid of the one essential quality that gives life and meaning to these things? They were full of self-complacency, trusting for their justification to these showy performances, very satisfied indeed with themselves, and so sure that the Lord regarded them in the same favorable light. In their dealings with the common people, these hypocrites were hard as flint. Over their bended backs they held the iron rod of God's threatened wrath, if they dared refuse submission to their condition of subservience.

Our Lord looked straight into the hearts of these blinded men and read there their secret sins. Quite well He knew that if He wished to curry favor with them, the way to go about it was to adopt a conciliatory attitude by condoning the vices of these smooth-faced hypocrites, abetting their harsh treatment of the common people and flattering their sanctimonious pretences. But Jesus embarked on a diametrically opposite course. His soul loathed all this galling insincerity. These double-dealers must understand clearly that He will be no party to their evil ways.

Gentle methods are of no avail here. In these hearts of granite there is no finer instinct to which He can appeal. All He can do is tell them, in straight and manly language, that they are in a desperate state, that it is sheer madness to try to pass themselves off as pleasing in God's sight when all the time He sees into their souls and knows that they are "full of hypocrisy and iniquity."

In their case the barrier erected against the charity of Christ was envy and jealousy. Their little hearts grew venemous when they were brought face to face with Christ, Whose teaching was calculated to foster true freedom, freedom from the irksome shackles and the strait-laced traditions of the ancients, the glorious liberty of the children of God.

But in spite of their fury they have not the power to put Him out of the way, for they are the serfs of Rome. So to Rome's representative they drag their victim, and here we come upon the second type with whom Jesus was to prove a failure. Pilate was a man whose motto it was to get on well with the world at all costs, to make sure that he would stand in a favorable light with any who wielded worldly power and worldly influence. A glance at the prisoner before him was enough to show him that Jesus was, in all probability, an innocent man, and that these Jews had arraigned Him before the tribunal merely because of some personal grudge against Him.

This impression gains ground as the trial proceeds, for Our Lord gives to His judge four very special warnings. First of all, the majestic bearing of the prisoner showed Pilate that this is no common felon. The words spoken by Christ, so full of dignity, so ready to explain to Pilate anything he wants to know, were his second warning. A third warning came from Pilate's own wife: "Have thou nothing to do with this just man, for I have suffered many things this day in a dream, because of Him." Finally, even the mob itself, all unintentionally, gave another prick to the judge's conscience. For, when the rabble came back to him from Herod, they shouted up to Pilate, as he stood looking down upon them from his balcony: "This man ought to die, because He made Himself the son of God," and the words which follow are full of significance: "Now when Pilate had heard these words, *he feared the more.*"

So he does not want to have the responsibility of pronouncing sentence on an innocent man, but neither does he wish to incur the wrath or displeasure of the great Caesar by failing to quell the very first rumors of a rising among the Jews. If he is reported to Rome by these infuriated people, he may well lose all chance of promotion, may even be recalled altogether. Still these ominous warnings rankle in his brain. There is Pilate's dilemma. A strong man, independent of human respect, would not hesitate. But Pilate was weak, so he began to jib and to compromise, and to embark on a whole series of shameful subterfuges, all designed to extricate himself from this awkward corner, and at the same time salve his conscience. His final condemnation of Jesus was the culmination of a life of shuffling. One ruse failed after another, and ultimately Pilate was morally forced to do a deed which his soul loathed. *Fecit tamen*—he did the deed, none the less, because he wanted to secure worldly advantages and he considered these more worth while than what he knew to be right in God's sight.

Immense graces bombarded the soul of Pilate on that fateful Good Friday, but they left the citadel of selfishness still standing. Why? Because he opposed the barrier of worldliness to the appeals of Christ's love, and to those four reiterated warnings which sounded in his ears.

5. A Diplomatic Move

The first of the shameful subterfuges by which Pilate tried to save Jesus, or at least get Him off his hands, was to send the prisoner to Herod. Herod was tetrach of Galilee, and it happened most opportunely that he was in town just then. This move, thought the Roman, will effect many happy results. If Herod condemns Jesus, then with Herod, not with Pilate, will rest the responsibility. If he acquits the accused, the Jews cannot blame Pilate. Most important of all, Pilate can very easily dispatch to Rome a glowing account to the Emperor, and he will not spare ink and paper in dilating on his own vigilance and promptitude in putting down rebellion. All this, he fondly dreams, will be secured by the simple device of sending Jesus to Herod. But he failed ignominiously. The only happy result was the reconciliation of Pilate and Herod, who up to this had been enemies one of the other.

You will notice that, in all this chain of reasoning, there is not a whit of consideration for the prisoner Himself. He does not count. He is only a pawn in the game. Anything is good enough for Him. And so it comes about that Jesus finds Himself standing face to face with Herod—the most humiliating scene in the entire Passion. For Herod, you see, was a man whose only ideal in life was to enjoy himself. Pleasure was Herod's god, and if God's law stood in the way of Herod's pleasure, why, so much the worse for God's law! On this festive occasion it is fair to suppose that he was serving his god, and that there was wine, and music, and dancing, and women. Presently in the midst of the celebrations the Roman soldiers appear at the door and lift their arms towards Herod in sign of salutation. Herod, they hope, will pardon this intrusion. They feel quite confident that he will as soon as he learns its object. Outside the main door, standing in the center of a group of soldiers, with His hands securely tied behind His back, they actually have Jesus of Nazareth. More still. Pilate has sent Him over to Herod, and Herod can do just exactly whatever he likes with the man.

Intrusion indeed? Why, this is just exactly what Herod is wishing for. He had been most anxious, and for a long time, to meet this wonder-worker, and now provide a most pleasant interlude for Herod and his gay friends. They were quite breathless after their revelries anyhow, and Jesus will amuse them for a while. So he stops the dancing and the music, gathers around him the merry-makers, and, with a knowing smile and a chuckle, imparts to them the great news. They will all adjourn to Herod's throne-room where they will be more at leisure to watch Him performing for them, and if they want to ask any questions, it might be interesting and diverting to hear His replies.

But Jesus stood before Herod, stood there in all the dignity befitting His position as Son of God. He stood, in His strong manly way, before His judge, without fear, without respect. He stood there and looked straight into the eyes of this cowardly, cowering creature before Him, and answered him never a word.

I wonder why. Simply because He saw it was no use trying to help. Herod has abused grace after grace, and by now he has reached a stage when he no longer needs even to be tempted. He has settled down to a life of vice, and he has learned to laugh complacently at virtue, and to poke fun at those who profess to practise it. But he cannot long endure the searching white light, shining full upon him from those eyes of the Christ. "What fellowship hath light with darkness?" In that light the blackness of his soul, reeking with sin, stands out in bold relief. He does not see, because he does not want to see. He refuses to think. He will not examine the state of his soul as revealed in the rays of that pure light. He is ill at ease in this company. Inwardly he is fuming with rage, and he recalls that this is the man who spoke about him as "that fox." Well does he understand that opprobrious epithet. Then, too, he feels he is rather making a fool of himself. What are his fine friends thinking? And after the pleasant entertainment he had led them to expect! He never bargained for this, for contempt from this countryman from Galilee.

He refused to be converted, but neither would he suffer his pride to be put to the blush. He beckons to a slave who advances, bearing in both hands a white garment lying on a silver salver, and kneels before his master. "Crucify Him?" asks Herod sneeringly. "Put *Him* to death? Not at all. I would not dream of doing such a thing. You see for yourselves just what He is—a harmless imbecile!" This flippant creature, whose soul was a cesspool, picks up with two fingers of each hand the white garment from the silver salver, and, hiding his fury under an indulgent smile, he flings the cloak loosely over the shoulders of Our Lord. It is the attire of a fool. The company is quick to take the cue, and presently Jesus is set at naught by the whole army. They will "play up" to Herod's vanity. That is the important thing to make sure of, for they depend upon his good will. Jesus does not matter. Him they owe nothing. He is only the fool. His mind is deranged!

Let the love of Christ be all-embracing, so comprehensive as to show itself prepared to restore even this reprobate. Let His love be compliant, selfless, throbbing with life. Let it be all this and much more, and still it must fail with Herod. Why? Because he deliberately elects to prefer his gutter life. So he only laughed that day, when he found himself face to face with Christ's immaculate purity. He was merely amused when he saw the reproach in those eyes of Jesus. Purity had long since become rather a joke with Herod, so, having held Christ up to ridicule, he sent Him away, and returned arm in arm with his boon companions to continue the dance and the fun where they had left off, and to soothe his anger with the hope that the unpleasant incident would thus be soon forgotten.

Perhaps the saddest failure of all was Judas Iscariot. What marvelous chances were given to Judas! What noble and lasting work for souls he might have accomplished had he corresponded with his graces! In another place we shall try to sketch his career. He is introduced here, merely to complete the four types with whom Jesus was a failure. Such golden opportunities as Judas lost! Such high hopes all dashed to the ground. Called to be an Apostle, he became a traitor. A fisher of men, and he himself suffered woeful shipwreck. An intimate friend of Jesus and he wrote a story of treachery, the blackest that ever disfigured the pages of history. Had he but persevered on the path upon which his feet were set, he might have broadcast Christ's message to the uttermost parts of the earth. He might have won legions of souls for heaven. He might have had the supreme honor of ending this glorious life by shedding his blood for Christ. But he only died by hanging himself with a halter, avowing in hoarse and husky accents that he had sinned by betraying innocent blood. And all because he was blinded by lust for money.

The charity of Christ failed to win the pharisees and scribes because they were swelling with pride and self-sufficiency. The charity of Christ did not penetrate into the heart of Pilate because it was crusted over with love of the world. The charity of Christ only provoked Herod to a display of ill-timed mirth and buffoonery, because the heart of Herod was glutted with the unclean sin. And, saddest failure of all, the charity of Christ knocked long and loud at the door of the heart of Judas Iscariot but the door remained bolted and barred in Christ's face, because Judas loved money too well and Jesus too little.

6. They Hate Him Still

Pride, worldliness, impurity, avarice—these four are thus seen to have entered upon a conspiracy to get rid of Jesus and His meddlesome ways. Is there not a very remarkable re-enactment of that same identical conspiracy in these days of our twentieth century? Pride has arisen to trample on the humility which Jesus placed as the foundation of His kingdom. Jesus declared that between Him and the spirit of this world there was diametrical opposition. He excluded the world from His prayer at the Last Supper, and St. John adds: "If any man love the world, the charity of the Father is not in him." But love of the world, a mad race for unbridled pleasure, a good time at all costs, the ever-growing tendency to live as if this life was the be-all and end-all, and to pitch aside all thought of a hereafter and all preparation for it—why, this is the gospel preached at you from your daily paper and illustrated magazine, this is the attitude you see taken for granted when you turn on your radio or look at a film, this appalling apathy towards the supernatural betrays itself in the manners and conversation of many who are considered to be tolerably good.

And what of avarice, greed for gold? And what of the deluge of immoral living that has broken loose? Who will hesitate to admit that these, too, have contributed their quota to the conspiracy against Christ and Christianity which is one of the blots on the escutcheon of the twentieth century?

Now there is nothing easier than to apply all this to others, to point out the close similarity between the campaign today and long ago in Jerusalem. The parallel does indeed exist and it might be developed in greater detail than we have done here. But more has to be done. Jesus will never force His gift against man's free will, but He will argue, and plead, and reproach the soul with its indifference. Like a general going round the walls of a city, Jesus will lay siege to the heart of man and try to *win* it. But it can maintain its resistance. It can, and we have seen that it often does.

Holmann Hunt painted the well-known picture, *The Light of the World.* In it he shows Christ, with a blazing lantern hanging from His hand by His left side, while, with His right hand He knocks at a door. That door is overgrown with brushwood. It represents the soul which He longs to flood with the light of His love and His grace. "But there is a flaw," said a critic to the artist. "You have forgotten to paint the latch. There is no handle to the door." "No," came the reply. "The handle is not forgotten, but it does not appear in my picture for it cannot be seen. There *is* a latch, but it is on the inside."

V. Two Test Cases

"Take heed to yourselves. If thy brother sin against thee, reprove him and if he do penance forgive him. And if he sin against thee seven times in a day, and seven times in a day be converted unto thee, saying: 'I repent,' forgive him."—St. Luke xvii. 3, 4.

1. Cock-Crow

"Forgiven sin," writes Fr. Considine, S.J., "is no bar to intimacy with Jesus." Certain it is that the fire of Our Lord's love shines out most brilliantly when it gathers into itself the sorrowful heart of the prodigal and makes him realize that its flames have completely burned up every trace and every memory of his sin. The soul then understands that Our Lord fulfils, as no one ever did, as no one ever shall, that fine definition of a friend—a man who knows everything about me and loves me just the same. The welcome back springs spontaneously from the Sacred Heart. There is no censure, no complaint, no aloofness, no formality. It is no time for formality when the welcoming Christ is overflowing with joy that His child is beginning at last to understand the utter truth of His love.

"It is just at this moment, too, when the sinner stands before this forgiving Christ, stands and looks at his own selfishness and his meanness, that he best appreciates Our Lord's generosity in forgetting all about it. Of course, he is forgiven; he knows quite well he is. But he has deliberately hurt a friend, and the remembrance of his ingratitude and the pain he has caused burns into his brain and brings to his eyes tears of sweet repentance. In the light of his sin he understands better than ever before how much Christ loves him. The very sincerity of the welcome back serves only to bring, hot from the heart, acts of sorrow and protestations that he is fixed in his determination to efface the past by a life of utter loyalty to that friend in future. This is how this extraordinary Lover of men takes the sinner's load of crimes from his shoulders, and from it welds, all the stronger and closer, the golden chain binding the sinner's heart to the Sacred Heart. Christ will make, even of his very sins, stepping-stones to higher things.

St. Peter learned this, and the story of his schooling is a drama in three acts.

Peter and the others are seated with the Master at the Last Supper. Our Lord is sad tonight, and, to these friends of His, "His own," He reveals part of the cause of His sadness. For the last time, He knows it, He is in the midst of His own whom He loves so well. He is longing to make them understand Him, to give them at least some insight into the affection He has for them. Above all, He wants them to be loyal to Him. He wants to be able to lean on them for support during this terrifying Passion that is about to break in on Him tonight. But they are going to fail Him, and He knows it. He looks around the table sadly, looks from Peter to John, from John to Andrew, and so round about the entire group. Quite quietly, quite deliberately, He stretches out both hands in a comprehensive gesture, and, including the whole twelve, He tells them: "All you shall be scandalized in Me this night. . . . One of you will even betray Me. . . . The hand of the traitor is with Me on the table."

For a moment they are struck dumb with horror and surprise. Scandalized in Him! Ashamed of Him! Traitors! Never would that be said of them, His very own, chosen out of the whole world. The Master must surely be mistaken. They can trust themselves that much at least, that they know they love Him and are ready to follow Him even to suffering and to death. Especially is Peter's generous heart chilled at the suggestion. "Lord," he says, when at length he finds his speech, though still his voice is hoarse under the strong emotion, "Lord, *I* will never be scandalized in Thee. The other eleven? Well, they, perhaps. But Peter? Even though all should be scandalized, yet not I." He means it indeed, but the Lord knew Peter. "Peter," He tells him, "the cock will not crow till thou deny Me three times." This is piling agony upon agony, and Peter cannot believe. It is not possible. "And he spoke the more vehemently: 'Lord, I am ready to go with Thee to prison and to death. Even though I should die together with Thee, I will never deny Thee.' And in like manner spoke all His disciples."

2. Danger Zone

A few hours lapse and the scene changes to the barrack-yard outside the palace of Caiphas. Our Lord has been arrested down in Gethsemani and dragged through the street, and now He is inside, standing His trial before Annas. The night is cold, and out in the yard the soldiers gather round the fire to discuss the latest happenings. They have secured this man Christ at last. For a long time He has been a source of trouble to the authorities, but tonight will seal His fate. What chance has He between the cunning Annas and the unscrupulous Caiphas? Indeed, truth to tell, on other occasions He had made away and nobody seemed able to say how. But tonight they have made sure of His capture. Where so many others had failed they have succeeded, and they hope their masters will not forget that for them. Although, when all was said and done, the night's work had been a simple enough task. There had been practically no resistance, for the man's friends had scampered away at the first sign of danger. One of them, indeed, had made some show of defence. In a sudden flare of zeal and anger he had drawn a sword, but presently the flare had died down again, and he, too, had deserted his Master and had run off with the others.

In this strain the conversation continues—the men sitting there with their hands spread out towards the grateful blaze of the fire, and regaling themselves at intervals with a draft from the bottles dangling at their belts. And, of all the people in the world, seated there, right in the midst of these soldiers, is Simon Peter—his face white with fear, his heart in his breast frozen with terror lest they notice him. What they are saying is true indeed. He it was who had drawn that sword and afterwards had run away when he saw the Master a prisoner. He had retraced his steps, however, and, sorrowful and ashamed of his cowardice, he had succeeded in gaining admission to this courtyard, whence he might follow Jesus afar off and see the end. But now misery is eating into his very soul. What a fool he has been! Better never to have come back! Why did he not remain in safety with the others? Instead, in his impetuous way, he has rushed into the jaws of danger. He has had the foolhardiness to come into this place where he can do nothing at all to help the Master, and where every moment he is incurring the risk of being himself suspected and imprisoned. He must watch his chance and make good his escape before it is too late.

His thoughts are rudely interrupted. Clear and loud above the coarse mutterings of the men rings out the shrill note of a girl's voice. "Why," she cries, "here is the very man you are talking about. Here is the friend of your Christ who drew the sword down in the garden." And she points an accusing finger in the direction of the Apostle. For one agonizing moment fear for himself and love for his Master have a fierce struggle in Peter's heart. He stands still, with head bent, undecided, quite taken by surprise. But already they are gathering around him and scrutinizing his features more closely in the glare of the firelight. He must save himself at all costs. "It's a lie," he mutters. "I do not know Who you are talking about! Never met Him in my life."

But they are not to be put off so easily. "A lie!" they repeat mockingly. "No, friend of Christ, if there is a lie it is on your side. Why, even your very accent betrays that you are a Galilean. And did we not see you in the garden with Him?" Peter dare not gainsay these arguments, and so he has recourse to cursing and swearing. Three times he declares he knows nothing of this Christ of theirs, and then, cloaking his fear under show of indignation, he rushes from the fireplace and his accusers, determined to get away at once before there is any more trouble.

He has about two-thirds of the way covered between the fire and the gate when all at once he stops dead and stands staring blankly before him like a man changed into a block of marble. What has happened to mesmerize him like this? At the farther end of the yard there is a balcony leading from the house of Annas to the house of Caiphas, and, just at that very moment,

Our Lord is being led across. For a few seconds only, their eyes meet—the eyes of Jesus and the eyes of Peter. "And the Lord, turning, looked at Peter." There is a whole world of pathos in the Evangelist's simple words. That look of Christ seemed to choke Peter's heart with sorrow. Light shone down from those eyes of Christ and penetrated into the deep places of Peter's soul.

It was like the flash of lightning that dazzles one in the midst of a black night. In an instant the flash was over, but it had lasted long enough to show the whole horrible truth to Peter. He had betrayed his Friend! He, Peter, who had been so loud in his protestations of loyalty only a few hours ago. Peter who had left all things to follow Christ. Peter, for whom Our Lord had prayed especially that his faith might not fail. Peter who was to confirm his brethren, to be their prop and their model. Peter, to whom had been made that promise that he should be lifted up to the high eminence of head of Christ's Church. Peter had betrayed Christ. All Christ's lovable ways stand out in his memory more lovable than ever now in the light of his fall—His patience, His thoughtfulness, His unfailing courtesy, His unselfishness. And Peter had betrayed Him! Not once either, but many times. And not by a simple denial, but with cursing and swearing that he never knew Him. And all because of the accusation of a whimpering servant-girl. The remorse of it! Echoes start suddenly in the man's tortured brain. "Even though all should deny Thee. . . ." "I am ready to go with Thee to prison and to death. . . ." "*I* will never be scandalized. . . ." "And the Lord turning, looked at Peter. And Peter remembered the word which the Lord had spoken: 'Before the cock crow, thou wilt deny Me three times.' And going out he wept bitterly."

3. Absolution

The clouds of the Passion have rolled away. It is early morning. Peter and the others have been out in their little boat all night fishing the waters of the lake. They have had a wearisome night of labor, casting their nets and hauling them up again, and they are very tired.

As they draw near, in the first grey streaks of dawn, the figure of a man is just discernible standing on the seashore. They take no notice of Him at first, preoccupied as they are, tugging at the oars, and eager to reach home and secure their much-needed food and rest. But that figure on the shore has attracted the attention of John. He peers intently out over the side of the boat, and then, reassured, he bends down and whispers into Peter's ear. "That disciple, therefore, whom Jesus loved, said to Peter: 'It is the Lord.' " Peter's heart gives a bound of joy. Nets, boat, tackle, the labors of the night, his weariness and hunger—straightway all these fall from his mind. One thought only obsesses him—Jesus is there, standing on the shore, and Peter must get to Him. The boat is too slow. Indeed, they have not far to go, but Peter's impetuous love cannot be held in check. "Peter, therefore, when he heard that it was the Lord, girt his coat about him and cast himself into the sea" to come to Jesus.

Then follows a scene so lovely that any words used to reproduce it must seem almost a desecration. The rays of the morning sun are just beginning to peep out of the east. The majestic figure of the Christ stands there on the white sand at the edge of the water; the little waves steal in and break only a small distance away from His sandalled feet. And, on his knees before Him, Peter, his clothes dripping with the water of the lake, slips his great rough seaman's hands into the hands of Christ, and stammers out his profession of love with all the simplicity of a little child. There is no embarrassment in Peter. He knows Jesus too well. Of course, everything is all right; the old loving relations are fully restored. Not only does Our Lord forgive, but Peter is quite sure that He will receive him in such a way that nobody looking on would suspect that He even knew about that terrible triple denial on Thursday night.

But, himself? Ah, he had inflicted a smarting wound on the Heart of a friend Who never had an equal. And a great sorrow and a great love and a big resolve to undo the past surge up in Peter's heart as he kneels here and grasps firmly the hands of the Master. And, once again, "the Lord turning, looks at Peter."

"Simon, son of John, lovest thou Me?" Peter looks up, and this time he gazes steadily into the eyes of Christ. "Yes, Lord, I do love Thee, indeed." A second time the same question: "Simon, son of John, lovest thou Me?" And a second time the same avowal. "Love Thee, Lord? Why, of course, I love Thee." Still a third time: "Simon, son of John, lovest thou Me?" and Peter is grieved. Is it possible that the Master doubts his love, seeing that He questions him thus three several times? More vehemently he declares it now. "Lord, dost Thou wish me to reassure Thee of my love? Lord, Thou knowest all things. Thou knowest that I love Thee." A triple declaration of love to blot out forever his triple denial, and the repentant Peter is lifted from his feet and raised to the highest pinnacle of greatness and honor that the loving Christ can find. "Feed My lambs; feed My sheep." The first Vicar of Christ on earth is Peter, who denied Him, but repented of his sin. Such is the love of Christ.

Peter never knew Our Lord so well as when he had caused Him pain. He knew Christ best in the infinitely tactful, infinitely gentle, infinitely forgiving, infinitely loving welcome back, given him that morning on the seashore. He had found Jesus Christ to be a friend—a man Who knew everything about him and loved him just the same. He looked up into the eyes of Christ, and it was good to know that he was trusted still. And the face of Christ is radiant, for He has found a man who is beginning to understand the sincerity of His love. The light in Christ's face blots out for Peter the brilliance of the morning sun, and he looks up wistfully and reads there the story of a love so great that words are only poor, feeble instruments to express it, a friendship so utterly genuine that no treachery or falsehood can alter it.

4. A Festering Sore

Among the twelve at the supper table that night, a man was sitting in whose heart a secret was festering like a horrible sore. Judas Iscariot was a sensible, hard-headed man of the world who had found Christ and His ideals to be a disappointment. Everything had looked so promising two years ago. Christ's name was on everybody's lips then, and the crowds followed Him everywhere, and Judas, too, had begun to take an interest in the man. People were saying that He had come to found a kingdom, to restore the splendor of the ancient Jews. There was no denying that the man had a wonderful power—there was power in His words to draw the multitudes; in His touch there was power, for with his own eyes Judas had seen lepers cleansed by that touch, sight restored, even the dead raised to life. Then He had the majestic bearing befitting a King. Perhaps there was truth in the reports that were current about Him, and, if so, Judas would want to be on the Man's side, for he loved power dearly, and he worshipped money for the power it put into men's hands.

So Judas had become more and more interested in Jesus of Nazareth, and more favorably disposed to listen to His teaching. Accordingly, he had been vastly pleased that morning two years ago when the Master had singled him out of the multitude to be His special disciple. The scene was still fresh in his memory. Jesus had spent a day by the shore of Lake Genesareth and from every side the crowds had gathered and thronged about Him. They brought to Him all that were sick, those possessed by devils, lunatics, palsied. And He, laying His hands upon them cured them all. "Power went out from Him," the Evangelist was to write later—that power coveted by Judas who was scanning every movement of Christ. That night Jesus went up the mountainside alone to pray—it was often His custom at the end of a day—and next morning the multitudes gathered again. And Christ, standing there before them on the brow of the hill, looked out over them, indicating clearly that He had some special concern this morning. Twelve men are called aside from the crowd; one by one, in His quiet, deliberate way, He selects them Himself, mentioning each one by name and assigning to each his place near Him. Henceforth, these are to be "His own." Presently they sit down, Jesus and the twelve, and with the multitude facing Him and His twelve, Jesus opens His mouth and begins to teach. And among the twelve names called that day was that of Judas Iscariot.

For a while he had sat there by the Master's side, proud that he had been chosen so, and fully conscious that the eyes of many were fixed upon him with a holy envy. But all at once his complacency receives a shock. Jesus is speaking to the crowds, and what is this Judas hears? "Blessed are the poor in spirit. . . . Woe to you that are rich!" The words jar harshly on the ears of Judas. He had dreamed of a wealthy kingdom in which he would wield power, but here is the founder of the kingdom advocating poverty and denouncing riches as a snare and a danger-trap. Already his fears are awakened that there is something wrong.

Throughout the two years all Christ's teaching has been consistent with this Sermon on the Mount. Consistently He has told His followers to expect and to love poverty and suffering; to despise what the world values most highly, and to look for their reward, not in this world, which is only a passing show, but to "lay up treasure in heaven where neither rust nor moth can consume nor thieves break through and steal." Gradually it becomes more and more clear to Judas that he has made a mistake. And lately there has been even a more serious development, for Christ has lashed with merciless rigor the pharisees and the scribes—the very men who hold the power! He has pursued them with relentless logic and has unmasked their hypocrisy before all the people. Of course, they are enraged, and everybody knows they are only seeking an excuse to put Him to death. Yes, Judas made the mistake of his life when he took up with this man, Jesus of Nazareth. But is the mistake irretrievable? He is on the losing side for the moment, but a skilful and swift move can save him still—perhaps.

Dare he take that move? For at first he is horrified by the mere suggestion and he rejects it. But, for all that, it comes back again another day, and this time it seems not quite so horrible after all. Judas looks at the idea, and, in a hazy kind of way, begins remotely to think out ways and means. Perhaps the thing is just feasible. Anyhow, the facts are that Judas wants money very badly; that for two whole years he has followed about after Christ, Who is now clearly proved a visionary, and for his pains he has been told to love poverty and insult! He has had enough of such unsavory doctrine. On the other hand, there are the chief priests, the pharisees, and the scribes, the men with money, influence, and power. And these are Christ's implacable enemies. No doubt about it, if they could discover a man willing to hand over this Jesus to them, they would pay him handsomely. Was it not a chance for Judas who knew every move of the Master? An opportunity of recompensing himself for the disappointments and losses of the past two years?

But conscience? Well, what of conscience? Judas has sense enough to know that there are times when a man has to brush aside these petty conscientious scruples. Besides, he remembers that before this attempts had been made to effect the capture, but Jesus had passed through His enemies in some unaccountable fashion. It is quite possible that the same is going to happen this time too, but not until Judas has had his money! Anyhow, there can be no great harm in approaching the chief priests and finding out what their offer would be. Not that he is going to clinch a bargain with them! He will just throw out a leading question to give them a hint of what is passing in his mind and see how far they would be willing to go.

5. Playing with Fire

That decision once taken, the remaining chapters in Judas' story follow in rapid succession. That night, under cover of darkness, the wretched man slips down the street and knocks at the door of the chief priest's house. It is opened, and Judas is admitted to the chamber where Annas and Caiphas and the other great men are holding council. It is the interminable question—how are they going to silence forever this fearless Christ Who is destroying their prestige with the people? They are frankly surprised to see Judas, a known disciple of the man they hate. What can Judas want with them, and at this hour? He has no time for apologies or introductions, for he has been driven by a restless hankering for something, anything almost, other than Christ. Christ is not enough for Judas; Christ is a disappointment to Judas; what can Judas get instead of Christ? That is his quest tonight. "What will you give me," he blurts out, "and I will betray Him?"

They are taken aback. This was more than they had hoped for in their wildest dreams. Is there any mistaking Judas' meaning? They observe him shrewdly, and the lips twitching with nervous excitement and the eyes glowing with greed reassure them. In such a place and at such a time, "Him" can mean only Jesus, but that hallowed name is stifled in the throat of the traitor Apostle.

Sure of their ground now, and recovered somewhat from the first shock of surprise, it is only with an effort that they succeed in controlling their delight. Why, if Judas can guarantee his side of the bargain, they are willing to go to almost any price. But they are not going to say so all at once, for they are careful Jews, and if they can have the capture effected at a low figure, why pay more than they need? What would Judas say to thirty pieces of silver? That was quite a fair sum. He would recall that it was the price laid down in their book of Exodus as the price to be paid to a master if his slave was injured. And Judas, dazzled by the glitter of the silver, sweeps the coins into his wallet and signs the promise that he will hand Christ over to them. "And from that time he sought opportunity to betray Him in the absence of the multitude."

That is the horrible secret that is raging in the miserable man's breast as he sits tonight at table with Jesus and the other eleven. Ever since he struck that fatal bargain he has been ill at ease in this company. And now, as Jesus, in His quiet deliberate way, begins to speak to them, His words strike the ears of Judas like a thunderbolt. "All of you will be scandalized in Me this night. . . . The hand of him that will betray Me is with Me on the table. . . . The Son of Man indeed goeth . . . , but woe to that man by whom the Son of Man will be betrayed. It were better for him if that man had not been born."

It is a warning for Judas from the merciful Christ. But by this time sin has eaten its way deep into the soul of the wretched man, and he refuses to yield. Christ he has tried in the balance and found wanting. He prefers his bag of silver and the good graces of the men with power. Very soon he will be finished forever with this company of dreamers, but even with them he must be tactful and diplomatic to the end. He will face Christ and brazen out His ominous warning. What does he care? And so, when deep concern lines the faces of these true lovers of Christ, the traitor, too, feigns alarm. Christ, it seems, knows the secret of Judas' heart. What of that, then? And, with an insolence that is incredible, he looks up into the eyes of the Master. "A traitor, Lord? It is not I, is it?" And he points his index finger towards his breast.

A mighty grace has been offered and rejected, and the Heart of Christ is crushed with sorrow and pain. He will not force this wayward man; He never does. Judas will have his way. Christ, having tried in vain to save Judas from his sin, makes sure now to shield at least his reputation with the others. "Judas, what thou dost, do quickly." The eleven were accustomed to orders like this being given to Judas, for he carried the purse and was a trusted Apostle. Frequently the Master would have some special commission for Judas to execute. Accordingly, they thought no more about him when he left the supper room and went out into the darkness, bent, they believed, on some errand of mercy undertaken at the bidding of Jesus. The traitor's good name with the others is still intact. Of that much at least Christ's love has made sure, even if He has failed to save him from his sin.

"Judas, therefore . . . went out. And it was night." Darkness fell down upon the soul of the Apostle and he hastened recklessly to destruction. We find him next with a cohort of soldiers drawing near the garden of Gethsemani. With nervous tread he walks along, a little ahead of the rest. There is an undefined fear clutching at his heart—the warning note of conscience—which all his self-assurances and specious reasonings have not succeeded in reducing to silence. How can he draw back now, even if he wants to? Poor Judas! But even yet, even now, on the very edge of the precipice, will that Christ he has rejected make a final effort to arouse his sorrow and win back his love once more. Christ has been kneeling in prayer under the olive trees, but on the approach of the soldiers and their leader He rises from His knees and goes forward to meet them.

By now the traitor has become quite callous. Conscience is a delicate instrument, easily blunted. Let the Christ save Himself if He will and as best He may. Judas has made his bargain and he is going to stand by it. "Judas, therefore, gave them a sign, saying: 'Whomsoever I shall kiss, the same is He. Hold Him fast. Lead Him away carefully.'" And he brushes aside the branches of the trees with both hands and emerges into the moonlight. Yes, there is the man standing erect before him, the man who loved Judas and loves Judas still, but to Judas the man is a disappointment. "And he kissed Him." Is there any hope left for Judas? For, if there is still even a shadow of a chance of saving him, this loving Christ will avail of it. Will not Judas pause and think?

From His place there in the embrace of Judas, Jesus looks steadily into the traitor's eyes. Such a look does He give him as will afterwards break the heart of Peter. Peter's sin was a sin of weakness. Judas was more calculating. He had sat down and reckoned up the profits and losses, and had calmly and deliberately decided that the contract was worth while. Once more Christ will plead and warn, but He will not compel. Love must be won, not forced. "Friend, whereunto art thou come? Judas, dost thou betray the Son of man with a kiss?" "And he kissed Him." Again Jesus has verified in Himself that definition of a Friend—a man who knows all about another and loves him just the same. As He looks straight into the traitor's heart, every single incident, from the first dallying with the temptation to this terrifying consummation, is spread out before His eyes like the pages of an open book. And, even in the face of all this treachery and ingratitude, Christ loves Judas still; Christ pleads with Judas to think and repent even still, but Judas will not be won. "And he kissed Him."

6. Sweet Sin

There is a sweetness about sin as there is a sweetness about some poisons. That sweetness Judas had tasted. He had handled his money. He had ingratiated himself, parasite-like, into the favor of the men with power and influence. No doubt about it, they would remember it for him that they owed Christ's arrest to his co-operation and plans. He had felt the importance of his position at the head of a troop of soldiers who awaited his orders. That was all, that much made up the sweetness of sin for Judas Iscariot. What a miserable pittance for which to betray Christ! The bewitching of trifles! But the worst was not yet. Who tastes the sweetness of poison must surely pay a bitter penalty, and who takes sin into his heart holds an asp close to his breast. This, too, Judas discovered.

No sooner is his crime completed and he has placed the unresisting Christ into the hands of His enemeis, than Judas is torn with remorse. Back he rushes to the chief priests with the coins in his hands. "I have sinned," he cries, in a voice hoarse with despair. "I have sinned in betraying innocent blood!" They smile upon him condescendingly. He has done his work very well. The bargain had been made and kept. They had paid the price settled upon, and Judas had secured their victim. Indeed he has been a useful tool in their hands, but now he is of use no longer. "Innocent blood! Why, Judas, that is your own affair. Look thou to it then."

Why did he not foresee all this misery? Why did he not heed Christ's warnings, repeated so lovingly and so insistently? He had dreamed of wealth, but now he has flung away even the thirty pieces of silver, for they were burning like coals of fire in his hands. He had fondly imagined that the betrayal would open the way to power, but these great men have just turned sneeringly from him. He is stunned at last into realizing that sin is a huge deception. A hatred seizes upon him, hatred for all men and hatred for himself. He must get away, anywhere, provided he be left alone. And as he rushes out, he knows not where and cares not, a vision rises up once more before his tortured brain—the face of Jesus of Nazareth; Jesus Who had said He was ready to forgive the repentant sinner not once merely, not seven times merely, but till seventy times seven times; Jesus Who had poured words of merciful forgiveness into the ear of Mary Magdalene and had made her the inseparable companion of His Immaculate Mother; Jesus Who had lifted up the woman taken in adultery and saved her from her enemies; Jesus Who had sat with publicans and sinners, Who had been accused of being their friend and had admitted the truth of the accusation; Jesus Who had looked so compassionately at Judas himself tonight and had spoken His warnings with so much gentleness and tact—the face of that Jesus haunts his brain now, but still Judas resists. "*My* sin is greater than that I should hope for pardon."

Blindly he hastens away to the lonely valley of Hinnon, trying to banish the vision of that merciful Christ from his mind. The blackness of despair envelops him and shuts out every ray of hope. To the end Christ is a disappointment to Judas. To the end he refuses to believe in Christ's mercy. To the end he cannot be convinced that Christ could know everything about him and love him just the same. "*My* sin is greater than that I should hope for pardon. *My* case is exceptional!" Despair ties the hands of an omnipotent lover. With his worldly ambitions dashed to the ground and with a sin which he persuades himself is too great to be pardoned, what is there left to live for? Better finish once and for all with this life of disappointments! Jesus will hang on the cross tomorrow and pray for His murderers. Judas will hang from the tree tonight and refuse to believe in His love and His readiness to forgive.

So ended the story of Judas Iscariot. Mistakes crowd into every chapter, but the fatal mistake, the mistake that was quite irremediable, was not Judas' love of money or even the horrible act of betrayal. The saddest mistake of all was Judas' refusal to believe that Christ *could* be such a friend, that He could still love Judas and still want Judas in spite of all.

One remedy could have saved Judas, as it saved Peter; one only remedy there was, but it was an infallible one. A humble confession of his sin and a cry for mercy would instantly have restored all the old loving relations between Christ and the traitor. Had Judas freed himself from the embrace of Christ in the garden, had he dropped on his knees there and then with an act of true contrition on his lips and in his heart, even at this eleventh hour all could have been put to rights. But that cry and that confession never rose from the lips of the Iscariot. He persisted in his refusal to believe in the mercy of Christ. "*My* sin is greater than that I should hope for pardon." The infinitely-forgiving, infinitely-loving Jesus of Nazareth had failed.

VI. Jesus Suffering Man

"They shall look upon Me whom they have pierced and they shall mourn for Him as one mourneth for an only son. . . . And they shall say to Him: 'What are these wounds in the midst of Thy hands?' And He shall say: 'With these I was wounded in the house of them that loved Me.' "—Zacharias xii. 10; xiii. 6.

1. He Need Not Have Suffered

At first sight it is, perhaps, somewhat surprising to find Our Lord enduring the pains of mind and body inflicted upon Him throughout His life, and more especially in His sacred Passion. Surprising, because, strictly speaking, suffering was not necessary for the fulfilment of His mission. He had come to break man's chains, to set him free from the thraldom of sin. The task that lay before Him was to unbar the gates of heaven and make them swing wide open, so that man, redeemed by the merits of his Saviour, would once more have the opportunity of securing the face-to-face vision with the eternal Father.

But in order to realize this plan fully Our Lord need not have selected the way of suffering. He was God, remember, equal in all things to His Father; His every act, therefore, was infinite in value. Hence, had He so chosen, He might have come into our midst, not as a little infant shivering in swaddling clothes, but as a full-grown man. He might have lived on this earth, not for thirty-three years, but only for a very brief period—a year, or a few months or weeks, or even for a few minutes. During that short space He could have offered to His Father, in reparation for our sins, one single sigh, or one single prayer, or a drop of His precious blood. Such an offering, made as it would be by one infinite in dignity, would have been immeasurably more than sufficient to redeem, not only this little world of ours, but countless other worlds which might afterwards be created.

None the less what do we find? Why, that He seems to go out of His way to discover ways and means of suffering. What took place in the last week of His mortal life was only the climax of a positive devotion to the cross which He had evinced during all the years preceding. That a course of action was hard, that it called for self-sacrifice or humiliation, always seemed somehow to be a reason for Him to adopt it, or if He could not, to allow it to escape from His hands with a sense of loss and regret which one experiences on letting go a valuable treasure. Why should this be? Why should He seek out suffering like this, when He might have redeemed us just as effectively with so much less cost to Himself?

There is another question that follows as a sort of corollary. When you study the lives of His best friends you find that to them, too, He invariably sends a large measure of suffering and a liberal share of the cross. Mary, His blessed mother, who undoubtedly held a place quite unique in the love of His Sacred Heart, was, like Himself, crushed and bruised and ground into the earth by a burden of sorrow. In the temple holy Simeon placed Him in her arms—He was only an infant that day—and he warned Mary to prepare her soul for a sword of suffering. On Calvary they brought Him to her again, and once more put Him into her arms. He is dead. She takes that lifeless form and a shudder passes through her frame as she feels with her hand the ugly hole where the nail had been, or removes from His head the crown of thorns, or looks with a mother's anguish into His face now nearly unrecognizable, even by her. Simeon's prophecy has been fulfilled indeed. "Thine own soul a sword shall pierce." All these years Mary has lived under the shadow of the cross. That Jesus loved her nobody can possibly doubt. That He could have spared her this torture, or at least much of it, would seem quite certain. Yet He did not spare her. On the contrary, there was no one, except Himself, to whom He measured out a fuller portion from the cup of sorrow. It is not so easy to understand, is it?

Coming now to the saints, those special friends of Jesus Christ, we find that they, too, were subjected to trials and persecutions, the most diverse and the most painful and humiliating. To some were given many long years of physical pain which kept them nailed to the cross. Others were victims of mental anguish, racked with scruples, abandoned by friends, humiliated by the disgrace of somebody dear to them, contradicted continually, distrusted, suspected without a shred of real evidence against them, falsely accused, misunderstood, misquoted, misrepresented. Want and dire poverty, incessant labor, hunger and sometimes even starvation—when you open out the life-stories of the best friends Jesus ever had, you find the pages covered with such things. Yet Jesus loved these friends dearly. Had He willed, He might have made their lot on earth much more even, much more pleasant. A strange way this, it would seem, to treat men and women whom He loved, and who were devoted heart and soul to Him. It may be difficult to understand at first sight, but this much at least we can deduce—that there must be in suffering lovingly borne some hidden value and power, seeing that it comes so persistently and so consistently into the lives of Christ and His friends. Can we hope to penetrate the mystery, to dig at least a little below the surface and discover the treasure hidden underneath?

2. The Reasons Why

Of course, it is quite true that Our Lord could have redeemed us without suffering, and had He deigned to do so, He would have conferred upon us a benefit for which eternity would be too short to thank Him. Redeem us—that is, confine Himself to what was strictly necessary in order to put into our hands the chance of escaping hell and securing eternal life—yes, that much Jesus could have accomplished without shedding a drop of His blood. But everybody knows that wherever there is a great love, there is always present also the urge to do more, much more, than is strictly necessary. Love does not pare things down nor measure out nicely just how far it is going to give itself. Love wants to give all, and that is why Jesus "emptied Himself, taking the form of a servant." Love will be satisfied only if it give a measure that is pressed down, shaken together, and flowing over. As long as anything remains ungiven, as long as any act of love that is possible to do is left undone, so long does love consider itself to have given nothing. True love would bear "all things" for the sake of the person loved.

That is the first and most obvious reason for the sufferings of Christ. If His sufferings, especially in His sacred Passion, do not convince man of the sincerity of God's love for him, then does it seem difficult to imagine what more an omnipotent lover can do to convince. "Greater love than this no man hath, that a man lay down his life for his friends." "What is there that I ought to do more to My vineyard that I have not done to it?"

Love helps to explain the trials of the saints and of those who strive to follow where they lead. Generous souls in whom the divine fire has been enkindled find in themselves a longing to give tangible proof of the reality of that love. "Love," writes St. Ignatius, "is shown by deeds rather than by words." But there is no proof of love more searching than willingness to suffer for the person loved. A mother will rush blindly into the burning house, and without a thought for her own safety will face certain death, because she sees the child she loves standing at the window surrounded by the flames.

Now the simple truth is that the saints had a love for Jesus just like that, and the longing consumed them to prove to Him how genuine it was. "Suffering is the badge of those who love" is a saying dear to St. John of the Cross, and to illustrate its truth he covers page after page to show how suffering will purify the soul, burning out of it all love of the world and of sin, and whetting its appetite for the things of God. A doctor will sometimes have to cause suffering to his patient, if he wants to save the man's life, or cure him effectively. The divine physician, too, sends sufferings to His friends, because suffering lovingly accepted from His hand draws off the poison from the soul and leaves behind a more vigorous and a more abundant life of sanctifying grace. In proportion as the life of sin and worldliness decreases in the soul, in the same will the divine life thrive; and suffering lovingly borne stifles sin and all attachment thereto and sets the affections of the heart free to expend themselves on God alone.

This is easy to illustrate. Take the case of a man who has been a sinner for many years, and now, under the influence of grace, makes a really good confession. Quite frequently it is through the cross that he comes to see his folly and ingratitude. While he enjoyed prosperity and good health he was inclined to slip away from God and lose his hold on the supernatural. But when the cross comes, in the shape perhaps of financial reverses or bodily illness, then he begins to see how tenuous is his hold upon the world and its toys, how quickly friends can forget when they see there is nothing to be gained for themselves by maintaining their friendship, how soon hard-earned money can be squandered or lost, how easily health can be shattered or how swiftly and unexpectedly death can swoop down and snatch away a loved friend.

If the man will now only open his eyes the lesson is plain to read. Since this world is so uncertain, why not transfer all his affections and longings to God and the reward exceeding great which He has promised to give? "Seek the things that are above; relish the things that are above." Why not make it his aim to lay up treasure in heaven where neither rust nor moth can consume and thieves do not break through and steal? The cross, you see, does this much for him. It leads him first of all to repentance, then it stirs up the desire to make atonement, and it lets him see that there is no more effective means of doing so, than to embrace what is hard from the motive of love. "Suffering is the badge of those that love."

3. Man of Sorrows

There is a second reason why Christ suffers and why He asks His friends to suffer with Him. Sin has for man, in his present fallen state, a truly terrifying fascination. Passion is seething in every human breast, and outside of every man there is the gay world which has long ago lost its sense of sin and bids us eat, drink and be merry, for tomorrow we die. So natural is sin to us in our present condition, that at times we find ourselves almost driven in spite of ourselves to ask if, after all, it is quite as bad and as wicked as we are taught to believe.

But the sufferings of Christ prove clearly how specious is any argument in favor of sin. In Gethsemani Jesus wrestled with sin and in the effort His sweat became as drops of blood. The pent-up hatred of sin against Christ was let loose and it scourged Him, all unresisting, at the pillar. In mockery of His kingship sin wove for Him a crown of thorns and pressed it upon His head. Sin flung the cross upon His bleeding shoulders and drove Him before it, a tottering, dying man, up the slope of Calvary. Into his hands and feet sin hammered the nails and raised Him up to be jeered at and taunted, as He hung there in disgrace. Sin stabbed His Sacred Heart and with a fiendish delight drew His precious blood. Glutted with triumph sin staggered down from that hillside and proceeded now to stalk throughout the world and make further conquests of the souls for whom He would die in vain. When sin wreaks its wrath upon the sinless Christ here is the result, or rather here is an infinitesimally small fraction of the result.

A steady look into the face of Christ in His Passion, such a look as passed between Him and Peter, will reveal as nothing else can, the true nature of sin. The world goes its way smilingly, telling you that sin is only natural, assuring you that the urge to sin cannot be resisted, saying you must see life and do your own sweet will, laughing away your childish scruples and pointing out that anybody with sense today understands that the Ten Commandments are a back number.

But turn away for a moment and look into the face of Christ. If the sinless Christ suffers like this because of sin, then, even though perhaps you do not see the answers to the world's arguments, you will surely admit that if there is one evil in this world, sin must be its name.

The prophet was permitted to graze the surface of the ocean of sorrow that inundated the soul of Christ in His Passion. "We have seen Him as it were a leper, a man of sorrows and

too hard, much work for souls remains barren of lasting results. The grain of wheat must die if it is to bring forth fruit.

Perhaps now, after all, it is not quite so difficult to see reasons for suffering. Love feeds on it, sin is unmasked in the light it gives, and when the apostle learns to accept it he may surely count upon an abundant harvest to his sickle.

For these reasons the saints have lifted up their voices to sing about the beauty and the power of suffering. It would be a simple matter to cull many eloquent and inspiring passages, but here one will have to suffice. It is a citation from the writings of the Jesuit Brother, St. Alphonsus Rodriguez (whose magnificent treatises on prayer and the interior life are all too little known), and here is what he says: "By means of sufferings the soul arrives at great holiness and at a close imitation of the crucified Son of God. Thence arise true peace of soul and continual prayer. Thence a genuine union of the soul with God, the perpetual presence of God, and purity and stainlessness of soul. Thence humble familiarity with God. Thence perfect charity, the love of God and of one's neighbor. Thence the seraphim's crown of glory. Thence great spiritual treasures and riches, which God is wont to bestow in abundance on souls in trials; and favors and heavenly secrets which God discloses to them, favors such and so great as are known only to God and the soul which receives them, for they are such and so great that they may be tasted but not told, for they take place between God and the soul alone.

"O sweetest Jesus, love of my soul, center of my heart! How comes it that I do not desire with stronger desire to endure pains and tortures for the love of Thee, when Thou, my God, hast suffered so many for me? O Sufferings, how I hope that you will come to me and make your stay within my heart, for in you do I find my repose, and I will go to the heart of my crucified Jesus, there to dwell in it with you. O Torments, how is it that you do not come to me who await you with open arms, that in you I may rejoice with my Jesus in torture? O Dishonor, why do you forget me, who never forget you, because I love you so much in order that I may behold myself debased by you and humbled with Jesus? O Ignominious Deaths, why do you not come upon me in thousands when I desire so much and wish so continually to sacrifice myself to my Jesus?

"Come then, every sort of trial in this world, for this is my delight—to suffer for Jesus. This is my joy—to follow my Saviour and to find my consolation with my consoler on the cross. This is my pleasure, this my delight, to live with Jesus, to walk with Jesus, to converse with Jesus, to suffer with and for Him, this is my treasure."

One is prompted to transcribe more, but perhaps this much will suffice to show the attitude of the saints towards the cross, and to enable us, who follow afar off, to fathom a little of the mystery of the sufferings which provide an outlet for their love.

VII. A Table of Contents

"Behold this Heart which has loved men so much that it has spared itself in nothing, even to being crushed and humiliated in order to win their love. Yet the greater number treat Me with indifference, by the coldness and sacrilege shown to Me in the most Holy Sacrament."— Our Lord to St. Margaret Mary.

1. Self-Sacrifice

We have heard what Our Lord and His saints have to say and to teach about love of Him, about zeal for souls and immolation of self in order to win them. If to us all this is a sealed book, and apparently an insoluble enigma, the reason is, very probably, that we never allowed the lessons of Calvary to penetrate into the innermost places of our hearts. Hence it will be useful, after having seen why He and His friends suffer, to go in spirit up to that cross and kneel there at Christ's feet.

The Sacred Passion is the most marvelous love story ever written, written in a language intelligible to every true lover, the language of sacrifice. St. Paul placed the title on the cover of the volume when he wrote: "Christ loved me, and delivered Himself up for me." The chapters contained within these covers Jesus has Himself filled in, and the ink He employed was His precious blood. It would be futile to attempt to read through the entire story; every detail needs to be lovingly lingered over, and even then, at the end of one's life, there is still an abundance to be meditated upon and made use of to stir in the depths of the soul a response to such a marvelous outpouring of love. So all we propose to do now is to take the volume into our hands and reverently peruse the table of contents. Even these we shall not exhaust. We shall have to be selective and confine our reverent attention to three such headings. Our position here, as we open out the book, is on our knees, for the ground is holy, drenched with blood, the blood of the God-Man.

I run my finger down the titles of the chapters and presently I pause. Here is a striking one upon which to delay some time. It is called: *The Self-Sacrifice of Jesus.* Sacrifice had always been a most notable trait in that perfect character, but on Calvary, and in all that immediately preceded Calvary, this spirit of Our Blessed Lord shone forth with more brilliant luster than ever. When you begin to think out the manifestations of self-sacrifice you conclude that it shows itself especially in two ways. A man possessed of this spirit, is first, unselfish, and because he is, he freely submits to suffering for the sake of another, when he could avoid it. Secondly, when he himself is enduring much pain, he is thoughtful, especially at such a time, for the needs and sorrows of others. He is not self-centered. The moment we begin to apply these two tests to Our Lord in His Passion we are at once faced with so many illustrations as to make it difficult to know which to choose and which to omit.

To begin with, we recall that throughout the pages of the Old Testament the prophets keep constantly stressing the fact that the coming Messias will suffer of His own free will. "He was offered," Isaias tells us, "because it was His own will, and He opened not His mouth. He shall be led as a sheep to the slaughter and shall be dumb as a lamb before His shearer, and He shall not open His mouth." Speaking in the name of Christ, David declares: "In the head of the book it is written of Me that I should do Thy will, O God. Then said I: 'Behold I come, that I may do Thy will.'" The spontaneity of the offering to suffer is here clearly expressed, and so perfectly did Our Lord fulfil that prophecy that St. Paul summed up His whole life by saying: "He emptied Himself, taking the form of a servant. . . . He humbled Himself becoming obedient unto death, even unto the death of the cross." Christ Himself has expressed in a single sentence the object of His life: "The things that are pleasing to My Father I always do"; and later, speaking to that Father: "Father, I have finished the work which Thou gavest Me to do." Christ's soul is the interior castle in which dwells all the fulness of the Godhead, and the key of that castle He has handed over, not merely with resignation, but with a loving eagerness, to the keeping of His eternal Father.

Looking back now, from our place on Calvary, over the events that are culminating here, it is the easiest thing in the world for us to see how steadily and how consistently Our Lord kept before His eyes the rôle of *voluntary* victim. The watchword of this sacred drama is: "Thy Will be done!" If, as we kneel here, our gaze could penetrate into the heart of the great sufferer, we might well discover those words stamped there in large characters. "Thy Will be done!"—His loving eagerness to suffer in obedience to the Father's Will is at least part of the explanation of the amazing patience He shows under such gallingly unjust treatment. When His enemies spat into His face and smote Him with the palms of their hands, when they jeered Him as He hung on the cross, and taunted Him and defied Him, when they pointed at Him in derision during those last terrible few hours, it was then in His power to cause the earth to open and swallow them; it was quite possible for Him to paralyse them with terror by descending from the cross; had He then willed to call down fire from heaven to destroy them (as His Apostles had suggested on another occasion), He could at that hour have done so. But none of these things happened. That divine power was held rigidly in check. The divinity hides itself, and Jesus hangs there, apparently unable to lift a finger to oppose them.

The self-sacrifice of Jesus freely permitted their insults and their tortures, because freely He had offered Himself to bear all this in satisfaction for the sins men had flung in the face of the Father. *Ipse voluit.* "He was offered *because it was His own will.*" He wants things to be just like this and refuses to have them otherwise when it was possible.

So much in general for the voluntary nature of His sufferings. But there crowd now into the chapter very many specific instances. Last night, as He lay on His face in Gethsemani, a great sweat of blood broke out in His sacred body. Fear had seized upon Him, as well it might, at the vision of the sufferings that were about to fall upon Him. A cry of terror broke from Him and sent its echo out into the tense silence of the dark night: "Father, if it be possible, let this chalice pass from Me." But instantly there is the insistence upon His willingness to drain that cup. "Nevertheless not My will but Thine be done!" The self-sacrifice of Christ!

After His prayer, He rises and goes forward to meet His enemies. He halts presently, and with majestic dignity, stands there in the moonlight awaiting their approach. By His side is Peter, and, close to Peter, John and James. Jesus points over in the direction of the oncoming soldiers. His three companions look and they see the glare of the lanterns and glitter of helmets and spears. "Behold," says Our Lord, "the hour is at hand. The son of man will be betrayed into the hands of sinners." Peter, in the impetuosity of his love, draws a sword to defend his Master. But Jesus will teach Peter that He accepts His Passion in the spirit of a voluntary victim. "Put up thy sword . . . thinkest thou not that I cannot ask My Father and He will presently give Me more than twelve legions of angels?" But did He ask? No. Very deliberately He refrained from doing so. One can almost see the angels ready to leap to His defence and Jesus signing them to stay. "He was offered because it was His own will."

Evidence of the same power is seen in the actual arrest. When the soldiers draw near He asks them a very natural question: "Whom seek ye?" But there is something in the bearing of this man that overawes them—a momentary breaking forth of the divinity, perhaps, through the veils of the sacred humanity which ordinarily hid it from view. "Whom seek ye?" And at last they stammer their answer: "Jesus of Nazareth." "I am He," He tells them, and instantly, though nobody has laid a finger upon them, they fall flat to the ground. They dare not take Him prisoner, you see, until He voluntarily hands Himself over to them. He is complete master of the situation. On other occasions they had tried to arrest Him, but in some mysterious manner He had passed through their midst. Why can He not do the same tonight? What is there to prevent Him walking away while the men are lying on the ground? "He was offered because it was His own will." The unselfishness of Jesus!

Next morning He stands bound before Pilate. The governor looks at Him and proceeds to vaunt the power he possesses over the prisoner. "Speakest Thou not to Me? Knowest Thou not that I have power to crucify Thee, and power to let Thee go?" At once Jesus warns him of the futility and emptiness of his boast. Any power Pilate holds has been entrusted to him by God. That is why Jesus obeys Pilate. He is exercising voluntary obedience to God in Whose hands Pilate is only an instrument. Truly then might Jesus declare, in view of all this: "I have power to lay down My life and I have power to take it up again. No man taketh it away from Me, but I lay it down of Myself. This commandment have I received of My Father."

This sublime folly, the folly of the cross, witnessed here on Calvary, is reproduced in some measure in His most faithful followers. The disciple is not above his master. He, too, must be a voluntary victim, keeping his eyes wide open for opportunities, perhaps especially little opportunities, of embracing suffering freely. He must be offered because it is his own will. The true friend of Christ looks around the world and sees how ready the votary of the world is to sacrifice himself for worldly gain. In the race for pleasure, worldlings will reckon light the sacrifice of a night's rest; it is regarded as a negligible price to pay for an all-night dance. Desire for big money will goad a man on to a ceaseless round of activity. Hatred of God and His Church endow people with a zeal and an energy that balk at no sacrifice.

Now all that readiness to face what is hard and go through with it is a challenge to the follower of Our Lord. He may not allow the children of this world to be wiser in their generation than the children of light. He will match sacrifice with sacrifice. He may not be expected by God to take on great penances and spend long hours in prayer. But, what is quite certain is, that God will strew his pathway with abundant opportunities of sacrificing himself in little things. Let him begin by schooling himself in these and later, if God so wills, he may perhaps be able to turn and consider the others.

Little opportunities. It is hard to bear a snub, to accept it with a smile, hard to treat the person next time as though nothing at all had happened, even as though you had not seen through the insult. It is hard to be patient under injustice—petty injustice, as when somebody touches up a story against you and makes you appear ridiculous; or bigger injustice as when he seriously injures your character or steals your purse. Others will be preferred before you; people will hint very clearly that they regard you as something of a simpleton; your opinion on any subject is beneath consideration and they shake their wise heads commiseratingly. It is hard, at times very hard, to bear, to keep silence about your grievances, even to turn the laugh against yourself; hard, and for that very reason Christ's friend will do it, or keep trying to do it. "He was offered," *voluntarily*, "because it was His own will."

Always Somebody Else

There is another manifestation of self-sacrifice in Our Lord's Passion—throughout it all, Jesus is always thinking of somebody else. When we are in pain it is our way, as a general rule, to allow ourselves to become preoccupied with ourselves and to look for more than ordinary consideration from those around us. A sick mother will regard as her right the extra attentions lavished on her by the children. A man with a violent headache, or just recovering from a major operation, will take it for granted that doctors and nurses and friends will go out of their way to be more than usually kind. If in anybody this attitude could be excusable, it surely was so in Jesus Christ throughout the torments of the Passion. "From the crown of the head to the sole of the feet, there is no soundness in Him, wounds and bruises and swelling sores. They are not bound up, nor dressed, nor fomented with oil." So we should not be surprised to find Him, judging by our own mode of procedure, so wrapt up in the thought of His own sufferings as to have no time or thought for the needs of anybody else. We would expect Him, if He was to act as we do when we suffer, to call attention to His pains and tell us how terrible they were.

That is what we might expect, but actually what do we find? Why, right in the very midst of tortures without parallel, Our Lord is all the time preoccupied with the needs of somebody else. All the time He is shielding others, rewarding others, warning others, praying for others. All the time He is silent about the agony of mind that is racking Him, and the wounds and scourgings, and crowning with thorns. Not a word escapes Him about these—except once when He complains of His thirst on the cross. But this complaint rises to His lips, the Gospel is careful to point out, in order that the scripture might be fulfilled. Moreover, on that occasion He spoke, not merely of the physical thirst, but also, and more especially, of His thirst for souls and their eternal salvation.

It was somebody else last night at the supper table. Already we have studied His exquisite tact in dealing with Judas. He knew well, as He showed with unmistakable clearness, the secret hidden in the soul of the apostate disciple. First, then, He warns the unfortunate man, and when His warnings meet with no response, He saves at least the reputation of the friend who has spurned His friendship. Judas went out, but "nobody knew" why. Jesus has been thinking of somebody else who at the very moment is guilty of blackest treachery.

When His enemies advance to arrest Him in the garden, some hours later, He tells them fearlessly Who He is. "I am Jesus of Nazareth. If then you seek Me, *let these go their way.*" He will not compromise these, His friends; even at the moment when His own program of suffering is beginning, He thinks most of others. They had seen that same thoughtfulness tonight already, when they were going with Him into Gethsemani to pray. "*Sit you here,*" He had told them, "while I go forward to pray." Them He would have in a restful posture, seated; for Himself, prostrate, He would kneel or lie flat writhing in agony. For His enemies as well, Jesus will be thoughtful. Peter in his impetuous way draws his sword and cuts off the ear of the servant of the high priest. Jesus heals the servant—always thinking of somebody else.

That same thoughtfulness is evident in His trials before Annas and Caiphas, before Pilate, and before Herod. His Sacred Heart is overflowing with compassion for their blindness and sin; this it is which constitutes the most poignant portion of His chalice of suffering. Tradition tells us about the meeting with Veronica on the road to Calvary. The good woman pushed her way through the crowd and took the veil off her head, and wiped from His face some of the blood and spittle. It was, after all, only what any woman, with a woman's gift of sympathy, would feel impelled to do. But His own torments do not so preoccupy the sufferer as to prevent Him from showing His gratitude and thoughtfulness. Imagine the emotions of Veronica when she reached her home, opened out her veil, and saw there before her eyes, quite plain to discern, the features of Christ—still thinking of somebody else.

On that same road there was also His thoughtfulness for the women of Jerusalem. No wonder they wept; but Jesus would have them think more of themselves and less of Him. Of Himself He has nothing to say at all, but for them He is filled with concern. "Daughters of Jerusalem, weep not over Me, but weep for yourselves and your children. . . . If this be done in the green wood what shall be done in the dry?"

Unselfishness lights up the gloom of this place where we are kneeling with Him in spirit on Calvary. Until the very end, Jesus is always thinking of somebody else. Round about Him stand His enemies, jeering Him, defying Him to come down from the cross. But most significant is it that even these very taunts are further evidence of the unselfishness of their victim. "He saved others; Himself He cannot save." Thus all unwittingly do they pay tribute to His unfailing thoughtfulness for others and forgetfulness of Himself. A pagan writer tells us that sometimes the agonies endured by crucified men grew so terrible as to extort frightful blasphemies from their dying lips. To stop this the tongue would be torn out as the man hung there. If we think of these enemies of Christ waiting half-expectantly to see if some such blasphemy will escape from Him, what will they hear? The most marvelous prayer for mercy—this is His way of retaliating. "Father, forgive them; they know not what they do."

It may well be that this was the prayer which converted the thief at His side. And this deathbed conversion affords still another opportunity for exercising the thoughtfulness of Christ. "Amen, I say to thee, this day thou shalt be with Me in paradise." Still is Jesus thinking of somebody else. Next He looks down through the blood and spittle that nearly blinds His eyes, and He sees Mary His Mother. "There stood by the cross of Jesus His mother." By her side is John, the disciple whom Jesus loved. What provision can the son make for the mother, now that He is about to leave her? Even though He be Himself in such agony, even though nails pierce His hands and feet, even though the thorns are making His brow throb, even though He is sickened in His soul with mental anguish, even though there never was one who suffered as did Jesus at this moment, still concerning Himself He is silent, and when He speaks it is only to call attention to the needs of somebody else, and to provide for them. "When Jesus therefore had seen the disciple standing whom He loved, and His mother, He saith to that disciple: 'Behold thy mother.' After that He saith to His mother: 'Behold thy son.'"

Christ's friends have knelt long and lovingly on this hill and have absorbed this lesson of thoughtfulness for others. Self-effacing they are, and self-forgetting, and at the same time all eagerness to foresee the needs of others and anticipate their wishes. You will find them acting in this way even towards those from whose hands they receive but scant recognition. The truth is that it is an honor and a joy to serve Christ in His members. "What you do to these, you do to Me." Often He may be very effectively disguised but the eye of faith penetrates the disguise. Thoughtfulness then becomes the most natural thing in the world, and forgivingness, and hidden acts of kindness, and a readiness to keep on exercising oneself thus at every opportunity, almost without adverting to the other person's ingratitude.

2. The Loneliness of Christ

There was a strange darkness on Calvary. "Now from the sixth hour," writes St. Matthew, "there was darkness over the whole earth until the ninth hour." St. Robert Bellarmine invites us often to contemplate the dying Christ stretched out on the cross and enveloped in this darkness. The scene indicates the second chapter-heading in the story of Christ's love for souls, and it is called: *The Loneliness of Christ*. That loneliness is symbolized by the darkness closing in round about His deathbed, but indeed it is true that loneliness had been His constant companion all through the Passion.

Certain emotions the heart of man can endure which are too profound to be expressed in words, too deep to be entered into by even one's most intimate and sympathetic friends. Such may be a sorrow so intense as to leave the sufferer incapable of showing it by any exterior sign. The grief remains pent-up in the heart, and an outlet such as weeping would rightly be regarded as a relief. But the eyes remain dry and the anguish is all the more painful. "There are tears which at their fountains freeze." Sorrow like this cannot usually be shared with others, at any rate in an appreciable measure, and that is why the sorrows of the Passion leaned with their fullest force on Christ, and that even His blessed mother could not fathom their depths. Indeed, it may be said that everybody with whom He had contact, Mary not excepted, served but to increase His grief.

The result was that Jesus endured a most frightening loneliness. Centuries before, the prophet, speaking in His name, had foretold it. "I have trodden the winepress alone and of the gentiles there is not a man with Me. I looked about and there was none to give help; I sought and there was none to give aid." Not only would His people fail to enter with Him into His sufferings and be a source of at least a small measure of consolation, but they would deliberately turn their backs upon Him. "Hear, O ye heavens, and give ear, O earth, for the Lord God hath spoken. I have brought up children and have exalted them, but they have despised Me. . . ." "My people have done Me two evils; they have forsaken Me, the fountain of living water, and they have dug to themselves cisterns, broken cisterns which can hold no water."

These texts are a foreshadowing of what is happening here on Calvary and of the events which went before the crucifixion. Let me look back over the incidents which filled up the last week of Our Lord's earthly life and I see that throughout them all He has been accompanied by a sense of isolation. Palm Sunday was His day of triumph, but even though He was then in the midst of a jubilant crowd, He is alone. For this excited multitude has no understanding of or sympathy with His real aims and interests. There was consequent loneliness in His heart on that day.

On the following Thursday night comes the Last Supper, and He sits down to table with "His own," His "little children." In a torrent of eloquence and affection never equalled, He pours forth expressions of love for these twelve men whom He Himself has chosen out of the world. He gives them Himself in the Blessed Sacrament. He empowers them to do what Himself has just done—to change bread and wine into His body and blood. But they do not grasp it all. Even later, when He is risen from the dead, He will have to complain that they are still foolish and slow of heart to believe. So, even in the midst of His own tonight, and even for the last time, Our Lord must bear isolation. Their ideals and His, their standards of value and His, He has tried to bring into line, each with the other; He has tried and failed. They are still without understanding, and Jesus is alone, not only in the midst of His enemies but even when surrounded by His friends. "So long a time have I been with you, and you have not known Me?"

In the great agony a little later, loneliness crushed Him to the earth. He had invited three of His special friends to remain near Him, to stay with Him to watch and to pray with Him, for His soul was sorrowful even unto death. But their eyes were heavy and they fell asleep, leaving Him to carry the burden on His shoulders alone. "What," was the sad reproach wrung from Him in His loneliness, "could you not watch one hour with Me?" "I have trodden the winepress alone. . . . I sought and there was not one to give aid."

Throughout the rest of the Passion this same sense of loneliness clings to Him. Look at Him as He stands on the balcony of Pilate's palace immediately after the scourging, blood flowing down into His eyes, a purple garment flung around Him, a mock scepter in His right hand. In the street below Him the surging multitudes, on His right side the corrupt judge Pontius Pilate, and on His left Barabbas, the robber and the murderer. The governor points to Him and cries out: "*Ecce homo!* Behold the man!" They look up to the place where He is standing above them, a sea of upturned faces, and on no single face does He see anything except hatred and envy and a determination to compass His death by crucifixion. They thirst for His blood as wolves thirst for the blood of the innocent lamb, and all at once the streets and the archways re-echo with their cries: "Away with Him! Crucify Him!" The loneliness of Christ on that occasion! "I have trodden the winepress alone." "Hear, O ye heavens, and give ear, O earth. . . . I have brought up children and have exalted them, but they have despised Me . . . they have forsaken Me, the fountain of living water. . . ."

But not even yet has Jesus drained to the dregs the bitter chalice of His loneliness. During His lifetime, in times of contradiction or obstinacy shown by His enemies, or when His friends did not understand Him, He had always found a refuge and a consolation in the sense of companionship with His eternal Father. "I am not alone, for the Father is with Me." Often, in the stillness of the night, you might have come upon Him making His way all alone up the slope of the hillside. There He would kneel, motionless, His soul in most sacred and intimate communion with the Father, spending the whole night in the there have been falls in the past, His precious blood is able to

Calvary, even this seems to have been taken from Him in some mysterious manner. Even the Father has abandoned His Son today. He has withdrawn His protecting hand and has permitted this mob to vent its rage thus against His divine Son. Human friends had long ago deserted Him. Those who had remained steadfast were incapable of sounding the depths of the sea of His sorrow. All this seemed tolerable so long as He could depend upon the Father to sustain. But now the Father has abandoned Him! This is indeed the culmination of loneliness, and the piteous cry sends its echo out into the surrounding darkness: "My God, My God, why hast *Thou* forsaken Me?"

When Clouds Are Dark

A point most worthy of note in this connection is, that though apparently He is "forsaken," Jesus perseveres in prayer. It is quite easy to pray when consolations abound. Often at the outset of the spiritual life the soul is inundated with a heavenly joy. Everything looks so simple. Sanctity is seen to be so reasonable. The cross is embraced with eagerness, and the soul is resolved to refuse nothing to so loving a God. At such a time it is difficult to understand why all men do not realize a great deal more about the love Jesus has for them, and why they do not labor to make to Him a less unworthy return of love. All this experience in prayer is excellent indeed, but it is not meant to last—and it does not. In this state of happiness and appreciation of the value and beauty of souls, there is nothing more natural than that a man or woman seek God's face in constant prayer.

But if the soul persevere a change will surely come. Presently the sweetness will begin to evaporate—through no fault of the soul, as we are presuming. Despite the soul's fidelity to prayer and self-sacrifice, prayer is now very wearisome; all joy in the Lord is gone; the soul, like Jesus on Calvary, will be inclined to call out that God has abandoned it. "I gave you milk to drink," wrote St. Paul, "not meat, for you were not able as yet." In the beginning of the soul's journey Godwards He attracts the soul to love of divine things by giving it the "milk" of divine consolations. When it has grown a little stronger, He withdraws this, so as to ensure that the soul will seek, not His gifts, but Himself alone. Sweetness in prayer is all very well, but it is not God Himself, and the thirst of the soul is, not for God's gifts, but for Himself.

Has He forsaken the soul actually? Not at all. At first the soul is attached, without knowing it, to this feeling of consolation in prayer. How will it react when God takes away this satisfaction? It is of paramount importance at this time that the soul understand that no change whatever should be made in its resolutions or its determination to follow the guidance of God wherever He leads. For it is now that the Holy Spirit is preparing to open up the ways that point towards close intimacy with God. It is nothing short of calamitous if the soul turns back, just because it is deprived of its former consolations. St. Teresa, St. Ignatius of Loyola, and St. John of the Cross—all three of them, and many others, too—emphasize the truth that if at this stage the soul is unfaithful and goes back to the good things offered to the worldling or to the tepid, a life of sanctity may very well be marred forever.

Just when God is prepared to act directly on the soul, just as soon as He begins to detach the soul from all except Himself, the poor soul may easily believe, or be talked into believing, that He has abandoned it. Why? Simply because He has withdrawn sweetness and sensible comfort, in order to make sure that the soul should cling to Himself alone and not to His gifts. No wonder the saints write broken-heartedly, on seeing how often, through this fatal error, many remain all their lives merely good enough when God was inviting them to a place near His saints. Let a soul at this time go back again to what it has left—to its love of ease, to pleasure in idle gossip, to satisfaction in hearing and rehearsing the tittle-tattle of the daily news, to any of the thousand things which it has seen are hindrances to steady progress, though they are not grievous sins—let the soul do this and it will tie God's hands. Jesus prayed in the darkness, in the abandonment and loneliness of Calvary, in order to encourage such a tried soul.

Let the soul do the same, and it will advance more in divine love and true spirituality in a single day than in years which abound in sensible sweetness. More than this. Let the soul only continue to hold on and the sweetness will return, as soon as the work of purification is completed. But it will not now be the same. It will be much deeper, more soul-satisfying, because now, on account of its increased purity, the soul is able to draw closer to the source of all purity. Hence prayer has gone through a cleansing process during this period of apparent dereliction. The soul seeks now God alone, whereas formerly it sought His gifts.

It would be very easy to cite examples of this from the lives of the saints, for without exception they experienced it in themselves. They became saints through the cross, and the form the cross most often took was just the dereliction of Calvary. Long periods of utter dryness, during which it would have been so simple a matter to let go their hold on the spiritual life, were crowned by a triumph such as shone out when a rift was made in the black clouds and the sun once again lighted up the darkness of Calvary.

It is not sweetness in prayer that makes saints but the adherence of the will to God. And the most searching test of this loyalty of the will is applied when darkness covers God's face and the soul has to trust Him blindly. Calvary taught the saints at such a time to pray with all the greater earnestness, and because they learned well that difficult lesson, they afterwards rejoiced in a fuller possession, not of God's gifts merely, but of Himself.

3. The Failure of Christ

Our third chapter-heading is called: *The Failure of Jesus Christ*. The life of Our Lord, judged by the world's standards, is a complete failure, and in His death here on Calvary, that failure, so judges the world, sinks down to its low-water mark. For consider. He had gone around doing good, healing all manner of diseases, raising the dead to life, opening the eyes of the blind, feeding the hungry, loosening the tongues of the dumb. And men look on Him now and they are filled with hatred. Men's tongues today yell out for His death, and, now that that has at length been secured, they hiss words of contempt at Him. Today the victory of His enemies spells the failure of Christ. Annas and Caiphas stand here before the dying Christ and point at Him the finger of scorn. "Vah, Thou that destroyest the temple of God and in three days dost rebuild it! Come down from the cross!" But He did not come down, and why? As far as men could judge it was because He was not able. He was only a dreamer of dreams after all. It is the failure of Christ.

He failed likewise with His friends. He had preached the kingdom of heaven with a forcefulness and an eloquence that compelled attention, but His pupils remained slow of heart and dull of intellect. He had foretold to His chosen twelve the details of His Passion, and had warned them to arm themselves, by prayer and vigil, against being scandalized. They swore they would die together with Him rather than abandon Him. But where are they today? In His hour of direst need they have forgotten His warnings, they have forgotten their promises—all they thought of was their own safety. They have fled from His side and left Him branded before His enemies as the world's greatest failure.

It is well worthy of note that that same failure is reproduced in Christ's mystical body, the Church. How many times, in nineteen centuries, have her enemies told the world that she, too, was dead! Like Annas and Caiphas, they pointed to her in derision at what seemed indeed to be her last hour. They seduced her own children to betray, even as Judas was seduced. They scourged her and crowned her with thorns. They nailed her to a cross and drove a spear into her heart.

That has been her history for nearly twenty centuries. And today we have the truly terrifying picture of mighty armies of men, marching in massed formation across the world, marshaled in organized and orderly fashion under the black flag of satan, and proclaiming to the ends of the earth that God is a myth, that religion is the opium of the people. For twenty long centuries the world has been wrapt about in a fog of lies and superstition, but our self-constituted prophets have found the light at last. They have made the remarkable discovery that man, after all, is little more than an animal; wherefore let him be satisfied to settle down and live like one. The Church is a hypocrite and an impostor, and it has been reserved for the high priests of modern atheism to tear the mask from her face and expose her deceits before the eyes of the whole world.

As for Jesus Christ—"we will not have this man to reign over us." Let Him come and proclaim Himself God, and we answer that we bend the knee to none except the god of "massed humanity." We are enlightened enough to adore that alone. We smile indulgently when to us Christ speaks about rewards or punishments in a future life. Sensible men have long since outgrown that hoary nonsense. Christ preached love and peace; we bring fire and the sword. Hatred is our watchword; our kingdom *is* of this world, and to consolidate its foundations securely we are prepared to wade knee-deep in blood, human blood. We want anarchy and we are going to have it. We want wild license, and who is going to say us nay?

That this is a correct picture of the state of affairs is plain to all who have ears to hear and eyes to read. Christ was a failure on Calvary, and He is a failure today in the lives of millions who either do not know Him at all, or because they know Him only imperfectly, are fired with mistaken zeal against Him. Like her divine founder, the Church is on the cross; perhaps, like Him, too, she may be inclined to call out in the midst of the darkness and ask if even God has forsaken her. For all that, she looks down from her cross on the faces of her enemies and there is calm and assurance in her gaze. For she is certain of ultimate success, and that certainty never for a single moment falters in her breast. Her history is exactly the one Jesus told her to expect when He founded her two thousand years ago.

Her survival in the teeth of such diabolical opposition from without and disloyalty from within—what does it prove? Surely it furnishes a most cogent argument for her divinity. Could any merely human institution have come through what the Church of God has endured and be still alive? But she is not merely alive after it all. Though she is bleeding in some of her members, she is extending her sphere of influence and it may be affirmed with confidence that today her priests are more zealous and learned, her lay apostles more keen, her work on the mission fields better organized, and her devotional life more fervent. She is not dead, but risen. She never *can* die, for she carries within her heart the seed of a life which is divine. She lives with God's own life imparted to her by Jesus Christ.

So it is clear that Christ's standards of success and failure differ widely from those of men. "My thoughts are not your thoughts, and My ways are not your ways." It is immensely comforting to think of this when we are inclined to regard our own lives as a failure. What a disappointing record is strewn behind us! Resolutions broken, deeds of shame, others led by us into sin, graces and warnings unheeded! Now it is well to recall, as we kneel here on Calvary, that the gaze of the all-seeing Christ penetrates into those secret places of our heart. Not a single thought, not a single act, done even under cover of darkest night, but He knows all about it; knows about it far better than we ourselves. He looks down from the cross and reads every detail of the life behind us like the pages of an open book. He has received those protestations of our sorrow, knowing that we would again betray Him, perhaps at the very first opportunity. All that He knows and understands much more clearly than we do, and yet, knowing it all, and understanding it all, He shows us here on Calvary what He still considers us to be worth. It is not He who has changed since those days when there was holy familiarity between Him and us. The change has been all on our side, and His friendship has stood the test of our repeated betrayals.

Is it possible to be despondent about one's failures in the face of all this? An utter sincerity shines in those eyes, a sincerity built upon the love He bears for our souls. A message of comfort falls from those lips, assuring us that, though there may be temptation ahead of us, His grace will be there to strengthen; though there have been falls in the past, His precious blood is able to wash away our sins; though that love of His has been despised and flouted, yet all those years, like the divine hound of heaven, He has been pursuing that soul of ours, so set upon winning it that He longs, even yet, in spite of all there has been, to pour into it in abundant streams, the torrents of grace issuing from His Sacred Heart. A soul must indeed be a pearl of great price, seeing the value set upon it by God. How easy He is to forgive sin, how ready He is to brush aside breaches of friendship, how long He is willing to wait for the sinner to understand and to allow Him to pardon all! In such an attitude, one can glimpse the value and the beauty and the destiny of an immortal soul.

It is not so much what we achieve or fail to achieve that He regards, as what we become. It is not so much what we do that matters, as why we do it. Calvary, indeed, is the triumph of failure.

The *Self-Sacrifice* of Christ; the *Loneliness* of Christ; the *Failure* of Christ. These are our three chapter-headings and it is clear that they open the way to many avenues of thought and reverent contemplation as we kneel on Calvary. Other chapters might be studied: the humility of Christ, for instance, or His absolute self-mastery, or His power throughout the Passion, or His union of soul with the Father in prayer. But the truth is that the story is inexhaustible, for the Passion is evidence of a love that is infinite, and every chapter-heading furnishes fresh proofs of that love. The three chosen are thus meant to be provocative of further search and further development. There have been saints whose prayer centered around the Passion for years, and for even a whole lifetime, and at the end they considered themselves to have done no more than master the alphabet of the language in which the story is written. Perhaps indeed, not even so much.

VIII. Three Attitudes

"God forbid that I should glory save in the cross of Our Lord Jesus Christ, by whom the world is crucified to me, and I to the world."—Galatians vi. 14.

1. Unless . . .

Sanctity is tested, principally, by one's attitude towards the cross and suffering. The reason for this must be apparent in view of what we have seen in Jesus and in those who were most intimate with Him. For sanctity means close imitation of Christ, and in our last chapter He showed us the love He always had for the cross. Sanctity, too, means a sharing in the divine life, which sharing we call sanctifying grace. But grace flows into the soul in the measure of the closeness of the soul's union with Him Who is its very source, Jesus Christ. One of the effects of the cross and suffering is to help to remove obstacles which would either kill the divine life in the soul, or at least impede its full development. Hence the attitude towards the cross which the follower of Christ adopts is going to play a vital part in the work of his sanctification.

Now when we look around the world and study different types of men and women, we discover three attitudes of mind towards this stern and uncompromising teaching of Jesus Christ concerning the cross. "Unless the grain of wheat die, itself remaineth alone, but if it die it bringeth forth much fruit. . . . Unless a man renounce everything that he hath, he cannot be My disciple. . . . Unless you do penance, you shall all likewise perish." Terrible words indeed, and they who hear them react very differently, and on their reaction depends, in large measure, their growth in holiness or their failure to grow.

The first attitude is undisguised rejection of the cross. In every heart there is a natural liking for what is naturally pleasing to the senses, and a natural shrinking from what is unpleasant and difficult. Most men acquiesce unthinkingly in this state of things. This is the attitude of the person who speaks and sleeps and thinks and goes to a show and is kind or unkind, just exactly according as the mood of the moment happens to lead him, a person whose decisions and choices are largely the result of caprice or impulse. When to such a person a thorn-crowned bleeding Christ presents Himself, and bids him deny his appetite, practise self-control, choose quite deliberately what naturally he does not like—when Christ lays a program like this before a worldly-minded man, He is looked upon with blank wonderment, and perhaps even with utter contempt. Why, what is the use of life if you cannot enjoy yourself in it? "Eat, drink and be merry, for tomorrow we die."

For such a person, then, suffering in any form is an unmitigated misfortune, a most unwelcome visitor if it comes to the doorstep, an evil which must be dispatched without ceremony or apology at the very first opportunity. That is the world's philosophy of life. It rejects Christ, therefore, *because* of the cross. "Away with Him; we will not have *this* man to rule over us." This attitude is entirely opposed to the teaching of Our Lord and it explains why He calls worldly people blind and leaders of the blind, why He excluded the world expressly from His prayer at the Last Supper, why He told His followers to expect to be hated by the world. "Wonder not if the world hate you. If you had been of the world, the world would love its own, but because you are not of the world, but I have chosen you out of the world, therefore the world hateth you."

The second attitude is the one adopted by those who indeed follow Christ and accept His teaching, but this they do *in spite of* the cross. They will tell you they are prepared to put up with suffering, that God knows best, and they bow in humble resignation to His blessed will. Since He has seen fit to let this heavy cross fall upon our shoulders, welcome be His holy will! We would much prefer He had not done so, but faith tells us He knows best. This we believe firmly, and accordingly, we stifle all questionings or complaints. We are *resigned.*

Of course it is clear that this second attitude is immeasurably nearer the attitude of Christ than the first one. When a crushing load of sorrow is pressing a man's heart down, when loneliness or disappointment or protracted illness is wearing out his powers of endurance, then to lift up his eyes to the heavenly Father and say with sincerity: "Thy Will be done!"—that surely is proof of one's anxiety to reduce to practice the lessons taught on Calvary.

2. Third Degree

But is there anything higher than mere resignation? Do His best friends stop short here? We might suggest that the answer will be found in St. Ignatius' golden little book of *Spiritual Exercises.* In one place he speaks about three degrees or kinds of humility, and, for our purpose, we want to discover what he means by the third of these degrees. In general, humility is the virtue which makes a man subject himself to God, and, in the mind of Ignatius, the "third degree" is the most perfect form of this subjection. Let us try to illustrate his meaning.

Suppose two courses of action are open to a man—one of them pleasant to his natural taste, and the other unpleasant, but neither of them sinful. On a beautiful summer evening, for instance, he can enjoy himself playing a game of tennis, or he can spend three or four hours visiting tenement houses—a work for which, let us suppose, he has no natural liking. From either course a certain amount of glory will accrue to God by the man's action. If he chooses what is unpleasant, God will receive from him, in the hypothesis placed by St. Ignatius, not a greater amount of glory, but the exact same which would have accrued had he selected what was easy and pleasant. Granted that this man is established in the spirit of the third degree of humility, his habitual bias will be towards the harder course, and he will habitually choose it. Does this mean that he will never do what is naturally pleasant? That he must always keep torturing himself, always contradicting himself, always renouncing every innocent enjoyment in favor of penance and self-denial? Undoubtedly there have been saints for whom the life of the third degree meant just this uncompromising attitude and they went through that life with iron and determined perseverance.

Others have not been so stern with themselves in rejecting everything that accorded with their natural taste. St. Francis of Assisi loved to look upon the beauty of nature, and delighted in the song of the birds, and St. Francis de Sales contented himself with taking with equal indifference what came his way—accepting it as from God's hands. But where one finds saintly men taking the pleasanter course, you will see that they are guided by the conviction that, in this specific instance, this pleasanter course will give to God, not the same glory as the unpleasant one, but a greater glory. They are still biased in favor of what is hard but here they recognize that they are faced with a state of things in which He will be more glorified if they accept what is pleasant. Hence their choice is not determined by impulse or caprice. They take the easier course, not merely because it is the easier one, but because it is the one they are sincerely convinced God wishes them to take just for this occasion.

The worldly man, to return to him for a moment, when he comes up against something hard, something demanding self-sacrifice, will instinctively ask himself: "Why *should* I take it?" That is, his instinctive reaction is to escape from it if possible and to seek out arguments against it. For the earnest disciple of Christ, the mere fact that a thing calls for a spirit of sacrifice is a most powerful argument in its favor. He reacts instinctively too, and his question is: "Why should I *not* take this hard thing?" He demands arguments, you see, to prove to himself that he should *not* have it, for the very fact that it is hard marks it at once as something to be allowed escape him only if there are preponderating arguments on the other side.

The motive underlying the philosophy of the third degree stares a man in the face when he kneels at Christ's bleeding feet at Calvary. "*He* humbled Himself becoming obedient unto death, even unto the death of the cross." *He* chose to redeem the world by the hard way of the cross when the hard way was not strictly necessary, and that fact alone is motive sufficient and superabundant for His follower to be prejudiced in favor of what is hard. This is no mere resignation to crosses and sufferings. It is eager, active acceptance. The saints cried out in complaints to God, not when they were laden with the cross, but when everything was going smoothly from a natural point of view. They feared at such times that God was forgetting them, and told Him so quite plainly.

Christ needs *saints* today. And why is it that there are so many good people, but comparatively few saintly people? Is it that these sincerely good men and women neglect prayer or sacraments, or that they often fall into grievous sin? Is it that they are forgetful of the all-important purpose of their existence in the world, or careless about preparing seriously for the journey hence? No. These are not the reasons. Christ has few saints because there are few who take literally the hard lesson of acceptance of the cross and suffering. As long as the soul leaves this hard saying in the region of dry theory, so long will it loiter on the road that leads to high holiness.

Christ offers us the cross and we can reject it with disdain. He offers us the cross and we can take and drag it after us; this is resignation. Christ offers us the cross, and we can accept it lovingly, knowing that His choice is always the best, understanding that suffering is the badge of those who love. This is the attitude of His saints and they have learned it by steeping themselves in the spirit of Calvary. This is the third degree of humility.

IX. Our Debt to Christ

"There [in heaven], we shall be at rest and we shall see. We shall see and we shall love. We shall love and we shall praise. Behold, what shall be our happy lot at the end, without end."—St. Augustine.

1. To Give Life

NAZARETH IS THE first place men begin to "learn Christ" by contemplating His sacred humanity in the mystery of the Incarnation. Then, on Christmas night, "Mary brought forth her first-born child and laid Him in the manger, because there was no room in the inn." Shepherds and Magi came and knelt down before Him in adoration. The little Infant cannot speak as yet, but later words will fall from those lips of His, which will be weighted with a wisdom and a power to stir men's hearts. He will deliver to the world a message which will revolutionize its history.

And what is it, that message? It is most noticeable that Our Divine Lord insists that His mission is to give *life* to the world. "The thief cometh," He told the Jews, "but to steal, to kill, and to destroy. I have come that they may have life and may have it more abundantly." Earlier still we find Him seated at the well of Jacob and talking to the Samaritan woman. She is a sinner and He explains to her that He has come to restore life, the life of grace, to her soul. Making use of the water at their feet to illustrate His heavenly doctrine, He says that He wills to give to mankind another water which will become in man a very fountain of water, springing up to life everlasting.

Nicodemus, too, was taught the same lesson about a new life. "Unless a man be born again of water and the Holy Ghost, he cannot enter the kingdom of heaven." "How can this be?" asked the astonished man. "Must he enter again into his mother's womb in order to be reborn?"

Finally—we are taking instances only at random—there is the same refrain in Our Lord's solemn words to Martha: "I am the resurrection and the life; he that believeth in Me, even though he be dead, shall live; and everyone that believeth and liveth in Me shall not die forever."

If, then, we speak of our debt to Christ, it seems clear that we must try to understand what He meant by this new life which He came to impart to the world.

Suppose you look from out a window across a field. The grass on that field has life, and the shrubs and the flowers in the garden have life, and the trees which put forth leaves and fruit in the summertime. From your place you can hear the song of the thrush in one of the branches. That thrush has life, too, and so has the cow seeking shelter under the shade, and the butterfly and the humming bee. And you who are watching, you are conscious that you possess as your most valued treasure the gift of life. You next lift your eyes above this world to recall the angelic spirits; they, too, have life. And over and above all there is God, from Whom all life descends as from its source.

So there are various degrees and grades of life. The tree lives, but it cannot move or speak. The bird lives and manifests its life by flying from branch to branch and by pouring forth its song. But the flower and the tree cannot walk nor can the bird and the animal speak intelligently and reason. This a man can do, for he possesses a grade of life higher than tree or beast. If a man comes to a fence that blocks his path, he will understand at once that he can either climb over or remove the obstacle or open the gate. A cow will stand there in front of the same fence and stare vacantly, incapable of making the conclusion that is obvious to the man.

Now if you did discover a tree that was capable of walking, or a cow endowed with the power of intelligent speech, you would have a prodigy that would dumbfound the countryside. If the cow could bid you good-afternoon as you walked past, or if the tree could of its own accord tear itself up by the roots and proceed to move about the field, you surely would blink with amazement. Why? Simply because the sort of life that belongs by right to the tree or the animal has no claim to be able to perform these acts. A cow is possessed of all the qualities that constitute it a cow without being able to argue or speak. A tree or a flower is fully a tree or a flower if it grow and blossom, and if it were to be endowed with power to walk about, its very nature would have to be raised to a higher degree in the scale of life, a degree to which its nature has no claim.

When our first parents were created, God gave them every quality that belonged to them by right in order that they should be human beings. But He did much more over and above. He actually raised them to a scale of being to which their nature had no right, so that, instead of being simply human beings, they were made real sharers in God's own life. A process was thus effected incomparably more amazing than would be needed to give the tree power to walk or the bird or cow power to speak.

It was this life, this actual sharing in God's life, to which man's nature had no sort of right, that was lost by Original Sin. And it was this same gift of God to which Jesus referred when He said that He had come among men that they might have life and have it more abundantly. He came, therefore, to restore grace to man, to raise him up once again to the level of God and fill him with this new kind of life by which he really participates in God's own divine nature. This sharing in God's life is called *supernatural* because it transcends all the natural claims or exigencies of mere human nature.

It may help me to visualize what this elevation implies to conceive of the life of God and the natural life of man as flowing along two parallel planes, one above the other, which can never meet. The only means of bringing one into contact with the other is either to raise man's life up to the plane of God, or to bring down the life of God to man's level. It was this second marvel which Jesus Christ accomplished in the mystery of the Incarnation. "He descended from heaven," says the Creed, "and became incarnate." He came into this world, true God and true man, and therefore He brought with Him this "more abundant life." More wonderful still, He *is* that life. "I *am* the resurrection and the life. . . . I *am* the way, the truth and the *life*."

To express the indebtedness of the human race for this act of infinite love and condescension is indeed a task that baffles the powers of human language. For consider. God in the very first instance was in no way bound to confer this life, supernatural life, on Adam and Eve. That He did so was an act of the special love which He had for man. His plan was, so to say, to plant the seed of this new life in man, and that seed was to develop and expand. For life is a growth. When divine life in man had attained to the measure of growth He had destined for it, then man was to be transplanted to paradise where he would be confirmed forever in his possession. But when sin entered in, man wantonly flung aside his most precious treasure. He bartered away God's gift and completely upset the plan God had made for him. He was free to do this because God had created him free. The sad abuse of his freedom results in this—that he is helpless to get back what has been lost, that he is irrevocably excluded from heaven, *unless* God Himself makes atonement for sin, gives back grace to His creature again, and with it man's title to the possession of God in eternity. This is just what God did. "God so loved the world as to give His only-begotten Son. . . . He who spared not His own Son, but delivered Him up for us all, how hath He not, with Him, given us all things?"

This divine Son brought back into the world the gift of God which had been squandered. He atoned for man's sin, as He alone was capable of doing, seeing that He is God. He also stored up infinite, inexhaustible treasures of grace merited by His Passion. These treasures He placed unreservedly at man's disposal, and it is His greatest anxiety that man should draw from these treasures, the only limit being man's capacity to receive. His saddest complaint is that man is so blind and senseless that he does not understand what loss he is sustaining when he refuses to avail himself of his supernatural privileges. "You will not come to Me that you may have life." "I know you, that you have not the love of God in you."

2. What Is a Saint?

Hence it follows that if our souls are to grow in holiness—by which is meant the developing of the life of God within them—our vitally-important task is to make sure to establish and maintain contact with Jesus Christ. For Jesus is the head from which the lifestream flows into the members, vivifying them. He is the vine and we the branches. Just as the sap flows from the parent stem out into the branch and in this way communicates its life to the branch, so does sanctifying grace flow from Him into us. The more freely it flows and the more fully we share in it, the greater will be our holiness. Holiness consists precisely in the possession of the grace poured into the soul by Christ, and the measure of the soul's holiness is in exact proportion to the amount of grace it possesses.

Outside every city you have a great reservoir, the purpose of which is to keep the place supplied with water. The reservoir is connected with the city by means of many conduit pipes through which the water is borne along till it reaches the spot required. Now the hill of Calvary is something like that reservoir. In it are contained all the merits of Christ's sacred passion and death. Because He came and atoned for our sin, the heavenly Father's just anger has been turned away from us and sanctifying grace has once more been given back to us. But how is the grace of Christ to be borne from Him into our souls? Our Lord has laid down "conduit pipes" for this purpose. These are His Seven Sacraments, visible signs instituted by Him for the very purpose of uniting us with Himself, so that grace may flow from Him into us, as the sap flows from the vine into the branch. This is why we are constantly urged to receive these wonderful sacraments worthily. If we have not yet received divine life it is given to us in Baptism. If we have the misfortune to stifle that divine life by the soul-suicide called mortal sin, it is given back to us by penance, and the very same measure of it which we had before sinning. The other sacraments help to foster and to strengthen this life, coming most opportunely at times of crisis in the soul's journey, in order to give it the extra vigor and confidence it requires at such a period. Thus there is Confirmation to impart courage to Christ's soldier at the crisis which meets him on passing from childhood to youth. There is Extreme Unction to soothe the passage into eternity. Matrimony and Holy Orders enable the recipient to face the difficulties of a new state of life. All the sacraments give a grace peculiar to themselves, as well as increasing what they find already in the soul.

This we owe to the love and compassion and mercy of Jesus Christ our Saviour. This is why we are directed by Holy Church to make all our requests "through Jesus Christ Our Lord." This is why Jesus tells us: "No man cometh to the Father except through Me." This is part of our debt to Christ.

So far we have contented ourselves with a plain statement of the doctrine of grace. But if the implications of this teaching be seriously considered and meditated upon prayerfully the result must surely be to inflame the heart with love and immense gratitude for such stupendous generosity to us on the part of Our Lord, and to fill the mind with wonderment that God, being who He is, should set His heart on His creature in this fashion. "What is man that Thou shouldst be mindful of him? Or why dost Thou set Thy heart upon him?"

This is the reason why St. Luke declares that "the kingdom of God is *within you.*" This is why St. Paul describes the soul as God's temple. "Know you not that you are the temple of God and that the spirit of God dwelleth in you? Now if any man violate the temple of God, him shall God destroy. For the temple of God is holy *which you are.*" This is the explanation of the marvelous promise made by Our Lord Himself: "If any man love Me, My Father will love him and we will come to him and take up our abode in him." Here you have stressed the idea of permanence —not that God will merely make a passing visit to the soul, but that He will actually settle down there, in much the same way as a man who goes to live in his home. "I live," says St. Paul, "now not I, but Christ liveth in me," and with all the vehemence of his great heart he longs that all should be like himself. "My little children, for whom I am in labor again till Christ be fashioned in you!"

All these wonderful texts are readily understood as soon as we begin to grasp the doctrine of man's supernatural life by the possession of sanctifying grace. God lives in the soul, sets up His kingdom there, restores that kingdom when man's perverse will has shaken it to its foundations. On man's side his one task is to co-operate with grace so that the divine life may expand in him more and more and he attain to the stature designed for him "according to the measure of the giving of Christ."

3. Let Light Be!

When the Son of God grew to man's estate, He walked into the highways of life and He found men seeking for happiness—just as they are seeking it today—but to Him they seemed like people groping and stumbling along a dark road. He saw that men sinned, but this they did under the sad delusion that sin gives happiness. If man piles up money he does so because he has convinced himself that a sense of security and the abundance of the good things which money can bring will satisfy this craving for happiness. He struggles against poverty, he labors to shake off sickness and rid himself of pain, because, in his philosophy of life, health and wealth and happiness go hand in hand.

When Jesus Christ saw men acting like this, He proclaimed that they were blind and that He Himself, as light of the world, had come to show them where they would infallibly find the object of their unceasing quest. He told them that He held in His hand the key to their problem. "I am the light of the world; he that followeth Me walketh not in darkness." He would guide them to the fountains of living waters at which, and at which only, their thirst would be satiated.

Have you ever lost your way on a dark road at night? Full of anxiety you stumbled along for an hour, and then to your joy you saw a light streaming into the darkness from out the window of a cottage. New hope arose in your faltering heart and your pace quickened as you walked towards that light. Or perhaps a car came up behind you, and for a minute or so two great headlights shone out and illuminated the place ahead of you, and you sighed with relief for you recognized the spot and you knew exactly where to go—once you had the light to show you. Or the clouds parted over your head and the moon's rays let you see just where you were, and now that you had your bearings your mind was at ease—since the light came.

Our Blessed Lord is such a light showing the path that leads unerringly to the possession of the happiness for which men crave. To be sure, the good things of this world, used with moderation and with due regard for God's law, can *contribute* towards man's happiness, but they can never *constitute* that happiness. The truth is that man is made for an object which transcends the good things of this world as much as eternity transcends time, or the Creator surpasses the thing He has created. "A man's happiness doth not consist in the multitude of things which he possesseth." In what then? In nothing less than in God Himself. And he is to seek for God and find Him, where? In the depths of his own soul! "The kingdom of God is within you." To possess sanctifying grace in the soul is to possess a share in God's own life and with this the beginnings of the "peace of God, surpassing all understanding," for which men hunger and thirst.

"I live, now not I, but Christ liveth in me." Hence a true follower of Our Lord will not seek his happiness in anything external, but he will look for it and find it in the secret places of his own soul. He seeks companionship with God, and prayer opens the way to this companionship. Indeed, prayer is nothing else than a loving and continual attendance on the divine Guest Who dwells in the soul. The tendency to give this attention to Him grows continually until a happy state of affairs is arrived at, in which the conscious contact between these two, God and His creature, is virtually uninterrupted. This is part of our debt to Jesus Christ.

But there is much more. How great soever be the soul's splendor through grace in this life, and how deep soever be its happiness and how spiritual and how genuine, Jesus teaches that here in the land of exile the soul has tasted only the crumbs that fall from the table. The light shining in the face of Christ reaches out far beyond the confines of time; it is raised immeasurably high, above the little interests of man till it falls full upon the gates of eternity. There, He sees, is happiness, indeed, for the soul created to enjoy God. If grace be a light in the soul, it is only like the faint flicker you see at early dawn. Gradually the dawn increases and spreads until you have the dazzling radiance of the noonday sun. In a somewhat similar way grace will develop until it reaches its perfection when it is changed into glory in heaven. So the happiness of the soul and its beauty here below, though true and deep and lasting when founded upon the possession of God by grace, are yet only a prelude to another joy that will be entirely without alloy.

Turn again to the immortal St. Paul and see how thoroughly he grasped this lesson. "I reckon," he writes, "that the sufferings of this present time are not worthy to be compared to the glory to come which shall be revealed in us. For that which is at present light and momentary of our tribulation, worketh for us, beyond measure exceedingly, an eternal weight of glory." The wildest flights of the imagination fall hopelessly short of the reality of the joys prepared by a loving God for the home-coming of His children.

When Our Lord moved in and out among men, His gaze was ever fixed upon that place of happiness. It is easy, then, to understand how small all else must have seemed in His eyes by comparison. With the truth of the happiness and the nearness of heaven always uppermost in His mind, it must have been difficult for Him, speaking in our human way, to bear with the wranglings and disputes about trifles which preoccupied the thoughts of men, their absorption in the toys which they were so soon to throw away forever. "You know not of what spirit you are," He told them, and even after the Resurrection, and even with "His own," he had still to complain: "O foolish and slow of heart to believe!"

4. A Glimpse of Heaven

What then is heaven? What happens when grace gives place to glory in a soul? We have made a feeble effort in another place to stammer out an answer—to stammer, for language is halt and inadequate when one attempts to describe that abode of unspeakable bliss. The task baffled St. Paul himself, as we saw. The divine expert explained to us that heaven is a state the *raison d'être* of which is to pour happiness into the soul, according to the capacity of the soul to receive it.

While here on earth the soul, which is now on the point of entering heaven, enjoyed the possession of God by grace, but now it is going to see Him face to face in the full splendor of His glory. The soul will possess God now exactly in the proportion to the measure of sanctifying grace which was in it at the moment of death. The object placed before the soul is infinitely knowable and infinitely lovable. "Quantum potes tantum aude, quia major omni laude, nec laudare sufficis." The beautiful words may be applied here, too. "Praise Him as much as ever you dare, for He is above all praise, so that you can never praise enough."

To Moses it was granted to converse with the Lord on Sinai, and when he returned to the children of Israel he had to veil his face lest the brilliance of the reflected light should blind their eyes. To Isaias was given a fleeting glimpse of the Godhead and he cried out that the vision was overpowering, that he was a man of unclean lips utterly unfitted to speak about what he had seen. On Tabor Our Lord's three chosen Apostles saw for a moment the unclouded beauty of the divinity as it shone through the sacred humanity. What was the result? The men were beside themselves in an ecstasy of delight, so transported with joy that Peter exclaimed that they would remain here forever on this mountain, and never again go down into the drab valleys below. To St. Paul was vouchsafed a like vision and he knew not how to tell us about it, saying only that he could not find words, and that, so intoxicated was his heart with the sight, that he was unable to decide whether he was "in the body or out of the body." St. John at Patmos saw the beauty of God and His wonderful heaven and he spoke about it in language so subtle as to seem to our dull minds almost unintelligible. The truth is that all words and all images and all turns of expression must fail, of necessity, when they are employed to describe the ineffable perfections of the infinitely holy God.

Jesus assures me that as a result of what He has done for me, as part of my debt to Him, I am now destined—and quite soon —to behold this wonderful God, to lay hold of Him, to possess Him, to contemplate unceasingly His beauty. All this, not for a flashing moment, like the chosen souls mentioned, but throughout the endless ages of eternity. This is the full flowering of the life of grace developing into glory. This is the life more abundant, the seed of which is sown in my soul by the hand of Christ here, and is intended to fructify in this marvelous manner hereafter.

In order to be able to see thus into the perfections of God, man's weak power of vision has to be strengthened. He cannot look with naked eye upon the sun at midday, even for a few minutes. With how much greater reason is it impossible for him to gaze upon God's beauty throughout eternity unless he receive some new power! So God will give to man, on his entering into heaven, "the light of glory," a greater keenness of perception as a result of which he will be enabled to look into the face of his God and not be overpowered by its loveliness or blinded by its splendor. "In Thy light we shall see light."

Omniscience, we saw, planned it. Omnipotence executed it. Infinite love threw it open and eagerly invited God's children to enter and possess it forever. And, as the object all-sufficing and all-satisfying, God gives Himself, His familiar, fatherly, face-to-face presence and companionship, to be united in close union with the enraptured soul and to be to the soul the source of everlasting bliss. But all had been lost. This design of a loving

Father had been foiled by the perversion called sin. Without Jesus a remedy could never have been devised. Without Jesus there would have been no restoring of the divine life here or hereafter. This is my debt to Christ.

5. Title-Deeds

To many people today all this is a fairy-tale. None the less the "fairy-tale" is most marvelous in this, that it is all the sheer, unadorned, unadulterated truth. We know in whom we trust. We have the word of Our Lord for it that Heaven is a fact, that the wall separating the soul from the staggering reality is becoming thinner every day.

"I am come that they may have life and may have it more abundantly." Through Jesus Christ my title-deeds have been put back into my hands. If I die with my soul pulsating with the life of God, I am certain that that life will endure throughout eternity. The path to heaven was lost, but the light shining from the face of Christ has shown it to me again. The road was blocked by sin and all advance was impossible, but Jesus has pushed aside every obstacle and the soul now but needs to walk behind Him where He has led the way. What all men together could not do, Jesus alone has done, and done super-abundantly, because He is God. Man knows the way now, but he is still weak and inconstant. So Jesus has gone farther; He has given to frail human beings His wonderful sacraments to pour wine and oil into their wounds when they weary of the way, even to raise them from death itself if they lose their supernatural life by mortal sin. This is our debt to Christ.

Suppose you are out in a small row-boat and you place a little thimble on the surface of the water. It floats about for a minute, then fills with water and sinks. Next suppose you place on the surface a wooden tub. It, too, drifts about for a while, but by degrees the water finds an entrance, and when the tub is filled it sinks to the bottom. Let me suppose next that your own tiny craft springs a leak and begins to take in water. You are alarmed and you call out excitedly to your companions in another boat near you to come to your assistance. They row over, take you on board, and only just in time, for regretfully you watch the water fill your vessel and send it down. Lastly, suppose a great transatlantic liner is dashed against a rock; the waters rush in and the boat founders.

All these different vessels on the ocean are *completely* filled with water, but they are by no means *equally* filled. The thimble cannot hold as much as the tub, nor the thimble, tub, and boat all together anything like as much as the liner. They are each as full as they *can* be and the amount they contain is measured, not by the water—which is all round in abundance—but by the capacity of the vessel to hold the water.

In some such way we may say that each soul in heaven will see and enjoy God, being each perfectly happy, each completely filled with the entrancing vision and all-sufficing knowledge of God, each reflecting as full a measure of God's glory in itself as it is possible for it to reflect. But all will by no means be equally happy, for the amount of grace contained in the soul at the moment of death determines the soul's capacity to possess and enjoy the Beatific Vision. "One is the glory of the sun and another the glory of the moon and another the glory of the stars, and star differeth from star in glory."

In God are *all* the treasures of wisdom and of knowledge, and it will be the soul's ineffable privilege to see, to know, to love, to possess. Regret in heaven is an impossibility, but if it were possible, it would be the thought that so much more might have been secured if only the soul, during its earthly career, had been more assiduous in cultivating the seed of sanctifying grace sown within itself on the day of baptism.

An old Jesuit, when nearing the end, was heard to say: "If there is anything that will cause you regret when you are lying on your deathbed, it is the thought that you have ever spared yourself in the service of so good a God." "If there could be sorrow in heaven," writes Cardinal Merry del Val, "it would be the thought that there is now no more left to do for Jesus." These are the men for whom the supernatural world is the great reality. For such as these grace is the only treasure and sin the only misfortune. The soul is the pearl of great price, and their one longing is to grow themselves in grace, to set up God's kingdom in the souls of others or to consolidate it if it be there already. This is the standard by which they assess the value of one's existence on earth, and they are well persuaded that their standard is the correct one. For these ideals they live, for these ideals they fight right up to the last ditch, for these ideals they are prepared to suffer all things, even to lay down their lives, for they have grasped, in some measure, the immensity of their debt to Jesus Christ.

Here is the kind of language in which such souls speak of their ideals and their strivings:

> "I have but one desire, Jesus.
> One fear, to lose Jesus.
> One to rest on, Jesus.
> One home, the wounds of Jesus.
> One occupation, to converse with Jesus.
> One charge, to do the will of Jesus.
> One joy, to possess Jesus.
> One hope, to see Jesus.
> One grief, compassion for Jesus.
> One witness, the eye of Jesus.
> One consolation, to suffer for Jesus.
> One glory, to be despised for Jesus.
> One rest, to labor for Jesus.
> One refuge, the heart of Jesus."

X. Who Art Thou, Lord?

"I know whom I have believed and I am certain that He is able to keep that which I have committed unto Him, against that day. Hold the form of sound words which thou hast heard from me, in faith, and in the love which is in Christ Jesus."—2 Tim. i. 12, 13.

1. Early Schooling

Saul was his name, Saul of Tarsus. As a boy he had been brought up in the narrow, straitlaced ways of the pharisees. His teacher Gamaliel trained him from the cradle to hate and oppose in the domain of religion anything that savored of innovation. The boy proved to be a strong, indomitable character with a will like a bar of steel. He developed into a truly religious man, but his religious sense was sadly misdirected.

So when he came to hear about this new prophet named Jesus, and when he was told that He had some fantastic ideas which were intended to supersede the traditions which had been handed down, when Saul first learned the name of Christ, the blood in his veins boiled with indignation. Nor is this to be wondered at, considering his education. One day news was brought about some fanatic called Stephen who had declared himself a follower of this Christ and had insisted on preaching His newfangled doctrines. But Saul's masters were quickly on the scent; they would track the man down and silence his blasphemies forever. Stephen was seized and stoned till he fell before them, begging even in death that God would deal mercifully with his murderers. "Lord," he prayed with his last breath, "Lord, lay not this sin to their charge." It was the echo of the prayer of another dying man, who lifted up a thorn-crowned head, and who parted lips that were dried and soaked in His blood in order to implore forgiveness for those who had crucified Him. "Father, forgive them, for they know not what they do."

It seems likely that this prayer of Stephen made its impression on Saul. But the ardent youth did not want to be impressed.

Serve the fellow right, he thought. He had been there watching Stephen's death, and while the older men flung the stones Saul held their coats. This would teach them, the rest of the gang, to stop their nonsense. Let any of them breathe the name of Jesus or attempt to preach His Gospel and they, too, would be dealt with thus summarily. Let them dare now persevere in their efforts to overthrow the established religion!

These were the ideals, and this was the atmosphere, in which young Saul grew up into manhood. One day—he was about thirty by then—this fire-eater was riding at the head of a band of soldiers into the city of Damascus. An exasperating report had reached him. It seemed quite certain that at Damascus there were men who professed themselves Christians. So the movement was spreading like an infectious disease, despite the efforts of God-fearing men to arrest its progress! Well, Saul volunteered to deal with this situation. At his own request this battalion of soldiers had been placed at his disposal by the Sanhedrin at Jerusalem, and Saul, breathing out threatenings and slaughter, swore that he would bring back in chains every Christian he could lay hands on, or if need be, he would slay them on the spot.

"And it came to pass that as he went on his journey he drew nigh to Damascus. And suddenly a light from heaven shined round about him. And falling to the ground he heard a voice saying to him: 'Saul, Saul, why persecutest thou Me?' Who said: 'Who art Thou, Lord?' And He: 'I am Jesus Whom thou persecutest. It is hard for thee to kick against the goad.'

"And he, trembling and astonished, said: 'Lord, what wilt Thou have me to do?' And the Lord said to him: 'Arise and go into the city, and there it will be told thee what thou must do' . . . And Saul arose, and when [although] his eyes were opened he saw nothing. But they, leading him by the hands, brought him to Damascus." This is the concise and vivid account given in the inspired word of this astonishing event on the Damascus Road.

Saul stood up a new man. The light shining round about him

had sent its rays into the innermost secret places of the man's soul and had revealed him to himself. In a flash he understood the folly and the injustice of the course of action pursued hitherto. But he saw something more in that light. Dazzled though he was as he knelt there on the dusty roadside, he still could shade his eyes with both hands and examine the source from which the light was emanating. It was falling upon him from the face of Jesus Christ, from Him Who is the light of the world, that light which Saul in his infatuation and blindness had been trying, all these years, to extinguish.

But today he sees his mistake. Today he has caught a glimpse of that countenance and he recognizes that it is radiant with a beauty which is divine. The Christ Whom Saul was persecuting is, in very truth, the anointed Son of God. "Who art Thou, Lord?" Saul knows the answer, and presently we shall see the transforming effects of his knowing.

Nothing short of what has been called "an audacious grace" could win such an unbending character, but once won, all the old fire of zeal and enthusiasm would blaze up with mightier power than ever, the energy of the man would be let loose again, and Saul, now become Paul, would be eaten up with an insatiable longing to din the message into the ears of every man on the face of the earth, and to enkindle in the hearts of all that flame of personal attachment to Jesus Christ which had begun to stir in his own on that fateful day.

The great Jesuit missionary, St. Francis Xavier, is often compared with St. Paul, and Ignatius used to say that Xavier was the toughest clay he ever had to handle. Both men belonged to the type that must be great. They would not, could not, be satisfied with half-measures. Put them on the avenues that lead to forbidden pleasures and they will run until they have tasted every sinful delight. Set their feet on the road to God and nothing will daunt them. Greatness they must have, and the higher the pinnacle and the stiffer the climb, the more do they revel in the effort. Let the way bristle with difficulties; these exist only to be overcome.

Yes, Paul would be great, and great now with true greatness. Jesus, Whom in his ignorance he had persecuted, now becomes, in this new-found knowledge, the friend and the lover by Whom he is completely captivated, the model Whose every action and word he will labor to imitate, the God the truth of Whose message must ring throughout the length and breadth of the world, to be preached in season and out of season, even if the preacher must pay for his preaching by shedding his blood. Jesus Christ is God. Jesus Christ, who is God, loves men and His love has drawn Him to live in the midst of men, to speak and eat and pray and toil and suffer and die in the midst of men. This is true! "God *so* loved the world as to give His only-begotten Son!" The profound and stunning implications of that sentence! No wonder when it began to dawn on the mind of Paul that the sheer reality of it swept every other interest clean out of his life. If this is the truth, if God loves thus, if Jesus is true God and true man, then indeed life has one purpose, one mighty all-engrossing occupation—it is the one and only opportunity given during which to share with others this light, so necessary, so revolutionizing, so far-reaching in the importance of its results.

2. Transformation

And this is Paul's mission! Jesus, Son of God, has singled him out, called him by his own name, and assigned to him the task of bearing His Gospel to the ends of the earth. He is the vessel of election; he the bigot, the hater of Christ, the persecutor, the man whose face had been set like flint against any who professed allegiance to Jesus Christ! Such a choice! Of such a person! And by such a leader! This is the truth, staggering and almost incredible though it must have seemed to him. But in face of it what else can Paul do now except allow his heart to be inundated with joy at the immense honor of being thus chosen? What can he do but strengthen that already strong will of steel, to face every sacrifice, any sacrifice for the love of Him Whom he has learned, or begun to learn, in the light on the Damascus Road?

Will he hesitate to regard everything valued by this near-sighted world as so much rubbish to be ruthlessly cast aside, provided that thus the fire of divine love be enkindled in his great soul, enkindled and expanded till it spreads from him into the souls of others? This all began to happen as soon as Paul was gripped by the reality of Christ's personal love.

Nothing is easier to illustrate than the hold which this love of Christ secured on Paul's heart, for the name he once hated is ever on his lips now, and in his letters he uses it more than two hundred times. He loves to write it, for now it stands for the Man Whose divinity and Whose perfect manhood are the subject-matter of his unceasing meditations. The more Paul knows the more does his longing increase to know, and the more does an overmastering desire to share his knowledge with others galvanize him into action. He might be said to have been transformed into Christ; indeed, as we shall see presently, he uses this very phrase of himself. He can speak of nothing except Christ, and His love, and His designs for the souls of men. The mind of this erstwhile bigot and persecutor is now filled with one thought only—how to further Christ's kingdom in the souls He died to save. Turn over the pages of those wonderful epistles for confirmation of all this. Every page seems to vibrate with the intensity of the passionate devotion to Christ which now consumes the heart of Paul.

Do you ask him what now he values most of all? "The things that were gain to me," he answers, "these same I have counted loss for Christ. Furthermore, I count all things to be but loss for the excellent knowledge of Jesus Christ, my Lord. . . ." Question him about his hopes for the future, and he tells you that he looks forward to heaven—"our conversation is in heaven." And in heaven what is he longing to see except the face of Christ in its unclouded beauty, the same he glimpsed one day on the road to Damascus? From heaven "we look for the Saviour, Our Lord Jesus Christ." Paul has to suffer much, as we saw is true of every follower of Our Lord. And it is the memory of the suffering Christ that sustains him. "If we suffer with Him we shall also glory with Him. . . . As the sufferings of Christ abound in us, so also by Christ doth our comfort abound." He preaches with eloquence and conviction—why? Because his words are inspired by Jesus Whose love has captivated him. "And I, brethren, when I came amongst you judged not myself to know anything but Jesus Christ and Him crucified." . . . "Jesus Christ, the power of God and the wisdom of God." "God forbid that I should glory save in the cross of our Lord Jesus Christ by Whom the world is crucified to me and I to the world!"

He can say no more than that he lives with the very life of Jesus Himself: "I live, now not I, but Christ liveth in me. . . . To Me to live is Christ." At the end of his eighth chapter to the Romans, Paul's language of devotedness reaches, perhaps, its climax in a passionate outburst: "Who then shall separate us from the love of Christ? Shall tribulation? Or distress? Or famine? Or nakedness? Or danger? Or persecution? Or the sword? But in all these things we overcome, because of Him that loveth us. For I am sure that neither death nor life, nor angels, nor principalities, nor powers, nor things present, nor things to come, nor might, nor height, nor depth, nor any other creature, shall be able to separate us from the love of God which is in Christ Jesus our Lord."

Thus the knowledge and love of Jesus Christ have become the core and center of Paul's existence. A truly marvelous change, for could you have imagined a more unlikely subject for this deep attachment than the pupil of Gamaliel the pharisee? Remember who Paul was. He had sworn to exterminate the name of Christ, and here is the result, an unconditional surrender, an act of whole-hearted and unqualified submission to the Christ Whom once he hated! There is much to think of here, for the very fact that Paul was of this sort, a determined enemy, and that yet he reached such a point of zeal and enthusiasm for the Man he once hated—this illustrates what the grace of God can do in my own case, too. So my own past sins and failings are not to be permitted to deter me.

3. Christ Means This

Christ is, first of all, the model of Paul's external behavior. He kept his eyes always fixed upon this Man. He scrutinized every single detail pertaining to His life, and then he set himself the task of re-living that life in its external manifestations, in so far as this was possible for mere man to do. The image of Christ moved always before his eyes, and the question ever foremost in his mind was: "What would *He* do if He were in these circumstances? If He had to treat with this sinner, what would His treatment be? If He were kneeling here in prayer, what manner of prayer would He use? If Jesus were bound a prisoner here with me in prison, how would He act towards His enemies? If He had to encounter the sly, insincere, carping hypocrites who attack me now, what would He say to them? Would He lash them with invective, as He did in the case of the pharisees and scribes, or would He keep silence before them as when He stood in front of Herod?"

And so, in every detail—waking or sleeping, at home or on a journey, eating or fasting, alone or in company—in all these things Jesus kept constantly moving before the eyes of Paul, and he bent all his efforts to reproduce in himself what he saw in that perfect character. "Be ye imitators of me," he cried, "as I am of Him." Just as a child tries to imitate the teacher, just as an amateur studies the technique of the professional, so did Paul make it his one aim in life to act in all times and places as he believed Jesus would have done in the same circumstances.

Lastly, Paul, having discovered the blessed sweetness of belonging to Jesus, having come now to realize the treasures he himself had been missing for so long a time, was "urged" by the love of Christ burning within him to share his treasure with others. This is the explanation of his boundless zeal; of the hunger for souls that consumed him day and night, which made him regard as dead loss a day in which he had not used the opportunities occurring, to make Christ known and loved; that fixed him in his resolve to slave, as long as there was life in his body, in the effort to bring Christ to souls and souls to Christ.

It is well worth while re-reading his letters and seeing how each of these three great truths dominates the mind and heart of the Apostle. Jesus, the model towards which he always looked for direction in his external conduct, in much the same way as the mariner keeps his eye on the compass; Jesus, the source from which Paul drank into his thirsting soul the waters of divine life, those waters of sanctifying grace which spread themselves and gradually took possession, ousting the life of sin and selfishness; Jesus, the inspiration of Paul's zeal, the memory of Jesus haunting his mind, the love of Jesus inflaming his heart, the craving, the aching anxiety that men should not miss this knowledge and this love. All this Jesus became for Paul.

It is hard to refrain from insisting again on the sort of man he had been, the man toughened by his early education, toughened by a character that naturally was strong and determined—think of all that and you are not surprised that his conversion struck the countryside like a thunderbolt and that many suspected his sincerity. Ananias, a man living in Damascus at the time of the vision, on being told by the Lord to meet Saul and restore him his sight, thought fit to expostulate: "Lord, I have heard by many of this man and how much evil he hath done to Thy saints in Jerusalem." The inhabitants of the town, on learning that Saul was preaching and giving himself out as a Christian, were undisguisedly skeptical. "Is not this he who persecuted in Jerusalem those who called upon this name, and came hither for that intent, that he might carry them bound to the chief priests?"

4. Tough Clay

Every detail in the history of Paul's conversion is calculated to fill the reader with encouragement. To begin with, I suppose we could scarcely discover a more unpromising subject to be transformed into a saint and ardent lover of Christ. He rightly calls himself a sinner, the greatest of sinners, and reminds us how he persecuted the Church of God and wasted it "beyond measure." Now it is quite true that there are many saints in the Church's calendar whose lives do indeed edify us greatly, but perhaps discourage us, too. We read of those who never sinned grievously, who seem to have been saints in the cradle, and they almost make us despair of ever attaining ourselves to any appreciable height along the mountain of sanctity. But not here does Paul belong. He had a bad record, and the memory of it is our encouragement.

Sinners we have been, and by all means we strike our breasts with sincere humility about it. But, with the example of Paul before our eyes, far be it from us to deceive ourselves into the silly belief that our past must be a handicap to our future. Rather is it true that it can help us powerfully. Saul possibly would never have been constrained by the love of Christ to toil as he did, had he not been constantly mindful of what he had done in the past against this greatest lover. There was indeed sorrow for the past, but no distrust about the forgiveness. There was the longing of his ardent nature to atone. Life was not all wasted yet; there still was time granted to him and never did man fling himself more whole-heartedly into the work of making reparation.

"Dearest children," writes St. Augustine in his sermon on Our Lord's Ascension, "let this be our task, that as Our Lord on this day of ours ascended with His body into heaven, so we, in so far as we can, may rise up with Him through hope, and follow after Him with our heart. . . . Let this ascent be made even through our very vices and passions themselves. For if each of us strives to subdue his vicious habits and trains himself to trample upon them, what will then happen is that he will make for himself a stepping-stone by means of which he will succeed in climbing higher still. Our very sins will lift us up to greater heights if they are under our feet."

That was just what Paul did. And that is why he beckons encouragingly to us to follow and imitate.

But, of course, he did not get there without many a struggle. So far we have talked about the extraordinary graces that were vouchsafed him. The memory of these might be misleading, for one might be inclined to argue: "It is all very well to hold him up as a model, but look at the exceptional graces and helps he received. Small thanks to him to reach the heights, seeing that he was born thus powerfully! God revealed Himself to him on the road to Damascus. When he describes his visions he exclaims that he was wrapt to the third heaven. He was permitted to see into divine secrets for the expression of which mere human language was quite inadequate. All he can say is that eye hath not seen, nor ear heard, neither hath it entered into the heart of man to conceive what things God hath prepared for those who love Him. Small thanks to a man so privileged to slave for Christ and for souls!"

Now there is a modicum of truth in the argument. It is quite correct to say that Paul did receive those extraordinary graces and helps, and that he was destined for a height of sanctity to which it might be presumptuous for another to aspire. But always remember that he was "a soldier of Christ Jesus." No soldier wants to spend his life marking time, and Paul was surrounded on all sides by enemies—traitors within and foes without—who gave him no respite. But the man that was in him exulted in the fight.

In proof of this we have only to turn again to his account of those stupendous visions with which his soul was favored. He tells his Corinthians, it is true, that his soul was so flooded with divine light that he did not know whether he was in the body or out of the body. But what he did know was that God revealed to him secrets of heaven of so intimate and exalted a nature as to ravish his whole being and set his heart on fire with love. That is true, but if we read on we find—for our comfort—in the very same passage, that he next proceeds to describe a persistent and fierce temptation, which he says, was given to him "lest the greatness of the revelations should exalt me." An angel of satan came to buffet him, a sting of the flesh injected its poison, or tried to, and three times he cried out in anguish to God, begging for deliverance. What a consolation to hear this! If Paul was favored with visions and ecstasies he was also tested in the furnace of tribulation.

Does he allow himself to lie down and be discouraged? Not a bit of it. In his distress he turned to God in prayer, but God refused to answer him. God saw fit not to set him free from this temptation, but He promised him grace to fight it and win through. "My grace is sufficient for thee, for virtue is made perfect in infirmity." As though He would say: "Unite your own weakness with My strength, and this temptation, so far from hindering your soul's progress, will turn rather to your eternal advantage." And Paul is heartened all the more for the fight. "Gladly therefore will I glory in my infirmities that the virtue of Christ may be manifest in me. . . . For when I am weak, then I am strong." He recognizes, indeed, his own weakness, but, what is of at least equal importance, he sees most clearly that he has Christ's own strength to lean upon for support.

Such a combination between strength and weakness, such an elevation on the one side and such human frailty on the other, cannot but prove a powerful encouragement and incentive to the soul that feels, as we all do from time to time, that it is quite impossible to keep going on any longer.

There are many men and women who are good enough Christians who would be somewhere near the saints only for a cankerworm called human-respect. They are ashamed to act up to their conscience, afraid of being laughed at, or held up to ridicule by those who object to taking religion too seriously. Under such criticism a weak character will capitulate and abandon principles, but it is precisely in face of cynicism or sarcasm sustained that sanctity develops and grows to maturity. "What doth he know that hath not been tried?" Hostility should not make a man testy or irritated; opposition is like the blow of the chisel on the block of marble, its purpose is to bring to light the latent beauty.

All this is easy to see in St. Paul. His one concern is to be right in the sight of God; what men say of him or think about him, matters not at all. "To me it is a very small thing to be judged by you or by man's day. . . . I am not conscious to myself of anything, yet not herein am I justified. He that judgeth me is the Lord." So he went on his even way, refusing to be beaten when men laughed at him for his bad Greek, as when he preached in the Areopagus; yielding not an inch when he was well aware that false brethren were spying upon him; persevering with heroic constancy in the teeth of a whole series of persecutions and trials which he catalogues for the Corinthians. "Of the Jews five times did I receive forty stripes save one; thrice was I beaten with rods; once was I stoned; thrice I suffered shipwreck; a night and a day I was in the depths of the sea. In journeyings often; in perils of waters, in perils of robbers, in perils from my own nation, in perils from the Gentiles, in perils in the city, in perils in the wilderness, in perils in the sea, in perils from false brethren. In labor and painfulness, in much watchings, in hunger and thirst, in fastings often, in cold and nakedness . . . at Damascus . . . through a window in a basket was I let down by the wall and so escaped. . . . I please myself in my infirmities, in reproaches, in necessities, in persecutions, in distresses—for *Christ.*" There is the all-sufficing motive—for Christ! "I seek not the things that are yours, but you. . . . I most gladly will spend myself, and be spent, for your *souls*. . . ."

Admittedly it is hard to stop quoting the repeated testimonies of this intrepid soldier who faced all this undauntedly for the sake of that Christ Whom he had glimpsed on the Damascus road and for the souls so dear to Him. But enough has surely been said to establish the truth that he had to fight, and fight to a finish, despite the visions and special graces granted to him. His one preoccupation is Christ and the spread of the Gospel. Personal sufferings do not matter. Opposition will not be allowed to put him down. He does not care so much even—as he writes from his prison in Jerusalem—if some who preach Our Lord are actuated by imperfect motives. The main thing is that at all costs He be preached and that men should be won to Him. "Some preach out of envy and contention, but some also out of goodwill . . . some out of charity and some not sincerely. What then? So that by all means Christ be preached . . . in this I rejoice and will rejoice."

And he would not be deterred in his efforts by lack of talent. He relies for success, not upon the persuasive words of human wisdom. "Brethren," he tells the Corinthians, "when I came to you, I came not in loftiness of speech or of wisdom. . . . I judged not myself to know anything among you but Jesus Christ and Him crucified. . . . We speak the wisdom of God in a mystery . . . which none of the princes of this world knew."

There you have him, this giant of God, beginning with such a huge handicap, enlightened indeed and strengthened by very special graces, but buffeted and attacked on all sides by trials and hardships and contradictions.

5. Reasoned Enthusiasm

What sustained him? Why did he become an Apostle? Was it that he stood to gain materially by his apostolate? We have seen that, from the point of view of wordly advantage, it brought him nothing but contempt and suffering. Was it that he tired of the very prosaic existence of the pharisees and grew weary of their hair-splitting arguments over points of their Law? Did he go out on his missions in order to win renown for himself, to be looked upon by the common people as a sort of hero? No. Not for any of these things did Paul care a whit. He became an Apostle because on the Damascus road he "learned Christ."

On that never-to-be-forgotten day Paul was seized upon by the love and lovableness of Jesus of Nazareth. "Who art Thou, Lord?" He found the answer; he understood that Jesus was God. Everything else right and left of that one single fact fell away. Paul saw the reality of life; that it was sheer waste of time unless it was employed in loving Christ and laboring incessantly to make Him known and loved. This was substance; hitherto he had been chasing shadows. The love of Jesus devoured his great heart; hungrily he fed his soul on the personal knoweldge and personal love of the God-Man; the yearning to make others see Him and understand Him and love Him, as he himself now sees and understands and loves, became a kind of torment; Paul could never be the same again, never again could he be even moderate in his loving, in his quest for souls. Personal gain or misfortune, or reputation, or prison, or death itself—why these things mattered not at all; what did matter was that at all costs Jesus should be known, Jesus should be preached, Jesus should be loved passionately, Jesus should not be offended. If only Paul could call an assembly of the entire world and din into men's minds the gigantic truth he had learned himself, and awaken in their hearts the response for which Jesus longed!

We have chosen Paul for the subject of our concluding chapter because he is such a splendid example of what happens when a man attains to the personal knowledge of Christ which it has been our effort to foster in these sketches. There is need of his spirit today. Saul the persecutor proves that there is no such thing as a hopeless case. Paul the man of prayer, lifted high up into divine light where his soul is bathed in the radiance of God, lets us see how a loving God forgives all and restores us to intimacy if we allow Him. Paul standing, sword in hand, manfully doing battle against the hydra-headed enemies of his soul and the souls of others, gives us to understand that temptation need not alarm us nor opposition surprise us—on the contrary it must be part of our expected program as members of the militant church. Paul so brave under trials of every sort, refusing to be beaten, exulting in the very thick of the fray, shows us that it is an honor indeed to be asked to give God something that really *costs*.

But it would be a mistake to imagine that Paul was swept off his feet by a blind and unreasoning enthusiasm. You will never make a Paul or a Xavier without enthusiasm, but it is the enthusiasm that appreciates thoroughly the sanity of the cause for which it is striving.

When Our Lord called for volunteers He insisted that, before offering themselves, they should first sit down and reckon what the cost was going to be. A king, He said, going to war, will inquire beforehand about the strength of the king who is marching against him. If he finds that he is going to be completely outnumbered and that the inevitable result must be wholesale slaughter of his men, he will be wise to sue for conditions of peace in good time. A man who sets out to build a tower must first of all calculate how much it is going to cost, and if he finds he has not sufficient money, he ought not begin to build it at all. Otherwise the half-built tower will excite the ridicule of the man's enemies.

So the king considers carefully, and the man estimates the cost of his proposed tower. And you, too, concludes Our Saviour, if you want to come and be an apostle, you must reckon what the cost will be. What is it? "Unless a man renounce *everything that he possesses* he cannot be My disciple." Never did any mere man make a claim like this, a claim which would be preposterous if Christ were not God. It is most true that He never allows Himself to be outdone in generosity. It is true that He encourages our frailty by holding for us to see a reward exceeding great which a just judge will surely give us at the end. It is true that He assures us most emphatically that even in this valley of tears the man who labors generously for Christ discovers, even here, a veritable corner of paradise. But all the time He never revokes the hard saying: "Unless a man renounce. . . ."

So the apostle sees very clearly indeed that in point of fact the saying *is* hard. But he discerns more, because a deep personal love of Christ gives him intuition. Zeal is not the result of mere intellectual conviction. It rests on conviction but it is also a fire that blazes up in the heart. Hence the apostle *sees,* and the apostle *loves,* and the combination of vision and love fixes him in his determination to root out of his own heart any obstacle to Christ's entire possession. Further, this same combination of conviction and love drives him forward to crush the enemies of God and to restore to Christ the souls purchased at such cost to Himself.

"If thou reliest," says à Kempis, "more upon thine own reason than upon the virtue which subjects to Jesus Christ, thou wilt seldom or hardly become an enlightened man. For God will have us wholly subject to Him, and to transcend all reason by an inflamed love." To *transcend* reason, but not to oppose it or contradict it; to transcend it in much the same way as vision transcends faith. No mere dry calculating service of God will ever lead a man to embrace the life of hardship we have seen in St. Paul. The conviction must be there indeed—as dry faggots are on the hearth—but it takes the spark of personal love and enthusiasm to set the fire ablaze.

So far our main interest has been in the element of enthusiastic love which is so much in evidence in the Apostle of the Gentiles. And now, what was Paul's intellectual background? What were the principles which controlled and directed this unflagging energy? I find that there are three—devotedness to the will of God; an understanding of the doctrine of the mystical body; and lastly, a keen appreciation of the necessity and the power of divine grace.

6. Fundamentals Again

"Lord," he said, "what wilt thou have me to do?" The question might well be regarded as Paul's fundamental principle in his apostolic work. All zeal is suspect, be its results ever so specious in men's eyes and successful as reckoned by men's standards, unless it is built upon a determination to accept God's will as criterion of right and wrong. Of course, obedience to that will as expressed in the Ten Commandments is here taken for granted. Devotion to the interests of Christ is counterfeit unless it be accompanied by at least a serious and consistent effort to avoid all grave sin. But enlightened zeal is quick to detect also what is called the Will of God's "good pleasure." A parent who loves does not want to be always issuing commands, and a loving child will be on the watch to do for the parent little gracious acts of thoughtfulness for the mere purpose of giving pleasure to the parent. Now God, our loving Father, has assigned each of us a vocation in life—the priesthood, or the religious state, or married life, or unmarried life in the world—and with it a certain profession or trade or round of duties.

The apostle will learn the art of "supernaturalizing" all these actions. In themselves they may be as insignificant as sweeping an office or cooking a dinner or writing a letter or polishing a pair of shoes. Or they may be tasks of utmost importance like the defence of a big court case, or the signing of a treaty between two nations, or the running of a very large business. But "to those who love God all things work together unto good." An apostolic man is not an apostle only when he is engaged on work that has to do directly with souls and their salvation or sanctification. Work and prayer and recreation and rest and duties of his state —all these, so to say, interpenetrate; in all these the apostle seeks to purify his motive from whatever savors of selfish interest and to guide himself by the single motive only of doing this task, whatever it be, in order to please God. He accepts it from His hand and sees it through because God wills it.

That zeal does not ring true which is exercised at the cost of sacrificing God's known will, even though its results may be quite spectacular. If God's will for a mother is to be giving breakfast to her children she would displease Him by being at Mass instead. If God's will for me is to sit in my office and type out those long lists of tiresome names and addresses, it is wrong for me to close down half an hour early in order to visit the sick or help the poor, or even try to reclaim a sinner. If God's will assigns me the task of breaking stones, He quite definitely wants me breaking stones rather than kneeling before Him in the Blessed Sacrament.

"Lord, what wilt Thou have me to do?" When Saul asked the question, Our Lord instructed him to go into the city, telling him that he would be informed there. At Damascus, Ananias came to meet him and to deliver to Saul the orders he had received. Why did Christ not tell Saul directly Himself? He might have done so, but for the increase of our merit He makes use of secondary agents. Saul obeyed Ananias as he would have obeyed Christ Himself. Small thanks to obey if Our Lord was sitting there in that shop or office and telling you what He wanted you to do. But when the instructions come through an impossible employer or a short-tempered and, perhaps, unjust master or mistress, then to obey cheerfully and bend one's will to this other, is indeed a searching test of devotedness to the doing of God's will.

Our Lord's unswerving loyalty to the will of His Father has

been dwelt upon in another place. Our study here is St. Paul as a man who had well "learned Christ," and here is the fundamental principle which governs and directs all his works of zeal. Like his great prototype he could say, with due reserve, of himself, that he too had come down from heaven in order to do the will of his heavenly Father.

The second principle is embodied in that question of Our Lord: "Saul, Saul, why persecutest thou Me? . . . I am Jesus Whom thou persecutest." Herein is revealed to Saul the doctrine of the mystical body of Christ which ever afterwards was to be so dear to his heart, and the marvelous implications of which he would expound so lucidly in his letters and spoken word. The truth dawns upon him as he kneels here in the light that all he has been doing—crushing those Christians into the ground, abetting their enemies—is actually being done to Jesus Himself. "I am Jesus Whom thou persecutest."

Why is this except that Christ and Christians are so closely united, that—to employ the analogy which Paul will later use himself—they form together one great organism, one only body? As in the human body there are many members and all the members help each other, and all the members are enriched with the same blood—so, in Christ's mystical body, composed of Him and us, the grace of God's Holy Spirit flows from Him into us, making us both one.

How well suited to the needs of our times is this lofty principle is abundantly proved by the masterly exposition of the doctrine in the Pope's Encyclical Letter on the mystical body. Written at a time when the world was torn in shreds by class hatred and war, that letter echoes the voice of Pius XII reminding men of their dignity as brothers of Christ and of each other, as sons of the same God and Father, and destined to share in the same birthright.

7. "My Commandment"

This sublime concept is not meant to be relegated to the land of forgotten theories. It has practical applications in our daily lives at every turn. No one of us escapes the annoyances, petty or great, incidental to life's journey. There are people who try our patience, whose mannerisms or exactions or foibles or acts of injustice irritate and make us want to explode with annoyance. What is wrong with my attitude towards that person, who, in point of fact, is quite probably a bore, or untruthful, or exceedingly selfish? No amount of talking will ever convince me that he is anything else, nor is it expected of me to be blind to his glaring faults and persuade myself that they are virtues in disguise. St. Paul said that charity was patient and kind, but he never told us it was blind. What has to be done, or at least seriously attempted, is to discern Christ in that person; to see and realize that the queer fads are permitted by Him; to work my mind round to the point of view which recognizes that they are in reality a vehicle of grace to my soul. Through prayer and meditation and patience, allied with the never-failing grace of God, this viewpoint can influence one's habitual manner of treating trying people and difficult circumstances. The greater such influence, the deeper has Paul's second great principle taken hold.

Nor will there be mere tolerance of another's weakness; there will be for that other, for every other, a deep and abiding love. For with this attitude, I look upon all men, not merely as human beings; I see in everyone an immortal soul destined to be God's tabernacle, very possibly His tabernacle at this moment. Thus is engendered patience with others, respect for others, genuine affection. This attitude prevents harshness or tale-bearing or unkind criticism or censoriousness or revenge—anything, in a word, that would cause another to suffer the slightest unnecessary pain. How could it be otherwise? If I recognize the implications of the sublime doctrine of the mystical body and realize that what I say or think or do, is done or said to Jesus Christ, then how can I fail to give to others a genuine love which will prove itself at every turn? If I am unduly harsh towards another, if I make life miserable for another, if I refuse to lend a helping hand and on the contrary do all I can to thwart and annoy, then, too, is it true that my victim can look up at me and say: "I am

Jesus Whom thou persecutest!" You are doing this to Jesus Christ!

No wonder Our Lord made this commandment of mutual love His own *par excellence.* "This is My Commandment, that you love one another as I have loved you; by this shall all men know that you are My disciples, that you have love one for another." No wonder it forms so large a part of the teaching of St. Paul who had "learned Christ." And no wonder that, like Our Lord and His faithful Apostle, a man or woman whose mind feeds habitually on this thought will be ready to face toil or hardship for another. And what is such readiness but zeal?

To see Christ in others no matter how effective be the disguise; to love Christ in others no matter how much they fail to express in themselves Christ's lovable qualities; to reverence Christ in others, to adore Him present in their souls, even when they think little of their dignity themselves, nay more, when they drag it in the mud; to serve others with a good grace, even when I see they are selfish and ungrateful and simply using me as a tool for their own ends—because in them I see Christ; to pass over a slight and pretend not to see or hear; to show special affection towards the one who I know has detracted me or calumniated me or ridiculed me in my absence; to act next time as though nothing had happened; to go out of my way to say a kind word to a person for whom nobody cares, to notice and speak to the man or woman whom another is seeking to ignore; to do these things because the love of Christ has seized upon the heart and because He is recognized in those whom we contact thus—this is the true zeal learned by Saul on the road to Damascus. This is his second principle, and by it alone may Christians hope to win the world back to sanity and to Christ.

8. Against the Goad

Finally, Our Lord told Saul: "It is hard for thee to kick against the goad." As though He would say: "Saul, I am offering to you today a grace so powerful, that, although it will leave you free, as grace always does, either to yield to Me or to persist in your own way, still so strong is it, that it will be very difficult for you to refuse it." There are times when a loving Christ appeals with more than His customary insistence. There are special moments when He seems to beg and importune us to avail of the graces He longs to pour into our souls. Such a moment may well be a time of sickness, or of a sermon, or when we stand broken-hearted over the mortal remains of one whom we loved as our own soul, and while standing there realize how precarious is our hold on life and whatever it reckons as precious.

At such moments it is hard to kick against the goad. Hard, yes, but it remains true that resistance is still possible. Divine grace will argue with us. It will plead with us. It will upbraid us with our sins and infidelities. But force our will—that is what God's grace will never do. After making the offer, God stands back and waits, and shows a deep respect for the gift of free will which He has bestowed upon His creature.

One day Our Lord sat upon the brow of a hill overlooking Jerusalem. He folded His hands upon His knees and turned a wistful gaze in the direction of the faithless city. "Jerusalem, Jerusalem, thou that killest the prophets and stonest them that are sent to thee, how often would I have gathered together thy children as the hen doth gather her chickens under her wings, and *thou wouldst not.*" He longed to deliver that city from the bondage of its sin, but He waited for the city freely to accept Him. And He waited in vain, and Jerusalem paid the frightful penalty of its rejection. "Thou wouldst not"—even Saul could have chosen to refuse.

"It is hard for thee to kick against the goad." There is still another way of interpreting these words. By them Our Lord would remind Saul that if he does resist he is going to be a very miserable man. "If you refuse this grace, the refusal will bring you nothing but sadness and unhappiness." Once again, experience bears witness to the truth of that word. Look at this man enslaved by passion, groaning day and night under a load of depression and self-contempt and remorse and shame. Happy, is he? "We fools . . . we have walked hard ways, but the way of the

Lord we have not known!" "Know thou and understand that it is an evil and a bitter thing for thee to have left the Lord thy God." "One truth at least I have learned," said an old man. "There is no happiness in sin."

We know that Saul did *not* kick against the goad. On that momentous day he yielded to the first promptings of grace within him. And according as the years went on he learned more and more about this life-giving gift of God to man. He has come to be styled "the doctor of divine grace."

Why? First of all because he understood so well his complete and absolute dependence upon grace. He has nothing of good in himself. "What hast thou," he asks, "which thou hast not received? And if thou hast received, why dost thou glory as if thou hadst not received?" Whatever good is in any man is there because it has been placed in him by God's loving hand. More than that. A man cannot have even a single good desire, much less carry that good desire into effect, unless he be helped all along the way by the sustaining grace of God.

Should this dependence make a man despondent? On the contrary, it is a joy to him to realize that he can lean on so loving and attentive a heavenly Father. And there is a complementary truth which also spurred on Paul in his work of self-conquest and in his efforts to win others. This is that, while on the one hand it is true that man is so helpless and useless, there is also the inspiring and comforting thought that through the grace of Christ he can beat down every enemy. "I can do all things in Him that strengtheneth me." In my own sickly, weakly condition I cannot stand, but the powerful hands of my Christ are ever ready to support me.

There are tremendous sources of strength at man's command, for all the infinite wealth of Christ's riches, "the unsearchable riches of Christ," are there to be called upon and to supplement his poverty. It is true that he is reduced to pauperism except a generous and merciful Christ give him alms. But, so far from giving grudgingly, He warns man to keep coming and to keep asking, and He goes the length of assuring him that he never will be refused or turned away.

The Will of God as the lodestar of his life; the realization that what he did to others was done to Christ; the need and the power and the superabundance of the grace merited by Christ—these are the three solid truths upon which rests the edifice of the holiness and the zeal and the enthusiasm of Saul of Tarsus.

With such an intellectual background it is easy to understand why he teaches that a generous service is the only reasonable service. With such deeply-rooted convictions half measures are impossible. The apostolate is pre-eminently the "reasonable service." "I beseech you, therefore, brethren, by the mercy of God, that you present your bodies a living sacrifice, holy, pleasing unto God, your reasonable service." Everything else is unreasonable. His mind was convinced. His heart was set on fire. The result is that he stands before us as a man of God, an intrepid warrior, a lover asking for one thing only—opportunity to prove the sincerity of his love.